I0061529

THE UNSETTLED SECTOR

ANALIESE RICHARD

The Unsettled Sector

NGOs and the Cultivation of Democratic Citizenship in Rural Mexico

STANFORD UNIVERSITY PRESS

STANFORD, CALIFORNIA

Stanford University Press
Stanford, California

© 2016 by Analiese Richard. All rights reserved.

No part of this book may be reproduced or transmitted in any form or by any means, electronic or mechanical, including photocopying and recording, or in any information storage or retrieval system without the prior written permission of Stanford University Press.

Printed in the United States of America on acid-free, archival-quality paper

Library of Congress Cataloging-in-Publication Data

Names: Richard, Analiese, author.
Title: The unsettled sector : NGOs and the cultivation of democratic
    citizenship in rural Mexico /Analiese Richard.
Description: Stanford, California : Stanford University Press, 2016. | © 2016
    | Includes bibliographical references.
Identifiers: LCCN 2015037995 | ISBN 9780804797986 (cloth : alk. paper) |
    ISBN 9780804799164 (pbk. : alk. paper) | ISBN 9780804799195
Subjects: LCSH: Non-governmental organizations—Mexico—Hidalgo
    (State) | Democracy—Mexico—Hidalgo (State) | Neoliberalism—
    Mexico—Hidalgo (State) | Citizenship—Mexico—Hidalgo (State) | Rural
    development—Mexico—Hidalgo (State) | Hidalgo (Mexico : State)—
    Rural conditions.
Classification: LCC JL1299.H5 R53 2013 | DDC 320.972/46091734—dc23
LC record available at http://lccn.loc.gov/2015037995

To the memory of Jose Luis Cordero

Contents

Acknowledgments

I began the field research for this book over a decade ago, when the seeds of neoliberal democracy in Mexico were beginning to burgeon. In the intervening years, I have accrued debts of gratitude to many people who helped bring this book into being.

My colleagues and friends in Hidalgo, Mexico, inspired me to undertake this research and contributed immeasurably to its outcome. I am grateful to the communities who welcomed me into their lives and homes, putting up with my faux pas and incessant questions with patience and humor. I am especially indebted to the Barron, Cordero, Fosado, Islas, Mancera, Ortiz, Perez, Rehberg, and Vargas families, whose collaboration and assistance proved invaluable during my fieldwork. In the United States, the Richards, Doucets, Martins, and Websters supported me throughout the long process of fieldwork and writing. I will always be grateful for their kindness, patience, and encouragement. They made the often-solitary tasks of analysis and editing easier to endure, and motivated me to keep on going.

Numerous friends and colleagues in the anthropology department at UC-Berkeley helped to refine this project and sustain its author through the years. I owe an enormous debt of gratitude to Donald Moore, Laura Nader, Gillian Hart, William Hanks, Laura Hubbard, Joshua Levy, Anke Schwittay, Dar Rudnyckyj, Sholeh Shahrokhi, Nancy Postero, Liza Grandia, Naomi Leite, Elana Shever, and Chris Vasantkumar. Detailed comments from my anthropologist colleagues in the School of International Studies at the University of the Pacific—Laura Bathurst, Ahmed Kanna, and Sarah Mathis—helped me to improve several chapters. Arturo Giraldez, Annlee Dolan, and Marcia Hernandez cheered me on through the final draft and provided worthwhile advice along the way. Ricardo Nurko graciously prepared and edited the photos and maps. Lea Popielinski did an excellent job copy editing a rough first draft, and Michelle Lipinski, my editor at Stanford, provided valuable guidance in preparing subsequent versions. I am also grateful to the two anonymous reviewers whose criticism and insights helped to strengthen the book immensely. Any errors that remain despite the tremendous support of all of these people are mine alone.

Acronyms

Mexican NGOs

CEMEFI	Mexican Center for Philanthropy (Centro Mexicano para la Filantropía)
FHAR	Hidalgan Foundation for Rural Service (Fundación Hidalguense para la Atención Rural)
FMDR	Mexican Foundation for Rural Development (Fundación Mexicana para el Desarrollo Rural)
HD	Hidalgo Development
UC	Campesinos' Union (Unión de Campesinos)
UDEC	Union of Catholic Businessmen (Unión de Empresarios Católicos)
SENEC	Secretariat for New Experiences in Community Education

International NGOs

ICNL	International Center for Not-for-Profit Law
SIPAZ	Servicio Internacional para la Paz

NGO Networks

CSC	Civil Society Council (Consejo de la Sociedad Civil)
MCD	Citizens' Movement for Democracy (Movimiento Ciudadaño por la Democracía)
MSN	Mexico Solidarity Network
Red TDPT	"All Rights for Everyone" National Human Rights Network (Red Nacional de Organismos Civiles de Derechos Humanos "Todos los Derechos para Todos")

Mexican Political Parties and Affiliates

PAN	National Action Party (Partido de Acción Nacional)
PNR	National Revolutionary Party
PRD	Democratic Revolutionary Party (Partido de la Revolución Democrática)
PRI	Party of the Institutionalized Revolution (Partido Revolucionario Institucional)
CNC	National Confederation of Campesinos National—PRI sectoral organ (Confederación Nacional de Campesinos)

Mexican Government Entities and Programs

BANRURAL	Rural Development Bank (Banco de Desarrollo Rural)
CONASUPO	National Company for People's Sustenance (Compañía Nacional de Subsistencias Populares)
COPLAMAR	Office of Nacional Plan for Depressed Zones and Marginalized Groups (Coordinadora General de Plan Nacional para las Zonas Deprimidas y Grupos Marginados)
DIF	Integral Family Development (Desarrollo Integral de la Familia)
IFE	Federal Elections Institute (Instituto Federal Electoral)
INEGI	National Institute of Statistics and Geography (Instituto Nacional de Estadística y Geografía)
INE	National Ecological Institute (Instituto Nacional de Ecología)
MINSA	Industrialized Maize (Maiz Industrializado, SA)
PIDER	Program for Integrated Rural Development (Programa Integral de Desarrollo Rural)
PROCAMPO	Program of Direct Rural Support (Programa de Apoyo al Campo)
PROCEDE	Program of Certification of Ejidal Rights (Programa de Certificación de Derechos Ejidales y Titulación de Solares Urbanos)
PROGRESA	Program for Education, Health, and Nutrition (Programa de Educación, Salud, y Alimentación)

PRONASOL   National Solidarity Program (Programa Nacional de Solidaridad)
SAM   Mexican Food System (Sistema Alimentario Mexicana)
SOMEX   Somex Bank (Banco Mexicano SOMEX)

US Government Entities

CCC   Commodity Credit Corporation

International Treaties

NAFTA   North American Free Trade Agreement

International Agencies

USAID   United States Agency for International Development
UNHRC   United Nations Human Rights Council

Other

CEB   Christian base community (comunidad eclesiástica de base)
ENSO   El Niño–Southern Oscillation
EZLN   Zapatista Army of National Liberation (Ejército Zapatista de Liberación Nacional)
INGO   international nongovernmental organization
ISI   import substitution industrialization
NGO   nongovernmental organization
SNA   social network analysis
SSP   specific social program

THE UNSETTLED SECTOR

Introduction

Valentina Herrera was the first female president of the governing board of Hidalgo Development (HD) and my first guide to the political and social changes that nongovernmental organizations (NGOs) like HD have helped to cultivate in rural Mexico.[1] Her life story parallels the rise and fall of Mexico's post-Revolutionary social order. Doña Valentina was the youngest of 17 children, a member of the new generation of campesinos born after the Revolution ended. A native of the tiny village I call El Ocote in the state of Hidalgo, she was born at a time when the Tulancingo River still flowed high along its banks, feeding the haciendas that provided the capital of Mexico City with livestock, textiles, and pulque,[2] the cactus beer that served as the elixir of the working classes. In the 1930s and 1940s, her parents and other relatives helped to found the *ejidos* of El Ocote, San Vicente, and San Isidro, fighting a long battle to wrest small, arid plots of land from wealthy landowners. They struggled together to build new agricultural communities and to forge the social networks that tied them to the outside world through the Catholic Church, schools, and the official state party, the Institutional Revolutionary Party (*Partido Revolucionario Institucional*, or PRI). They were desperately poor, Doña Valentina said, but in those days one could get ahead by working hard and counting on the labor of a large family. Her parents and siblings worked the communally held plot assigned to them by the *ejidal* council for subsistence and earned cash income by sharecropping on private lands in the nearby town of Alcholoya.

In the days before television's glow illuminated campesino homes, rural families spent their evenings engaged in storytelling. Doña Valentina remembered many of the tales her parents and grandparents told about the horrors of life on the haciendas—the backbreaking labor and piercing hunger, the treacherous credit arrangements at the company store, and the indifference of the priests who occasionally visited to conduct baptisms and burials. Recalling stories about one overseer who forced men to beat their wives in public for his amusement, she once confessed to me that had she been present, she might not have been able to restrain herself (*aguantarse*) as her forebears had. When I asked her how people endured such abuse, she answered quietly, "If they protested and were killed, who would look after their children?" Her parents were "hard people," she said, because they lived hard lives and sought to instill in their children the discipline and endurance (*aguante*) they would need to survive. As a girl, Doña Valentina's grandmother had spent her days on her knees, scrubbing the stone floors of the hacienda and grinding the maize for the hacendado's household by hand. But with the founding of the *ejido*, the campesinos' labor became their own. Because of her parents' sacrifice and hard work, Doña Valentina said, her own generation could take advantage of new opportunities.

In the late 1940s, the PRI launched a series of efforts to modernize agriculture and organize the campesinos politically. Many elderly *ejiditarios* associated the PRI with the memory of President Lázaro Cárdenas, who championed the agrarian reforms of the 1930s. However, for many members of Doña Valentina's generation, the gratitude they felt toward the PRI was mixed with resentment. In Hidalgo, as in other regions of the country, the dawn of nationalist development meant a shift in cultures of politics but not a major change in the composition of the political class. The party helped to create the *ejidos* but also used campesinos as political pawns. Although large landowners (for the most part) no longer exercised direct control over rural residents, the same ruling families now enjoyed prominent positions in the PRI hierarchy as well as in the state and municipal governments. In Hidalgo, a small number of powerful families have managed to maintain political control for extended periods through a combination of clientelism and violence. Indeed, Hidalgo has long been used as a training ground to prepare PRI functionaries for national posts or leadership positions within the party structure. Two important figures in current President Enrique Pena Nieto's administration, Interior Minister Miguel Angel Osorio Chong and former Attorney General Jesus Murillo Karam, are both former PRI governors of Hidalgo. Thus the party's incorporation of campesinos as citizens of the modernized nation through education and development programs seemed, to Doña Valentina, more like paternalism than an invitation to equal participation in public life.

El Ocote, whose tiny parcels of three hectares each had been wrested from large landowners in two disjointed tracts, suffered more than most from lack of access to water. As a child, Doña Valentina and her neighbors had to travel long distances to the Tulancingo River to wash clothes, water their animals, and fetch water for cooking and drinking. By the time she married at age 17, the *ejido*'s population had grown and land was already becoming scarce. The residents of El Ocote were not well connected to PRI brokers (*caciques*) in the state government, and so little of the new government aid for agricultural development reached them outside of election years. The government schoolteacher assigned to the village rarely appeared. By the 1970s, some of the younger men from El Ocote began to migrate temporarily to Puebla to work in construction and industry. Hard work and *aguante* were no longer sufficient to make a living and raise one's family, and little relief was forthcoming from government agencies or the church. Rather, a new institutional form—the nongovernmental organization—began to insert itself into the life of rural Hidalgans.

Hidalgo Development was the first to arrive in the late 1970s. HD undertook an intensive program of infrastructure and cooperative development projects that helped to transform the Tulancingo Valley into a small-scale dairy-producing region. It was HD that coordinated the project to perforate El Ocote's first irrigation well in 1986, enabling residents to access regular water supplies for the first time. A series of productive and educational projects followed, and Doña Valentina began to participate in HD's retreats, or *encuentros*. Doña Valentina's husband, Don Emiliano, recalled that as a young bride she had been shy and quiet. Now he complained that she was never at home because she was always out "getting involved in other peoples' affairs." Although she described herself as a housewife, through her participation in HD's various projects over the years she also became a catechist, a rural health worker, the organizer of a revolving microcredit cooperative, and eventually the leader of HD's governing board. For Doña Valentina, the arrival of Hidalgo Development marked a turning point both in the life of El Ocote and in her vision of herself as a citizen. Through her participation in HD projects, she told me, she came to relate her experiences and those of her relatives and neighbors to the struggles of rural people in other regions, and eventually even other countries. As she began to understand her life in a broader social, political, and economic context, her sense of herself as a social actor also shifted. Involvement in "other people's affairs" became something akin to civic duty.

I first met Doña Valentina in 1996, two years after the start of the Zapatista rebellion. On January 1, 1994, the day the North American Free Trade Agreement (NAFTA) took effect, indigenous rebels calling themselves the Zapatista Army of National Liberation (*Ejército Zapatista de Liberación Nacional*, EZLN) occupied several towns in the impoverished southern Mexican state of Chiapas. Denouncing the Mexican government's neoliberal policies, they demanded respect for indigenous rights, land reform, and democracy. Chiapas became the site of a low-intensity war in which the Mexican government attempted to wear down rebel support bases, invading civilian areas and unleashing a humanitarian crisis. As participants in a trinational NGO-based human rights observation mission to the conflict zones of Chiapas, Doña Valentina and I were assigned to the same delegation. Together we visited three Mayan towns, where we collected testimonies from residents and documented evidence of military incursions and human rights abuses. I admired her from the start—the way she took charge of a room, the way she dispensed advice in the form of proverbs, the powerful effect of her words. She only really got going *after* the official testimonies had been taken down, when she sat down in a circle with the women of the villages we visited to compare experiences and organizing strategies. The seasoned NGO leader I came to know through those visits bore little resemblance to the shy young bride Don Emiliano remembered. She felt a deep responsibility to listen to the concerns of her fellow citizens, to help ensure that their voices were heard, and to hold the government accountable both for the physical violence it perpetrated and for the years of systematic marginalization and neglect that had led to the rebellion.

In 2002, when I returned to the Tulancingo Valley to undertake this ethnographic study, I looked forward to visiting Doña Valentina first. Two years earlier, in 2000, a broad-based coalition of NGOs and social movements had helped to bring about the historic opposition victory of President Vicente Fox. By the time I returned to El Ocote, however, a mood of disenchantment had begun to set in. Many of the transformative possibilities promised by Mexico's internationally celebrated "democratic transition" had already been foreclosed or rerouted. The community was disappearing as the markets for maize and milk crumbled, forcing young people to move north in search of work. It appeared that campesinos were once more being pushed toward the sidelines of Mexican modernity, perhaps for the final time. In Doña Valentina's kitchen, we took stock of the changes together.

"*Ya no se de que esta hecha esta gente [I just don't know what these people are made of anymore]*," she sighed, gazing out of her kitchen window at the dried-up fields, the soil too hard to plow because the rains were so long overdue. She and I stood before the stove, making tortillas and reminiscing about our time together in Chiapas. A framed picture I took of her with children from one of the villages we visited hung over the table, next to the grade-school diploma she had earned at age 55. "It's hard to believe that was almost six years ago," I said. "So much has changed since then." "So much and so little," Doña Valentina replied. "Sometimes I wonder what it would take for revolution to come again. *¿Hasta donde aguanta la gente? [How much of this can the people take?]*," she sighed. "But now that the PRI is no longer in power, no one is sure who or what to rebel *against.*" As the heat from the *comal*, a flat, smooth metal griddle, overtook the warmth of the sun beaming through the kitchen window, Doña Valentina undertook a characteristically concise explanation of the problem. "It's like this, *mija*," she said, wiping her hands on her apron and sitting in a chair. "*Antes a los campesinos el gobierno nos daba atole con un dedo. Ahora ni te dan ni te dejan. Ahí esta el problema [Before, the government spoon-fed the campesinos. Now they neither give us anything nor allow us to do things for ourselves].*" The double meaning of her words became apparent over the course of my fieldwork in Hidalgo. Government divestment from the countryside and the neoliberal trade policies that accompanied it constituted a withdrawal of resources from rural communities while also limiting their ability to succeed at creating development alternatives by working with NGOs. At the same time, while the government engaged in less ideological "spoon-feeding" of campesinos, rural issues could no longer gain political traction according to the established rules of the game. Campesinos had gone from being treated as unruly children to being mostly ignored or regarded as folkloric relics by the political class. Nonetheless, it was clear that the work of NGOs from the late 1970s on had helped to cultivate changes in both ideas and practices of citizenship in rural Hidalgo.

What role have NGOs played in cultivating democratic citizenship? Since the end of World War II, our world has been shaped by struggles over the meanings and uses of democracy. With the fall of the Berlin Wall, democracy's triumph was proclaimed, but its problems and possibilities remained an open question. An ensuing third wave of democratic transitions in Latin America, Eastern Europe, and the Pacific failed to obey normative models, proving to be more complicated and ambiguous than anticipated, and ultimately prompting social scientists to hyphenate the concept itself.[3] At the same time the vitality of civic life in established democracies steeply diminished as a result of the growing influence of big business and increasing citizen apathy toward participation in traditional institutions and political processes (Gagnon and Chou 2014, 4). At the close of the twentieth century, NGOs announced themselves as new kinds of actors with the potential to transform the relationship between states and civil society on a global scale by strengthening civic engagement and supplementing traditional institutions. In the intervening decades, they have grown in number and reach to become normalized as global actors. NGOs have alternately been lauded as tools for empowering the poor and disenfranchised and critiqued as accomplices in the creation of nonelected forms of neoliberal governance. However, the NGO as an institutional form remains poorly understood. Although NGOs are often distinguished from state and market institutions, this study reveals the continuity in practice between public and private fields of power. Indeed, NGOs become instruments for producing such continuities through the work they perform on and through notions of public morality and active citizenship.

This book analyzes the often contradictory modes of civic and social engagement facilitated by NGOs during Mexico's democratic transition. The changes cultivated by these organizations cannot be properly understood without considering the relationship of NGOs to earlier historical forms of communitarian relations. Although NGOs may constitute a novel form of organization, the modes of engagement they foster are ultimately related to much older philanthropic, religious, and civic traditions rooted in the historical and cultural terrains of specific regions. This study analyzes the growth of the NGO community of Tulancingo, Hidalgo, from the 1970s on, examining the evolution of relationships to target communities, donors, international partners, state agencies, and political actors, and focusing on how the people behind them seek to make sense of and manage those connections. Uniform in appearance yet malleable in practice, NGOs bridge formal politics and public morality, citizenship and domestic life. Studying how they accomplish this yields fresh insight into the processes of democratic change.

Neoliberal Democracy

Latin America has been characterized as a global laboratory for neoliberalism, a testing ground for the utopian designs of neoliberal ideologues whose ability to carry out radical experiments in economic, political, and social restructuring was predicated on the region's indebtedness and backed by hemispheric US military hegemony (Goodale and Postero 2013; Grandin 2006). Not surprisingly, the region has also incubated some of the most formidable challenges to neoliberal orthodoxy, including the neo-Zapatista rebellion, the rise of Hugo Chávez's Bolivarian revolution, and the rewriting of the Bolivian constitution under President Evo Morales (Goodale and Postero 2013). Far from encountering a blank slate, the utopian plans of the Chicago Boys and the orthodoxy of the Washington Consensus were transformed by their encounters with complex, historically situated social and political terrains of specific regions.[4] While its South American neighbors struggle to articulate a postneoliberal regional project, Mexico has instead undergone a period of retrenchment, producing profound economic and social contradictions that threaten its very social fabric. Over the last two decades Mexican political figures from the right and the center have increasingly adopted the language of democratic citizenship as a political tool, but the earlier identification of democratic principles with social equality seems to have been left aside.

Whereas classic Western liberalism dictated the separate delineation and governance of social and economic spheres by a central state, neoliberal philosophy introduces the predominance of the economic over the social and the dispersal of governmental power through a variety of sites and establishments (Foucault 2000; Fraser 2003). The logic of the market comes to stand in as the organizing principle in the relationship between state and society. Although neoliberal reforms have often been presented as a natural result of the evolution of the global economy, "a bundle of economic policies with inadvertent political and social consequences," Brown insists on the importance of viewing neoliberalism as a "*political rationality* that both organizes these policies and reaches beyond the market" to reorganize society and culture (2003, 2, emphasis in original; see also Harvey 2005). However, neoliberalism does not just arrive in specific sites as a fully formed system and unfold according to its own inner logic. Instead, relations of rule must be worked out in a space of "cultural intimacy" (Herzfeld 1997) where neoliberal rationalities and techniques are combined with a sort of political and cultural savvy about how things get done and an intimate knowledge of the limits of state power. This is certainly the way the term is used in Mexican activist circles, where *neoliberalismo* refers to an economic model imposed by Mexican elites and technocrats with support and pressure from abroad, despite the widespread political opposition it has provoked and the deep social suffering it has caused.

In Latin America, neoliberal reforms have generally moved society in the direction of "market democracy" (Peck and Tickell 2002), in which the role of the state is confined to technocratic regulatory and security functions. Responsibility for social welfare and local governance is often decentralized and devolved onto private actors such as NGOs. This does not, however, lead to a withering away of the state. Throughout the period of neoliberal reforms, from the 1980s into the present, the state has retained its centrality as the primary reference point for citizen mobilization around political, economic, and social issues (Goodale and Postero 2013, 18–19). Indeed, as we shall see in Chapters 1 and 3, state agencies have become even more deeply imbricated in the lives of rural Mexicans, while forms of governance and of civic action have been diversified and decentralized.

The growth of the third sector in the neoliberal era has been accompanied by a displacement of narratives of national progress in favor of metaphors of social repair (Bornstein 2012, 16). Even in the homeland of Margaret Thatcher, who famously declared three decades ago that society as such no longer existed, increasing social marginalization (often associated with violence) and ecological destruction have given rise to the realization that mechanisms of social integration are not only valuable but also completely necessary. Hence the emergence of a new model of active citizenship in which individuals participate through volunteerism and philanthropic acts. In this paradigm, "citizenship is detached from its modern roots in institutional reform, in the welfare state and community struggles, and rearticulated with the more Victorian concepts of charity, philanthropy and self-help" (Hall and Held 1989, 16). NGOs have played important roles in this process by reworking existing practices of citizenship and communitarian relations. Because NGOs organize social action at multiple scales and across multiple contexts simultaneously, many times as intermediaries, the study of the NGO form aids in understanding the intersections of political, economic, and cultural transformation as well as the emergence of new forms of citizenship.

NGOs and Neoliberal Democracy

International organizations have existed in various forms since the nineteenth century; however, modern NGOs are a product of the post–World War II development era. The term "nongovernmental organization" was coined in 1945 during the constitution of the United Nations. Provisions were made in the intergovernmental organization's charter for entities that were not states, political parties, or for-profit businesses to observe and comment on the proceedings. However, it was not until much later that the term came into common usage. Brian Smith (1990) explicitly linked the appearance of NGOs (especially those organized as nonprofit corporations) to moments of crisis in capitalist expansion. In Western Europe and North America, NGOs became more numerous beginning in the 1970s with the reorganization of the welfare state. Their rapid expansion into the global south accompanied the neoliberal reforms brought about by the Washington Consensus; in fact, in Mexico and many countries, the promotion of NGOs was an explicit goal of the World Bank and USAID, which viewed them as supplementing the downsized social role of the state as well as catalysts for democratic civic engagement, a stabilizing force for societies in crisis. At the same time, global communications technology made it easier for NGOs in different parts of the world to work together on large-scale problems that transcend national boundaries. The 1990s marked the rise of transnational issues networks, organizing NGOs and social movements around the world to advocate for human rights (including women's rights and indigenous rights) and environmental issues (Keck and Sikkink 1998). They made their presence felt at the 1992 Earth Summit in Rio de Janeiro, Brazil, and organized the World Social Forum as a counter to the World Economic Forum held annually in Davos, Switzerland.

Global efforts by the World Bank, USAID, and private foundations such as George Soros's Open Society Institute to encourage democratization and rule of law during the 1990s and early 2000s all promoted the growth of NGOs,[5] based on the notion that a robust "civil society" could serve as a counter to the destabilizing effects of global economic restructuring. For states and corporations, the disembedding of social relations posed problems of governability and labor discipline. To communitarian activists, the problem was one of social anomie. For both these seemingly disparate camps, however, civil society marked the space of the changing social collective (Yar 2004). Global NGO networks were commonly theorized as representatives of an imagined global civil society, an autonomous space of creativity and resistance to the powers of both states and capital (Appadurai 1996, 2000; Comaroff and Comaroff 2000; Escobar 1995). For example, Appadurai argued that they

> emerged to contest, interrogate, and reverse these developments and to create forms of knowledge transfer and social mobilization that proceed independently of the actions of corporate capital and the nation-state system (and its international affiliates and guarantors). These social forms rely on strategies, visions, and horizons for globalization on behalf of the poor that can be characterised as "grassroots globalization" or, put in a slightly different way, as "globalization from below." (2002, 3)

However, this insistence on the emancipatory potential of NGO networks as communities of choice, both local and global, raises some important questions about power relations. It is difficult to argue that NGOs operate autonomously with respect to the states that regulate their existence and may provide them with funding, or with respect to corporate capital, which flows through both direct sponsorship and grant-making foundations. NGOs have become the preferred conduits for foreign development and humanitarian aid because they allow international agencies to bypass regimes they view as corrupt or inefficient and fit their proprietary aid models into local settings in a more direct way (Carroll 1992; Fischer 1997). Moreover, NGOs are simultaneously local and transnational, and their forms of intervention into the lives of local populations allow other transnational actors to circumvent states to enact their own programs of change. To challenge state strategies of rule, NGOs themselves may appeal to transnational ideals and networks (Fischer 1997). NGOs formulate agendas and organize social action in dynamic tension with both governments and corporations, remaking notions of citizenship and forms of civic action along the way.

Early attempts to theorize the proliferation of NGOs within a normative paradigm resulted in the elaboration of complex taxonomies and specialized terminology. Organizations were classified according to size and scale of operations (for example, local, regional, national, or global), as well as according to the kind of institutional relationships they participated in with governments and international organizations such as the United Nations and the World Bank. The fruit of these labors was an alphabet soup of acronyms (BONGOS, INGOS, GONGOS, and so on) that did little to clarify the practices and forms of thought that NGOs serve to facilitate in different contexts. While classical liberal state theory tends to imagine a clear divide between public and private fields of power, and hence between NGOs and the state, theories of governmentality have instead emphasized the continuities between state and civil society in terms of power relations. More recent studies tend to focus on the everyday practices of NGOs and what these reveal about the production of subjects and modes of expertise. Unlike classical liberal theory, these have also highlighted the unintended consequences of NGO projects and practices (Bernal and Grewal 2014, 4–5). I argue that despite the ways in which they are commonly distinguished from both state and market institutions within the normative liberal paradigm, NGOs work to supplement both states and corporate capital (Richard 2009).

To illuminate this aspect, I propose to analyze the NGO form as a quasi-object. The concept was originally elaborated by Michel Serres ([1980] 2007) and Bruno Latour ([1991] 1993) as a means of theorizing how objects constructed by human actors in turn come to act upon those subjects themselves. On the one hand, the quasi-object is a thing—a tool or form produced and deployed by human actors in order to accomplish a concrete objective. However, a quasi-object is not inert; nor is the human actor's influence over it unidirectional. Once deployed in a specific context, the quasi-object acquires a kind of indirect agency in the sense that its use influences the behavior and worldview of the actors who use it, thus helping to reshape social relations. I propose to apply this concept to NGOs in two ways: to examine how the NGO form comes to be standardized in response to pressure from states and funders to render operations legible at a distance, and how NGOs in turn come to participate in the rationalization of social and political change. My aim is to ascertain the forms of thought and action, of sociability and of politics, enabled by the deployment of the NGO form in this specific historical and cultural context.

In Mexico, as elsewhere, NGOs have functioned as intermediaries in the reconfiguration of citizenship. In fact, Mexico's NGO boom took place precisely at the intersection of a nationwide movement for democracy and civil rights, and a top-down program of neoliberal reforms that would dramatically alter Mexico's economy. During the 1980s and 1990s, a group of activists in the Tulancingo Valley founded NGOs dedicated to promoting rural development, human rights, and environmental conservation because the existing institutions (governmental and religious) appeared to lack the capacity or will to address the region's most urgent social problems: poverty, ignorance, disease, and environmental degradation. Through this work, they also sought to cultivate a new, more egalitarian vision of Mexican democracy. NGOs seemed to offer an institutional form distinct from but recognizable by the state, which they could use as a means of pressuring the state to fulfill the economic and political rights of marginalized citizens. Far from merely representing the preformed interests of a specific class or groups, however, these new Tulancingo NGOs became sites of cultural production—of practices, identities, and networks, and of the symbols and relationships that tie them to one another. Neoliberal democracy was brought into being through practice, involving the continual articulation of meaning and means.

Neoliberal Democracy and Mexico's NGO Boom

Although few scholars agree on the precise moment at which Mexico's transition to democracy began, most acknowledge the influence of the 1968 Tlatelolco massacre on the development of the NGOs, which would eventually lead the democratization movement of the late 1990s. Independent unions and student movements had been active for some time before this event, but the 1968 massacre marked a public loss of legitimacy on the part of the Mexican state. This was soon followed by a series of external blows to the PRI's monopoly on power, including the 1980s' debt crisis, which reduced the capacity of the corporatist apparatus to contain discontent through patronage, population growth leading to land invasions throughout the countryside, and a growing liberation theology movement that encouraged Catholics to question authoritarian hierarchies.

Mexico's experiments with neoliberal restructuring began as a project of elite technocrats and politicians within the ruling party. In the wake of the lost decade of the 1980s, groups within the economics ministry, many of them trained in US universities, sought to "modernize" Mexico's political economy by reducing state ownership and regulation while promoting trade and foreign investment. They sought primarily to leverage Mexico's connections to the United States and during the last twenty years have increasingly emphasized this relationship over their ties with the rest of Latin America (Rus and Tinker Salas 2006, 7). President Carlos Salinas (1988–1994) promoted NAFTA as the key to Mexico's entry into the first world, and even after the opposition victory of 2000, many of the tenets of his approach have been recycled by successive National Action Party (Partido de Acción Nacional, PAN) and PRI administrations. Political reforms were part of that package as a response to pressure from movements for human and indigenous rights and protest movements that resisted earlier rounds of structural adjustment, and as a response to the need to assure investors of the rule of law and political stability. However, Mexico's one-party state was able to push through painful economic reforms as a result of a near monopoly on political power. The institutional reforms advocated by even the most progressive branches of the PRI were limited to what Centeno (1994) has called "democracy within reason"—cleaner elections accompanied by the cordoning off of economic policy from political contestation. However, the relative autonomy of those elites in instituting their reform program was attenuated after 1994. The eruption of the Zapatista rebellion and the popularity it enjoyed both at home and abroad made it impossible for the government to ignore resistance to neoliberalism or to contain it via the conventional combination of repression and patronage. In addition, the devaluation of the peso and the concomitant US bailout meant that much of Mexico's economic policy would continue to be determined from without, according to Washington Consensus orthodoxy. Structural adjustment trimmed the legal responsibilities of the state for social services, and political reforms opened up new arenas for citizen participation in government.

The period of the 1990s was marked by an NGO boom in Mexico as organized groups sought to take advantage of these domestic openings and enhanced international funding opportunities. Various NGOs played a vital role in producing the democratic transition, but their modes of engagement with the state and international and domestic funders during this period and in the years directly following the 2000 elections would profoundly shape the future course of Mexican democracy.

Mexico is considered part of a larger third wave of democratic transitions that began in the late twentieth century. The transition paradigm launched during the Reagan administration aspired to provide a universal academic model for understanding political upheaval and change in authoritarian regimes. Democratization was portrayed as an orderly progression of key stages: opening (a period of political liberalization and struggle resulting in the weakening of the regime), breakthrough (the fall of the regime and the rise of a new system, marked by free elections), and finally consolidation (a slow process of institutional reforms and the strengthening of civil society and democratic culture) (Carothers 2002). Although this model was largely ahistorical, it was congruent with neoliberal orthodoxy, which proclaimed the primacy of economic freedom and implied that political freedom and stability would naturally follow. The transition model deeply influenced the agendas of major international foundations and funding agencies working in Mexico in the 1990s and early 2000s, especially with regard to projects aimed at supporting the consolidation stage. However, philosophical traditions dating back to the early days of the republic warned that entrenched relationships of social dependency posed a serious obstacle to the free participation of the marginalized classes in the public sphere, giving rise to a class of entrepreneurial political intermediaries (Hale 1989). Mexican intellectuals and international observers promoted the growth of a third sector composed of NGOs as an antidote to this problem of representation, a laboratory for producing active democratic citizens (Deakin 2001; Putnam 2000). Philanthropic and governmental efforts to foment civic engagement focused on developing an independent civil society as a step toward democratic consolidation (Carothers 2002). These efforts were often coterminous with economic development projects that encouraged various forms of participation by target populations as a means of organizing consent around and making recipients more responsible for project outcomes (Cooke and Kothari 2001). In this context, the proliferation of NGOs was regarded as an indication of the strength of civil society in overcoming corporatism and forging new forms of civic engagement (Olvera Rivera 1999a, 1999b; Verduzco, List, and Salamon 2002).

In practice, however, the political, economic, and social changes mediated by NGOs were much more complex and contradictory. Contrary to the assumptions of many transition theorists, civic associations have a long history in Mexico, predating both populism and revolutionary nationalism (Forment 2003). Carlos Forment argues that third wave transition models tend to overemphasize electoral politics and institutional change, obscuring some interesting continuities and long-term trends. Among them is the interaction between daily practices and institutional structures in the creation of a unique democratic tradition rooted in the idiom of civic Catholicism, which Forment describes as an ethic of reasoned self-rule enacted via a rich associational life, derived from the Jesuit doctrine of probabilism. He argues that civic democracy "understood in Toquevillian terms as a daily practice and form of life rooted in social equality, mutual recognition, and political liberty" (2003, xi) was already in existence in Mexico by the mid-nineteenth century, although it has sometimes coexisted and sometimes conflicted with authoritarianism. According to Forment, these civic democratic practices have at times enabled people to live "with their backs to the state" (xi). Although Forment's central purpose is to argue for a new historical understanding of democratization in Latin America, his insights can be applied to interrogate the relationship between modern NGOs and earlier associational forms. In twentieth-century Mexican history, as we shall see later, NGOs emerged precisely as a means for people to "live with their backs to the state" and later became a means of organizing to hold the state accountable to citizens. However, the articulation between NGOs and antipolitics also aided their incorporation as partners in projects of neoliberal rule in ways that ultimately limit their social and political autonomy. In fact, strong tensions have emerged between some social assistance NGOs and others with more radical political positions during a period of retrenchment in which class divisions have deepened sharply (Shefner 2007, 184). Entrenched inequality remains as great a problem in the posttransition era as it was for neo-Tocquevillian analyses of transition that emphasized the impact of traditions of dependency and deference on the development of a democratic public sphere. A more nuanced account of how neoliberal democracy has been cultivated and contested in rural Mexico is made possible by attending to specific regional histories of capitalist development in connection with multiple translocal trajectories of political, economic, and cultural change. Viewed from an out of the way place like the Tulancingo River Valley, continuities over time in forms of rule and modes of civic action become more visible.

Locating the Tulancingo River Valley

The southern border of the state of Hidalgo lies only forty kilometers away from the Monument to the Mexican Revolution, in Mexico City, but this proximity and the close economic and political links (between them) do not, paradoxically, prevent it from being a place unknown to residents of the capital, or to the majority of Mexicans.

— ARTURO HERRERA CABAÑAS,
Los Movimientos Campesinos en el Estado de Hidalgo

The data are illustrative in themselves; it is not even necessary to indicate them region by region; in Hidalgo there is more illiteracy, fewer services, almost half of the dwellings have only dirt floors, etc. It is clear that we are dealing with one of the most Third World states in our Third World country.

— IRMA EUGENIA GUTIÉRREZ,
Hidalgo: Sociedad, Economía, Política, Cultura

The territory that is now the state of Hidalgo formed an integral part of six major civilizations even before the arrival of the Spanish in 1521. It has long been regarded as a provincial enclave, central to the functioning of imperial states but always politically and economically subsidiary. This status has made the land fertile for the cultivation of utopian experiments by powerful elites. The city of Tulancingo (its Nahua name means "the place behind the tule reeds") lies in a large valley crisscrossed by multiple tributaries of the Tulancingo River, roughly halfway between Mexico City and the Atlantic coast, at the mouth of the Sierra Madre Oriental (Figure 1). Its location made it an important agricultural region as well as a trading center for the Toltec and Aztec civilizations. The ruins at nearby Huapalcalco are composed of multiple historical layers of construction and are thought to be some of the oldest in Mesoamerica. Since colonial times, Tulancingo has been the mercantile and religious capital of the region, hosting both a commercial center and the seat of the local archdiocese, one of the most conservative in central Mexico. It is known as "the refuge of the ancient conquerors." During the early colonial period, a son of the Spanish conquistador Hernán Cortés and the infamous Malinche owned an estate there. The outlying regions were later home to Pedro Romero de Terreros, the count of Regla, owner of the silver mines of the Pachuca region (now the state capital), and the vast system of haciendas that served them. Originally part of the state of Mexico, Hidalgo supplied the capital with raw materials essential to the life of the colony, including silver, wool, meat, pulque, and hides. Despite its designation as a separate state in 1824, geographical diversity and lack of transportation routes prevented Hidalgo from achieving any measure of internal territorial coherence until late in the twentieth century. Its five major regions—Pachuca, the plains of Apan, the Huasteca, the Mezquital Valley, and the Valley of Tulancingo—all related separately to the capital as enclaves but had relatively little interaction with one another. After the Revolution, Tulancingo's economy developed as a center of dairy and livestock production, and a medium-size textile industry accompanied by various food-processing operations rounded out the region's economic diversity. In the late 1960s the city's manufacturing base began to grow, and a new satellite facility was located there to broadcast the 1968 Olympic Games. It experienced a new population boom in the 1980s as people displaced by the Mexico City earthquake relocated there to newly built housing tracts.

Estados Unidos Mexicanos

①   Hidalgo
②   Valle de Tulancingo
③   Tulancingo

Figure 1. Map of Tulancingo Valley. Elaborated by Ricardo Nurko Ja-vnozon and Antonio Sanchez Ortega.

In the mid-twentieth century Tulancingo remained Hidalgo's second city, a conservative region ruled by a close-knit bourgeoisie, including landown-ers, merchants, and owners of local textile mills. The Catholic Church ex-ercised more political weight there than elsewhere in the state. The church hierarchy dictated both private morals and the public social agenda by set-ting the terms of social interaction. One older member of this provincial elite described her parents' generation to me as *comesantos*, or "saint-eaters," outwardly pious but strict in their observance of social boundaries. The term is derived from a local expression, *comer santos y cagar diablos* (to consume saints and shit devils), used to describe those of the upper class who took communion faithfully each week in the cathedral but would have a peon whipped for looking them in the eyes or wearing a hat in their presence. A local schoolteacher, the son of a campesino, spelled out the legendary conservatism of Tulancingo's upper classes for me over lunch one afternoon:

> During the Conquest, this was the home of Cortés' son and a center for Franciscan missionaries. During the War of Independence, Tulancingo was loyalist. When the French invaded, they welcomed Emperor Maximilian and his family. The house where they stayed is still standing to one side of the plaza. During the wars of the Reforma, Tulancingo was Conservative. In the Revolution, Tulancingo sided with Porfirio Díaz, and they declared public mourning when the Maderistas rode down out of the hills and took the town. The hacendados rejected the claims of the ejiditarios until into the 1940s, and then they gave them only the worst land. In the 1980s and 1990s the PRI murdered PRD [Democratic Revolutionary Party (Partido de la Revolución Democrática)] activists and organizers for the teachers' union.

This is the environment into which Hidalgo Development (HD), Tulancingo's first independent development NGO, was born. In the late 1960s and early 1970s, when agrarian violence unleashed by the forces of modernization threatened to spill over into the Valley of Tulancingo and upset this conservative social order, HD was launched by the sons of two elite families as a reformist civic improvement project. Agrarian issues once again became a major point of contention in Mexico's "democratic transition." As Hart (2002a) points out, agrarian questions that emerge from the enactment of neoliberalizing projects are not only about land or agriculture per se. They also speak to debates over disappearing social rights and redistributive justice that are often shunted aside or invalidated as official democratization projects become wedded to economic liberalization schemes. Ideological struggles over the fate of the countryside serve as "partial interpreters" of larger systemic shifts (Williams 1973, 294). By telling the story of the growth of Tulancingo's NGO sector and how its work helped to transform the social landscape of the region, this book reveals the complex roots and routes of change in neoliberal Mexico.

Fieldwork and Methodology

I first visited Tulancingo in 1996 and undertook preliminary research visits to local development project sites in 1998 and 2000. The primary participant observation and interviews for the project were completed in Tulancingo and the surrounding rural areas from August 2002 to August 2003, with brief follow-up visits in 2004, 2005, 2006, 2009, and 2013. The research was designed as a "vertical slice" of the problem of neoliberal democracy in rural Mexico, meaning that it entailed studying the various contexts within which the problem is situated in order to discover the connections among them (Nader 1980). I began at HD's headquarters in the city of Tulancingo, where I lived with and worked alongside the organization's staff. From there my research moved outward, working "up, down and sideways" (Nader 1969) to get at other components of how neoliberal democracy works in and through the countryside. Through archival and secondary research, I examined national discourses around and government strategies for accomplishing projects of economic and political liberalization. In addition, I looked at the history of and recent trends in the Mexican NGO sector as a whole by working with members of the Mexican Center for Philanthropy (CEMEFI) as well as participants in several of the larger NGO coalitions who were the power behind the prodemocracy movement of the 1990s (including Alianza Civica, Movimiento Cuidadano para la Democracia, and Red TDT). In a sideways move, I interviewed staff from six additional Tulancingo-based organizations to analyze the emergence and development of an NGO community there. In researching local organizations' participation in transnational NGO networks, I made use of HD's correspondence and funding archives. I conducted participant observation during four separate NGO solidarity tours to HD project sites, interviewing foreign delegation members and surveying past tour participants from Spain and the United States. I also interviewed HD staff members and tour host community members about their experiences. The work of situating NGO development efforts over the years also led me to various state and local government offices. Perhaps most importantly, I spent significant amounts of time in four of the eight rural communities in which HD maintained project sites, visiting the others on occasion. It was there that I learned the most about how life in the Hidalgan countryside has changed over the past several decades and how

NGO workers and rural people go about engaging those changes in meaningful ways. The names of these communities and of the campesinos, NGO workers, state officials, and others (with the exception of well-known public figures and politicians) who participated in this study have been changed or omitted to protect their privacy.

Cultivation: An Organizing Metaphor

The labor of cultivation is central to the historical identity of Mexican campesinos, encoded in the revolutionary Plan de Ayala as a condition of claims to territory and livelihood (*la tierra es de quien la trabaja*) and later transformed into the bedrock of a corporatist social pact that endured for seven decades. Despite the sweeping social changes of the last century, yearly cycles of planting and harvesting still guide the religious and social calendars of many rural communities, and their regularity or interruption serve as symbolic interpreters of the health of political and social relations. Metaphors of cultivation also appear in the discourse of NGO workers, who speak of new practices and ideas as seeds to be planted in the soil of rural villages or in the hearts of foreign donors. But beyond an understanding of how such folk terminology elaborates shared worldviews and moral economies, the metaphor of cultivation can also yield theoretical insights for anthropologists and others seeking to understand processes of cultural and political change.

As the semantic roots of the words themselves suggest, citizenship and civic virtues have traditionally been grounded in the lives of cities. Nonetheless, managing the relationships between cities and the agrarian hinterlands that supply the material conditions of possibility for such civilizations creates governmental challenges and struggles that come to influence ideals and practices of citizenship. The proper disposition of common resources, control over territories and populations, the extraction of labor, tribute, and taxes from rural communities, the creation and expansion of markets, and the promulgation of integrated development schemes—all are part and parcel of nation-building projects. A focus on cultivation therefore encourages us to adopt a deeper historical perspective, paying close attention to the sustained interactions between country and city that influence ideas about democracy and inequality over time.

Cultivation also draws attention to the cultural labor implied by the construction of subjects, institutions, organizations, and practices proper to particular visions of citizenship and civic life. Rural development projects in twentieth-century Mexico were broadly aimed at integrating rural people more fully into the life of the nation and transforming them into agents of national progress. Such projects ranged widely in scope and scale, but all relied on the cultural labor of a new sort of intermediary, whose own motivations, worldview, techniques, and frustrations are important to understand. Their ways of working are related to those of development technicians and NGO personnel in other places but have also been intimately shaped by Mexican history and cultural logics of intermediation. The work of cultivating and caring for relationships undergirds the work of development. While the former is constant, the pace of the latter is uneven, characterized by periods of intense activity followed by fallow periods when resources are scarce. Some terrains are more amenable to cultivation, while others require heavier investments of labor and resources. Shifts in political, economic, or natural climates all have the potential to reroute or derail projects of improvement. Cultivation changes the landscape over time, but not always in predictable ways, as the concluding chapter demonstrates.

This book is designed to present the complex dynamics of rural citizenship and public morality in Mexico's neoliberal democracy from various points of entry, exploring distinct aspects of the changes rural development NGOs have cultivated in the Tulancingo Valley. Chapter 1 traces the historical development of the citizenship question in postindependence Mexico, with particular attention to the ways in which the figure of the campesino comes to be reframed in local and national struggles over modernity and globalization. It contextualizes the role of modern development NGOs in helping marginalized groups to claim their rights as citizens and to participate in formal political processes, highlighting the complex relationships that develop in practice between these new organizational forms and earlier historical models of civic action. Chapter 2 examines the growth of Tulancingo's third sector, from its origins in the late 1970s until the end of the Fox administration, revealing important insights into the relationships between NGOs and the political class with whom they are intimately, if sometimes uncomfortably, engaged. In the 1990s, poor Mexican peasants came to be regarded as iconic victims of structural adjustment and free trade policies under the Washington Consensus. The Zapatista rebellion helped to draw attention to the human costs of neoliberal reform, but institutional and demographic shifts also meant that the countryside was losing its traditional political importance as a source of votes and as a symbol of national identity. Chapter 3 focuses on the lived experience of agricultural crisis in the Tulancingo Valley, exploring the way climatic anomalies and anthropogenic hazards have intersected with newly generated forms of social vulnerability to create a governmental disaster that served to foreclose traditional collective forms of political agency. In Chapter 4, the focus shifts from campesinos' experiences of change to those of NGO workers. This chapter examines the relationship of Tulancingo NGOs to more traditional forms of mediation and brokerage, highlighting the categories of social action through which NGO workers make sense of their own interventions. Examining this relationship to past cultural forms reveals the limits that civil society institutions face in the neoliberal era, as well as the ways in which NGOs, and not just their project participants, are rendered vulnerable by large-scale transformations. The capacity of Tulancingo NGOs to pursue their programs of social change in the countryside depends in large part upon their perceived legitimacy as intermediaries. While the history of the third sector in Tulancingo reveals the long-standing importance of international ties for local NGOs, relationships with partners from the United States and Europe have become increasingly crucial to the survival of some NGOs in a difficult political and economic climate. Chapter 5 reconsiders some unexamined assumptions embedded in the network metaphors that animate contemporary social theory, elucidating how transnational NGO networks are enacted by situated social subjects as they rework extant cultural forms for use in new contexts, in turn imbuing institutional relationships with new meaning and value. I examine how Hidalgan NGO workers perform the cultural work necessary to conceptualize, configure, and maintain the relationships between these disparate groups of peasants, activists, and professionals by reworking local notions of solidarity and reciprocity to produce a sense of transnational kinship. The concluding chapter considers the implications of these transformations, both for the long-term outcome of the democratic transition in Mexico and for the future of global civil society activism. It examines how cultures of capitalism intersect with evolving modes of social solidarity to produce new forms of governance.

CHAPTER I

Developing Rural Citizens

Old and New Liberalisms

The language of citizenship gained global prominence in the nineteenth century with the formation of modern nation-states. It was revived and re-worked in the late twentieth century as the capacity of those nation-states to manage the collective lives of citizens was challenged from without and within. The formation of citizens has traditionally been approached from two distinct perspectives. The first emphasizes citizenship as a corollary of state-building and economic development projects, which entail the produc-tion of particular sorts of subjects capable of animating new social worlds. The other examines how "sovereignty of the people" is enacted through associational life, generating practices and strategies that enhance the ca-pacity of citizens to generate social power within particular domains (Bel-lamy 2008). In Mexico, renewed attention to the citizen as subject and the practices of associational life have coincided with the reconfiguration of the rights and responsibilities of citizens during a protracted restructuring of the economy and formal political system.

Like those of many postcolonial nations, Mexico's liberal institutions have historically been built on regimes of exclusion that rendered indigenous and rural peoples citizens in name only. Their access to the formal rights and rites of citizenship has thus been limited in practice, despite their participation in other forms of local association and governance. In order to understand the role of NGOs in producing and responding to these changes, it is first necessary to examine the political and social contexts from which they emerged. Mexico has a long history of cultural revolutions in which contested projects of rule have been negotiated after extended periods of social upheaval (Corrigan 1994). At each of these historical junctures, different approaches have been proposed for balancing individual freedoms with collective entitlements, as well as for reconciling European and US political models with indigenous forms of government and social organization (Hale 1989; Lomnitz 2001). This chapter traces the historical development of the citizenship question in post-Independence Mexico, with particular attention to the ways in which rural denizens have been conceptualized as dependent subjects incapable of full participation in public life. It focuses on the historical interplay between liberal ideas of individuated citizenship and corporatist forms of solidarity and reciprocity, a dynamic that has shaped the outcome of cyclical political, economic, and social crises over the course of modern Mexican history. Both nineteenth-century liberalism and the more recent neoliberal reforms produced deep dislocations in the Mexican countryside, changing how rural people were incorporated into the body politic.[1] These ideas shaped the worldviews and strategies of early NGO organizers in rural Hidalgo, as well as Hidalgan campesinos' own understandings of themselves as political subjects.

Campesinos, Civic Values, and Public Morality

The campesino has long served as a symbolic anchor for public discourse around Mexican national identity and the nation's path to modernity. This symbolic value of the campesino in national political discourse draws from other values—moral, historical, cultural—purported to inhere in actual rural denizens, as well as from the economic and political value of the countryside to the city in the quest for modern capitalist development. The moral character and citizenship capacity of campesinos repeatedly surfaces in historical debates over Mexico's "agrarian question," a term that first appeared in economics literature in the late nineteenth and early twentieth centuries.[2] Byres explains: "In its broadest meaning, the agrarian question may be defined as the continuing existence in the countryside of a poor country of substantive obstacles to an unleashing of the forces capable of generating economic development, both inside and outside agriculture" (1991, 9).[3] During both of the fin de siècle crises under analysis here, the relations between country and city were played out in public discourse around the moral and civic character of rural people, whose supposed backwardness figured as a major impediment to the economic and political development of the nation.

In addition to the political uses of the campesino as public symbol, Joseph and Nugent (1994) point out that during each of the three major social upheavals in Mexican national history—the War of Independence, the Reforma, and the Revolution—powerful antagonists attempted to mobilize the support of rural people. Drawing on the work of Corrigan and Sayer (1985), they argue that in each of these historical moments, a complex articulation between popular cultures and projects of state formation has produced a cultural revolution—a transformation not just in how people are ruled and how goods are produced and exchanged but also in how people make sense of the world and their place in it. These cultural revolutions give birth to the idioms through which state power is organized and exercised and through which subordinated groups must struggle for emancipation. The production of meaning and the production of power relations are thus coterminous.[4] Accordingly, the Revolution was not the starting point for building the political idioms of modern Mexico; rather, many of the symbols and tropes that would later animate public discourses about the nation, including the iconic figure of the campesino, can be traced to earlier periods.

The concept of public morality is useful for deciphering the place of rural people in the citizen problematics of both the nineteenth and twentieth centuries because it reveals the often informal ways in which political and social change has been cultivated in rural areas. Escalante Gonzalbo (1992) argues that conflicts among competing republican, liberal, and democratic traditions forged the characteristic features of Mexican political order and public morality (*moral publica*) during the nineteenth century. He uses the concept of public morality to call attention to the regularities of conduct in public life through which civic values are manifested. Even in situations where governments are illegitimate or ineffective, institutions are discredited, or political values are not widely shared, public morality undergirds political order by enabling actors to interpret and predict the behavior of others. Although rural people were for the most part excluded from full participation in the formal political system for much of the nineteenth and part of the twentieth century, attending to the development and dynamism of public morality enables us to appreciate the ways in which they participated in the political order and were represented in public discourse during successive historical periods. This in turn sheds light on the operating assumptions of the early development NGOs that began working in rural Hidalgo in the 1970s. It also helps to explain how Hidalgan campesinos' own understandings of their political agency changed under neoliberalism.

Pastoral Predicaments: Nineteenth-Century Liberalism and Rural Hidalgo

Several important features of Mexico's competing great traditions of public morality emerged between 1821 and 1880, roughly the period from the end of the War of Independence until the beginning of a period of prolonged stability with the dictatorship of General Porfirio Díaz (Escalante Gonzalbo 1992). During this era, a violent political conflict emerged between the Conservatives, who favored the maintenance of the colonial power structure with minor modifications, and the Liberals, who sought to modernize Mexico by restructuring property relations, promoting private capital, and establishing the state as the manager of economic development. The nineteenth-century liberal vision, enshrined in the Reform Laws of the 1850s and 1860s, proclaimed an end to the legacy of the colonial era and the beginning of the new nation's first modernization project. However, governing the largely rural and indigenous population and fragmented territories that made up the new nation presented particular problems (Hale 1989). How was Mexico's government to articulate rural to urban and make modern citizens out of isolated communities dominated by the alliance of Church and hacienda? This grand undertaking demanded the creation of new mechanisms for political representation and participation, and the outcome set the stage for future debates around agrarian questions and the nature of rural citizenship.

From the beginning, matters of civic order and morality were intimately linked. The creation of a democratic political system was framed as a civilizing mission. Creole elites were convinced that Mexico could be remade as a member of the modern community of nations if only it could cast off its colonial legacy and find the correct model for creating a new political system. They looked abroad for inspiration, primarily to France, Spain, and the United States. "Almost everyone believed in good faith that this imaginary order was possible, that it was a fact in the 'civilized' world. They did not know, or did not want to know, of the violence of public life in Spain, French authoritarianism, or the corruption in the US. It was due to this . . . that pragmatism would always carry the stigma of being a transaction with barbarism" (Escalante Gonzalbo 1992, 18). Different political factions advocated for the adoption of different foreign models, but all of them concurred that Mexico's seeming inability to simultaneously foster popular sovereignty and maintain territorial supremacy stemmed from some basic moral failure on the part of the citizenry. Mexican liberals despaired of ever modernizing Mexico so long as they were forced to negotiate with large landowners, regional strongmen, and various intermediaries in order to retain effective control over the national territory.

Active Citizenship and Nineteenth-Century Liberalism

The creation of an active citizenry entailed a radically new conceptualization of the body politic. The civic model the liberals sought to institute during that formative period in Mexico's history rested on a particular definition of the citizen as the basic unit of social life. This citizen was imagined as a rational individual, constructed in explicit contrast to hierarchical and corporate structures of the type that prevailed in colonial society. This civic model distinguished between a private sphere, where self-interest ruled, and a public sphere, where individuals behaved in a responsible, solidary manner in addressing collective problems. The key to modernizing Mexico was seen to be the production of a modern citizenry.

In the early days of the new Republic, suffrage rights formed the core of political rights as a result of their central role in political representation. The ideals and rights of liberal citizenship were predicated on a series of constitutive exclusions, which were highly racialized and gendered (Alonso 2005). While property ownership and literacy were not erected as barriers to full political citizenship, women, slaves, servants, and others classified as economically dependent were disqualified from suffrage. Liberalism promised a home for all in modernity, but some subjects would need to be converted or elevated before they could be incorporated into the nation. Hence the production of rural citizens became, in many instances, a pastoral project. And while the progressive extension of suffrage was viewed as an expansion of the modern state, extended suffrage was also seen as a problem for the maintenance of political stability. Electoral practices often failed to conform to normative expectations. Sabato notes that "the key to electoral success was the creation and mobilization of clienteles in networks . . . Actual voters were far removed from the image of the autonomous, individual citizen in full command of his political rights, who attends the polls peacefully to cast his ballot" (2001, 1301). Instead, clientelist networks were mobilized as collective forces to participate in electoral processes characterized by violent confrontation and negotiation. Even so, in the mid-1800s only a very small percentage of Mexico's population actually participated in elections.

Forment (2003) and others have argued that too much emphasis has been placed on electoral politics, leading scholars to neglect the historical significance of other forms of civic action, especially the forms of association and sociability that developed in concert with these projects of political modernization. The roots of these institutions and practices can be traced to the late eighteenth century, when Western Europe witnessed the "spread of associations of a new type, based on the free will of their individual members, [which] inaugurated a whole new set of communicative practices presumably governed by the laws of reason" (Sabato 2001, 1305). The expansion of civic and voluntary associations was viewed as an ideal site for producing these new subjects and forms of collective action. In Mexico, however, membership in such groups was limited almost exclusively to elite and urban populations. Ideas about citizenship were diffused and debated in political clubs and by a growing number of newspaper readers but also circulated among members of Freemason organizations and *tertulias*, informal salons that met in coffeehouses and private homes.

On the whole, the Tulancingo Valley remained deeply conservative and staunchly Catholic throughout the Independence and Reform periods. In contrast, Pachuca's role as a cradle of Hidalgan liberalism is commonly attributed to its history as a mining center. The arrival of British mining companies in the early nineteenth century propitiated the immigration of English and Welsh technicians and operators. As their numbers grew, and especially after the 1857 Constitution established freedom of religion, they established their own Methodist congregations. Members included both immigrants and lifelong Pachucans, the majority of them educated. Among them was Marcelino Duran, a doctor who helped to found Hidalgo's first institution of higher education as well as a newspaper, *La Libertad*. These new congregations were later bolstered by the arrival of Methodist missionaries from the United States, who helped to expand church membership and found a series of schools in locations throughout the state (Menes Llaguno 2006, 190–191). The new civic associations they established, like the liberal paradigm of citizenship itself, were adapted from foreign models. The new forms of sociability that they fostered took root in a limited way in elite circles, while communal institutions and more traditional forms of sociability, such as religious brotherhoods or confraternities, held fast in the rural areas.

"The figure of the modern citizen proposed by the liberals—the abstract and universal individual, free and equal to the rest . . . overlapped with more traditional notions of the body politic that evoked the institutions of the colonial and even pre-colonial times: the pueblos, the communities, the subject, the *vecino* (neighbor or resident)" (Sabato 2001, 1292–1293). The process of cultivating citizens was a complicated one, an arena of negotiation rather than one of seamless unfolding. In rural areas, the project of political individuation often came up against entrenched forms of corporatism and intermediation, rooted in the moral economy of peasant communities as well as their protracted histories of spiritual and military conquest.

Civilizing Rural Society

To politicians and writers of the nineteenth century, the Mexican countryside was problematic terrain for cultivating Enlightenment values or democracy. Rural rebellion—rife throughout the period—presented resistance to both state authority and the rights of private capital alike. Urban elites hardly expected rural people to uphold a political order that had subjugated them for centuries, yet this also meant that the latter were suspected of lacking the will to identify with the new nation over and beyond their local and corporate loyalties, and hence to participate fully in civic life as rational individuals. The very marginalization of rural people from political life, it was thought, betrayed a lack of capacity for citizenship.[5] This was especially true in Hidalgo, which became infamous for the prevalence of armed banditry during and after the French Intervention (1861–1867). Apart from the treacherous terrain, rendered nearly impassable by floods in the rainy season, the insecurity of Hidalgan roads was legendary. Most of the main routes between Mexico City and the coast of Veracruz were controlled by organized groups who robbed and kidnapped travelers, often with the tacit cooperation of remote indigenous and mestizo villages that sheltered them. Property owners, officials, merchants, and mine operators traveled with uniformed companies of armed guards (Herrera Cabañas 1995, 18–19). Indeed, a nineteenth-century bandit hideout on the outskirts of Tulancingo, a hillside cave called the Devil's Hole (*el Hoyo del Diablo*), is still legendary among residents even though the thick forest that once hid it has long since been cut down. The national political class felt it incumbent upon them to "civilize" the rural and indigenous peoples and rid them of their relations of dependence on the owners of the great landed estates. Nonetheless, while campesinos were not regarded as potential citizens, they remained an important political resource for members of the political class and were to become a key symbol in the post-Revolutionary national pantheon.

Public Morality and Rural Society

Although campesinos were not thought to be endowed with civic virtue, they did possess their own idioms of public morality. Escalante Gonzalbo (1992) argues, following Wolf, that for rural Mexicans of the nineteenth century, the most important reference point was the community, imagined not as a straightforward demographic unit but rather as a kind of political structure. As towns and *republicas de indios*[6] during the colonial period, many rural communities had retained a measure of autonomy derived from control over their lands and the persistence of traditional forms of self-government. However, Spanish authorities converted the tradition of faena into a form of tribute. In place of the traditional mutual assistance functions of the *calpulli*,[7] Catholic missionaries introduced the confraternity (*cofradia*), a civil-religious association of laypeople devoted to the worship of a particular saint, relic, or sanctuary. *Cofradias* organized charitable works and provided for the observance of yearly rituals, under the close supervision of the Catholic hierarchy. Catholic missionaries also sanctioned the practice of *compadrazgo*, or ritual coparenthood, in association with baptismal rites, and it later expanded to organize a variety of reciprocal obligations for mutual aid (Foster 1953). Hence pre-Conquest self-governance institutions and forms of reciprocity were progressively replaced with social assistance mechanisms grounded in Christian ideas of charity and tightly controlled by the Church hierarchy. In the Independence period, Mexico's insertion into new global markets and the concomitant extension of market relations across new regions would further threaten the foundations of rural community autonomy.

Like agrarian societies elsewhere, these nineteenth-century communities were organized via an ethic of subsistence, with social action directed toward the reduction of risk. According to Scott (1977), reciprocal obligation forms the basic moral criterion of such communities and is applied between social equals as well as across social hierarchies. This same logic guided campesino political conduct, in that

> campesinos seek and prefer personal ties with hacendados or caciques, with whom they can maintain relations of reciprocity. By the same logic, the State tends to appear more as a threat than as a guarantee; in particular taxes, decreed by distant authorities, extracted rigorously and without regard for the particular necessities of each community, are frequently resented as unjust. (Escalante Gonzalbo 1992, 61)

Rural communities sought to reduce political risk by exploiting the competition among rival authorities, seeking the highest authority possibly to intervene as a mediator in local conflicts. The new national state was often too weak to serve as an effective intermediary but did possess the power to effectively extort them.[8]

Figure 2. Chapel (*sagrario*) of the Cathedral of Tulancingo.

The autonomy of rural communities, which stabilized the political dominance of regional elites, presented major problems for the organization of the new state. After Independence, rural communities and *republicas de indios* came to be viewed as relics of the colonial order in need of reform. The latter were reorganized into municipalities (*municipios*) in an attempt to transform the rural political order by taking away some of their autonomy and subordinating them to centralized state control. In many places, this also meant that indigenous communities became subject to mestizo authority. The liberal vision of a democratic and ordered society based on rational individuals was fundamentally at odds with the communitarian morality of peasants. As the state consolidated its power, the pueblos came to be seen as more and more of a threat to this centralized political order.

Relations between the state and rural communities were largely brokered via the work of regional intermediaries with whom local leaders maintained personal reciprocal relationships of mutual confidence and trust based on intimate familiarity (*confianza*). The basis for generating consensus and inducing compliance with state authority was reciprocity rather than ideological compromise or civic virtue. This meant that in practice, the stability of the post-Independence state rested firmly on its capacity for negotiating order rather than an abstract rule of law. Intermediaries did not so much guarantee the obedience of their clients as they brokered their disobedience. The influence of intermediaries depended in turn on networks of loyalties. "The intermediaries were not just charismatic chiefs, they were not representatives of the 'masses' nor of a simple 'pueblo'; they headed up a system of loyalties, organized into corporate bodies and communities. The network of an intermediary was a mechanism of corporative or quasi-corporative political representation" (Escalante Gonzalbo 1992, 111–112). Caciques were often incorporated into the state apparatus as a means of channeling resources to them and their constituents. Although politicians and journalists decried the influence of the caciques, they became even more essential during the mid- to late nineteenth century, a period of foreign invasions, rural rebellions, and bloody struggles over the political organization of the new nation.

Rural Unruliness and Liberal Reforms

Although peasant rebellions recurred throughout the colonial period during times of economic crisis, after Independence they were exacerbated by the promulgation of the Reform Laws, which led to the expansion of the haciendas at the expense of the communal properties of indigenous communities (Herrera Cabañas 1995, 9). The most important of these for rural communities was the Lerdo Law, which mandated the liquidation of all clerical and community property. Its object was to promote economic growth and individualize citizenship by creating a large number of private property owners, but instead it enabled the concentration of indigenous property in the hands of a small elite. According to Barry,

> While brandishing their ideals of individualism and private property, the Liberals set about furthering their own economic interests by occupying lands formerly held by the church and Indians. They further justified this expropriation by claiming that the Indians were an inferior race whose society and culture stood in the way of modernization. Behind the dispossession of Indian land also lay the need of the new agrarian bourgeoisie for an unencumbered rural workforce. (1995, 15)

These privatization schemes would deprive indigenous and peasant communities of 90 percent of their communal lands by 1910, leaving roughly 92 percent of the population landless (Barry 1995, 16). Mallon (1995) argues that local struggles over these reforms—the Lerdo Law in particular—laid the cultural and political groundwork that would enable later post-Revolutionary projects of state formation predicated on land reform and collective representation as "campesinos."

In Hidalgo between 1857 and 1865, only 7 percent of the Church's property was expropriated, reflecting the relative power of the Church in the region. Many of those properties were cemeteries, convents, and hospitals, which passed into the hands of the state. The indigenous communities, however, were dispossessed in short order using a variety of legal and extralegal means (Herrera Cabañas 1995, 31–32). Merchants, miners, and speculators alike invested in this new real estate market, which provided both a safe haven for surplus capital and a measure of social prestige. An estimated two-thirds of Hidalgan peasants lost access to their traditional agricultural lands during this period, forcing them to enter into the service of nearby haciendas as *peones* or to flee to the cities or silver mines to find work. Those who managed to remain on their land were nonetheless forced to pay for access to water, pasture lands, and forests that had formerly existed as community commons. This kind of enclosure led even free peasants to become indebted and dependent on the goodwill of large landowners. Eventually most of the expropriated land ended up in the hands of hacendados, whose private holdings were extensive and often enclosed several villages (Herrera Cabañas 1995, 26–27).

This expansion was also impelled by a shift in the economic orientation of the haciendas themselves. In the latter half of the nineteenth century, many haciendas began to enter into direct production for the market (often Mexico City) rather than serving as supply sources for the owners' other enterprises (such as mining). While the Church lost some of its official political and economic clout in the Reform, the expansion of the haciendas ultimately provided the Catholic hierarchy with a new base of indirect power. The clergy, deprived of their own holdings, found a refuge in the growing haciendas. The hacendados, eager to garner merit for themselves and "civilize" the *peones*, invested great sums in their chapels. The priests obliged by elevating the *peones'* drudgery to an act of worship, promising them a better life in the hereafter. Because of the relative isolation in the interior of the region during this period, hacendados eventually became intermediaries between now landless rural people and the cities. *Peones* on the haciendas depended on their masters for food, clothing, and shelter, and in many cases the hacendados wielded power over life and death on their estates. In the remaining indigenous villages, the caciques "exercised absolute power," negotiating with whatever authority sought to enter their territories (Herrera Cabañas 1995, 67). The Mexico City newspapers portrayed the caciques as the primary source of Hidalgo's insecurity. The only way to impose order on a territory "swarming with bandits," according to one publication, was to "extinguish the *cacicazgos* and feudalism, which still persist here more than in any other state" (quoted in Herrera Cabañas 1995, 68). Hidalgo thus acquired an enduring reputation for feudal backwardness, and its citizens, overwhelmingly rural and poor, appeared to exist outside of (and in many cases to endanger) civic order.

In 1861, during a brief period of peace after the end of the Reform wars, the districts of Tula, Tulancingo, Huejutla, Teotihuacan, and Texcoco petitioned the National Congress to create a new state named after the patriot Miguel Hidalgo y Costilla by partitioning the extensive territory of the State of Mexico. The unfolding of the French intervention interrupted their efforts, as French, British, and Spanish troops arrived at the port of Veracruz in response to President Juárez's suspension of payments on Mexico's foreign debt. In an effort to defend the national territory (and also to address the ongoing campesino rebellions in the Valle del Mezquital and Huasteca), Juárez divided the state of Mexico into three military districts. One of these would eventually become the new state of Hidalgo. While the French were initially turned back at the famous Battle of Puebla on May 5, 1862, they regrouped and managed to take the capital on June 7 of the following year. The commander of the French forces, Elías Federico Forey, named a governing council of 215 notable citizens, including Juan Bautista Ormachea y Ernáiz, bishop of the recently created Diocese of Tulancingo. The council decreed the creation of a hereditary monarchy and offered the throne to Maximilian of Hapsburg, brother of the Austrian emperor. Much to the surprise of Conservative factions, the new emperor confirmed the application of the Reform Laws and failed to restore the properties and privileges of the Church. On a tour of the Tulancingo Valley in 1865, Maximilian visited with the leaders of the fledgling textile industry of the city and stayed overnight in the same house once occupied by Agustín de Iturbide, now popularly referred to as the House of the Emperors. While Maximilian was received with great fanfare in Tulancingo, uprisings against the new imperial ruler broke out elsewhere in the region. When the French were finally driven out in 1867 and the Republic restored, Ormachea was exiled (Menes Llaguno 2006, 162–169). Accordingly, when the new state of Hidalgo was finally created on 1869, Pachuca was designated the capital instead of Tulancingo, which remained a seat of Church power.

The Peasant Problem and Public Morality in the Porfiriato

Under the rule of General Porfirio Díaz (1876–1910), Mexico developed a modern bureaucratic state (albeit with a limited reach) and launched a massive effort at economic development aimed at placing the country on par with Europe and the United States. Economic growth was constant during the Porfiriato, as massive infusions of foreign investment provided the capital necessary to build up the country's infrastructure in transportation, communication, mining, industry, commercial agriculture, and forestry. But export-driven modernization came at a heavy price for rural people. Having lost access to their ancestral lands, most were forced to work in foreign-owned mines and commercial plantations. Widespread hunger led to localized uprisings among the *peones* and workers, as well as major strikes in the northern states (Barry 1995, 17). The gaps between the upper and lower classes were not only socioeconomic but also increasingly regarded as moral.[9] The individual property owner was the ideal Porfirian citizen. While the former group represented the forces of progress, rural people were seen as miring modernization efforts, the result of their seeming disregard for technological innovation and their perceived lack of acquisitive ambition. Rather than attempt to incorporate them, the government resorted to the *pan o palo* method to control them (Buve 1997).[10] This practice would not only help to produce the Revolution but would ultimately frustrate post-Revolutionary efforts at state formation.

The problem vexing Mexico's nineteenth-century liberals was that in practice, "society produced an order alien to and enemy of state institutions, formal authorities, and the inflexibility of the law" (Escalante Gonzalbo 1992, 100). However, Escalante Gonzalbo argues that things were more complex than they appeared. The state apparatus also inadvertently served as an instrument for the consolidation and legitimation of local networks, facilitating the growth of *cacicazgos* but also enabling some communities to "live with their backs to the state" (Forment 2003, 154). Indeed, in rural areas, "there were no citizens because there were no individuals. Security, business, and politics were collective affairs" (Escalante Gonzalbo 1992, 290). This made it hard to conceive of a public interest that went beyond private interests of those groups and collective bodies. The real modes of participation available to rural peoples did not fit easily into the institutional forms of representative democracy. This is precisely the situation Escalante refers to when he says that peasants and other rural denizens during this period were regarded as a political resource by many actors but were not considered capable of properly practicing citizenship.

This was a question both of dependent status and of moral disposition. By the turn of the twentieth century, the ruling elites of the Tulancingo Valley had come to characterize the peasant problem as a Catholic pastoral predicament. Their views regarding the perceived backwardness of the countryside were shaped by a larger intellectual shift that took hold in Mexico during the 1880s and 1890s. General Díaz came to power after a protracted period of upheaval and internecine struggles over the political organization of the country, in which diverse liberal factions all shared the understanding that once political integration and institutionalization took place, peace and prosperity would naturally follow (Hale 1991). Under the

Figure 3. Monument to Benito Juarez in el Jardin
de la Floresta, downtown Tulancingo.

dictatorship, however, the problem of economic development began to take
precedence, and policy making was redirected toward the aims of guaran-
teeing stability through political conciliation. According to Zulema, "This
ideal of material progress was based on a particularly optimistic vision of
the 'inexhaustible' natural wealth of the country, which was contrasted to
the characterization of national economic backwardness, the explanations
and causes of which were continually discussed and debated" (1999, 60).
The political tenor of these debates was shaped by an underlying economic
transformation. As the price of silver softened on the world market and
global demand for agricultural products rose, Mexico began to move away
from mineral exports in favor of agricultural exports. The global demand
for tropical and industrial crops such as henequen, cotton, and coffee was
complemented by a push to achieve self-sufficiency in basic food commodi-
ties. Porfirian elites looked abroad for technologies and production models

that might expand agricultural productivity, seeking to modernize and ratio-
nalize Mexican agriculture. Organizations such as the Mexican Agricultural
Society (Sociedad Agricola Mexicana) spawned local chapters in nearly all
the states of the union, dedicated to disseminating the principles of scientific
agriculture and putting them into practice in particular regional conditions.
The *Bulletin* of the Mexican Agricultural Society's national office and the
published proceedings of state-level conferences provide keen insights into
how agrarian questions were framed in Hidalgo on the eve of the Mexican
Revolution.

Porfirian Pastoralism in the Tulancingo River Valley

The dioceses of Tulancingo convened the first Agricultural Congress
(Congreso Agricola) in the region in September 1904, inviting representatives from the national office of the Mexican Agricultural Society as well as
hacendados and civil authorities from the region. A second was convened
in December 1905, this time with ample representation from members
of the regional Church hierarchy, civil authorities, experts in health and
agronomy, mill owners, ranchers, and landowners. The tone and purpose
of the meetings was distinctly pastoral; the major concerns expressed by
the delegates were the need for modernization in farming equipment and
practices and the high incidence of alcohol use and informal domestic
partnerships among *peones* and other rural denizens. These issues were
distinct but related, as the modernization of Hidalgan agriculture was seen
to be endangered by campesinos' lack of moral and technical competence.
The opening speech given by the bishop of Tulancingo was described in
the official report as

> moving . . . with paternal benevolence and tenderness . . . a grand delinea-
> tion of the moral failings of the countryside's workers, whose regeneration
> was proposed at the initiation of these meetings . . . he insisted upon the
> truth that those peones who are the greatest drunkards and live in greatest
> demoralization are those who least look out for the interests of their pa-
> trones, ergo improving the customs of the servants would also bring about
> positive benefits for their masters. (Sociedad Agricola Mexicana 1906, 8)

If the private lives of *peones* could be brought into line with Church doctrine and the tenets of modern hygiene, the countryside might thereby be rendered more productive and tranquil. Hacendados and overseers were enjoined to provide their dependents with living examples of moral rectitude and the basic conditions necessary to live lives of piety. They were encouraged, for example, to invite priests to the hacienda chapel regularly to perform marriage ceremonies so that rural children might grow up in "honorable" homes, thereby avoiding the moral failures of their parents. Other suggestions included the establishment of primary schools, the provision of medical services to injured workers, and allowing *peones* to cultivate small plots of unused land for their own subsistence.

One of the least heeded recommendations, according to oral histories I collected, was that hacendados reduce the markup on goods sold in the *tienda de raya*, or company store. Isolated from regional markets, *peones* were forced to purchase cloth, medicines, and other goods from these proprietary outlets at inflated prices, at terms that often exceeded 100 percent interest. It was also common at annual holidays for hacendados to grant their *peones* "loans of habilitation" to clothe their families and participate in the festivities. While the rural residents I interviewed recalled both these practices as means for the hacendados to draw *peones* deeper into debt and thus ensure their compliance, the participants in the Agrarian Congress viewed the habilitation loans as contributing to public drunkenness and "lassitude." They characterized the *peones* as incapable of self-control and prone to criminality and violence once they had the means of buying pulque or *aguardiente*. As a solution, the Congress put forth a legislative proposal to stiffen the penalties for public intoxication, proscribing a sentence of one month in jail for a single incident (with or without witnesses) and three to six months and a fine of one hundred pesos for rowdy drunks (*cuando la embriaguez causare simple escandalo*) (Sociedad Agricola Mexicana 1906, 31).[11] While hacendados were enjoined to show greater benevolence toward their dependents out of a sense of patriotism and Christian duty, peasants were viewed as incapable of reason and in need of the collective medicine of a harsh legal regime. The Porfirian public interest was articulated as inhering in proper relationships of paternalism and deference between servant and master. Rural people were neither individuals nor fellow citizens.

Writing in the 1960s, amateur Tulancingo historian Roberto Ocádiz speculated that if the "admirable themes" of those meetings "had been taken into account by the hacendados, authorities, and liberal intellectuals of that time, perhaps they would have prevented all the blood, death and destruction of so many years of revolution" (1962, 28). This is doubtful. In fact, by this time workers and rural laborers in the Tulancingo Valley had already begun to organize themselves into independent groups, such as the Circle of Free Workers of Rio Blanco, to struggle for higher wages (Menes Llaguno 2006, 195).

Rumblings of discontent and rebellion surfaced regionally all over Mexico for years before progressive politician Francisco Madero launched a national campaign to overthrow Díaz in 1910. Sporadic revolts in the Tulancingo Valley were brutally put down; recalling his childhood as a hacienda peon in a testimony collected by HD staff in the 1970s, the oldest man in one Acatlán village told of eavesdropping on his father's whispered conversations with the other *peones* when they gathered in the fields for their midday meal:

> There came a rumor from the South that it was not true that God had intended the land only for the rich, for the hacendados. That the earth was not the property of humans, but our *madrecita* who provides us with food. And that the poor who belonged to the land should reclaim it, to work it and to feed themselves. Those words came to us on the southern wind, and when dawn broke the next day many of the men who had gathered to listen and who had spoken of these things were found dead and hanging from a tree.

While still effectively excluded from formal political participation, poor rural folk who were once the fodder for Porfirian modernization projects eventually become revolutionary protagonists.

One militant peasant leader from the state of Morelos (south of Hidalgo), Emiliano Zapata, refused to lay down his arms when Madero eventually became president. He converted the local struggles of rural villages in Morelos into a national platform via his Plan of Ayala. Zapata was eventually assassinated by the northern generals, who continued to struggle among themselves for power until well into the 1920s. He was not, however, forgotten. Zapata has since been enshrined in Revolutionary mythology as the champion of the poor, a symbol of national freedom and of campesinos' rights to land. His powerful legacy helped make land reform part of the constitutive agenda of the post-Revolutionary state. In popular iconography, Zapata is often depicted armed and dressed in campesino garb, surrounded by fields of maize.

Becoming Campesinos: Rural Subjects in Post-Revolutionary Mexico

Much of the historiography of twentieth-century Mexico has centered on the Revolution as the foundational event of the modern nation. Hence the role of rural people in the Revolution has been ground for important debates over the popular character of the revolt and the national state that grew out of it. Although the decade of violence that lasted from 1910 to 1920 was for many years conceptually condensed into a singular event, regional and cultural histories have emerged to challenge that view as well as conventional claims about the success of the cultural revolution that accompanied it. Out of a population of nearly sixteen million in 1910, around two million Mexicans died of as a result of violence or starvation before the Revolution's end (Handelman 1997, 35). The modern infrastructure that had been built up during the Porfiriato was all but destroyed, and the country's political leadership was wracked with violent rivalries. Given that the majority of the country's population remained rural and that most commerce depended on primary production, bringing Mexico's rural regions back under control became critical to the project of reconstituting the state. Seeking to mollify the mass movements mobilized by years of fighting and to render the nation governable once more, President Álvaro Obregón and his successor, Plutarco Elías Calles (whose administrations together were known as the Sonoran State by virtue of their shared roots in the populist-liberal middle classes of Northern Mexico), undertook a profound restructuring of the economy and federal bureaucracy. In order to prevent Mexico from sliding back into tradition and isolation, they saw the need to court the workers and farmers who would support their government and modernizing vision. Without challenging the structures of capitalism, they sought to garner support by redistributing land, promoting labor organization, and providing an unprecedented spate of benefits for common working people (Boyer 2003, 4). Article 27 of the new Constitution gave the state eminent domain over the land and water of the nation, which it was empowered to distribute in the public interest. It also set limits on land ownership as a means of preventing latifundia.

Boyer (2003) argues that "in articulating their vision of this new Mexico, the Sonoran presidents adopted a progressive, and at times overtly radical, discourse that was at odds with their increasingly conservative policies. In a sense, however, they had no choice but to do so" (4). After years of struggle, Mexico had become a hotbed of popular militancy. In order to contain popular demands and mediate between warring political factions (especially those associated with the conservative Cristero rebellion) that threatened to hurl the nation into political crisis once again, Calles adhered to an authoritarian style of leadership. In 1929, he founded the National Revolutionary Party (PNR) as an institutional means of unifying left, right, and center factions to win elections and marginalize political upstarts. From the viewpoint of the Sonoran presidents, land reform and labor organization were but temporary measures to quell popular dissent before undertaking a further modernization of the economy and privatization of land tenure. For revolutionary militants, however, the promises of the Revolution were ongoing; they fully expected a deepening of populist reforms with the passage of time.

Rural Citizens and the Revival of Corporatism

Nineteenth-century liberals campaigned against corporatism because they perceived it as an obstacle to modernization. Nonetheless, corporatism proved to be a valuable cultural and political resource for the post-Revolutionary nation-building project, where the political sovereignty of citizens was subordinated to a new model of social welfare. In seeking to correct the "excesses and exclusions of 19th century authoritarian liberalism," the new one-party state recuperated and reworked older corporatist forms, "offering abstract justice to all and participation to rural communities recreated as corporate *ejidos*, and to state-sanctioned trade unions, chambers of commerce and industry, etc. All were incorporated into a mass party and rule by presidents with powers that knew few limits, legal, political, or other" (Meyer 2007, 284). Although this transition was far from smooth in rural Hidalgo, it meant that eventually rural people would become more than a political resource—that they would achieve a measure of recognition as political actors and participants in Mexican modernity.

The post-Revolutionary state reached a crossroads in 1934 with the election of General Lázaro Cárdenas to the presidency. While the Revolution is widely regarded as the foundational moment of the modern nation, the Cárdenas presidency is legendary as the moment of consolidation, when the promises of the Revolution for the pueblo were finally fulfilled. Cárdenas encouraged rural people to organize and press their claims to the land despite the conflict this provoked within the party elite. Indeed, the Cárdenas *sexenio* is when most *ejidos* in the Valley of Tulancingo were founded. On average, *ejidal* claim processes began there in the mid-1920s but were held back by alliances between large landowners and state officials until the mid-1930s. Archival documents for the municipality of Acatlán record a series of long and arduous processes of surveying and resurveying endured by would-be *ejiditarios*, who hired engineers with their own scarce funds to stake their claims to land, only to have local hacendados deploy arcane legal procedures to dispute their claims or petition for exemptions. In many cases there, as elsewhere in Mexico, landowners sidestepped land redistribution by carving up their holdings into smaller plots that were then reregistered in the names of friends and heirs. Even when *ejiditarios* succeeded in pressing their claims, the lands they were assigned were often the least productive and most isolated. In the case of the community of El Ocote, the *ejidal* land grant consisted of two discontinuous, arid tracts, carved from two distinct haciendas. The hacendados in both cases retained sole control of all access to roads and water sources.

To the leaders of the post-Revolutionary state, rural folk represented both developmental potential and a governmental challenge. "As they appraised the countryside where three-quarters of Mexico's population lived, they saw a land of religious fanaticism, of masses impoverished by their refusal to participate in modern economic life, and of a people utterly unaware of their civic duties" (Boyer 2003, 36). Converting the rural masses into revolutionary citizens would require restructuring their allegiances to traditional institutions such as the Church and the village community and instilling a new sense of belonging and solidarity oriented toward the national state. Rural people had to be made aware of their rights and obligations as citizens. Palacios (1999) has argued that this political project entailed the construction of the campesino as both a political actor and an economic producer capable of contributing to the nation's political and economic development. Cárdenas viewed rural people as rightful heirs of the Revolution, but before they could be integrated into the nation, they would have to be "redeemed." Revolutionary citizenship not only conferred unprecedented rights on rural people but also imposed normative attitudes and modes of participation as a condition for those rights. The institutions of the post-Revolutionary state, including the corporatist party system, the *ejidos*, and unions, and the educational system, were intended to promote these new values and allegiances.

Compared to his predecessors, Cárdenas had a more radical vision for integrating Zapata's legacy into Mexico's path to modernity. He centralized political participation by creating a system of corporate institutions that organized key sectors of Mexican society, especially the military, campesinos, and workers, under the consolidated control of the official state party (now called the PRI, or the Party of the Institutionalized Revolution). His economic policy afforded campesinos a key role in agricultural production, setting up the *ejido* as a collectivized production unit charged with fueling the country's industrialization program.

During his six years as president, Cárdenas redistributed over twenty million hectares of land, an amount unprecedented in the nation's history. By the 1940s, *ejidos* held half of Mexico's cultivated land, and the number of landless rural people had declined from 68 percent to 36 percent. Cárdenas encouraged local campesino groups to organize, channeling the mass mobilization through the new National Campesino Federation (CNC), a corporatist organ of the PRI (Barry 1995, 23). Citizen participation was mediated almost exclusively through the organs of the official party, leaving clientelism and mass protests as the major modes of political engagement. In Hidalgo, the Cárdenas *sexenio* coincided with the governorship of Javier Rojo Gómez (1937–1941), who rose from humble rural origins through the party ranks. He oversaw the first significant land redistributions in the state as well as the installation of small irrigation works, dams, levees, schools, and a network of major highways. According to Menes Llaguno, this period of Hidalgan history was marked by "the proliferation of various cacicazgos, promoted by the anxiety caused as the land redistributions began to [affect] old landowning families, who took advantage of the ex-revolutionary military leaders who had not yet been rewarded with regional political posts"

(2006, 220). In order to exert greater control over these regional strongmen, Rojo Gómez granted many of them official posts in his government. As soon as their terms were finished, however, most of them returned to their former pursuits rather than taking up bureaucratic careers. The consequences of this development would become clear several decades later, as rivalries among them helped to fuel rural conflicts in the Huasteca region. In 1941, Rojo Gómez was named to a national-level post by newly elected president Manuel Ávila Camacho and was succeeded as governor by his brother-in-law, Jose Lugo Guerrero. Thus began an important Hidalgan political dynasty and a key PRI strategy. Hidalgo, located close enough to the capital to maintain close communication and resource flows yet still isolated enough to be ruled as a fiefdom, would become a proving ground for PRI politicians.

Cultivating Campesinos as Political Subjects

Through Cárdenas's deployment of Zapata's legacy, the figure of the campesino became integral to the symbolic composition of the imagined community of post-Revolutionary Mexico. Although it was later taken up by rural residents and deployed for their own purposes, Boyer (2003) argues that the social category of "campesino" was the ideological creation of the post-Revolutionary state. Two conflicting images of the rural masses animated contemporary political debates: the stoic face of tradition and the violent, disaffected rabble. Wolf (1959) argues that the first image, that of the campesino as an enduring repository of Mexican national history and folk traditions, is closely linked to the cultural value of displaying fortitude in the face of difficulty (*aguantarse*). The figure of the *campesino aguantador* (stoic campesino) is that of a victim who turns defeat into triumph by his calm and derisive acceptance of fate. That calm surface, however, is regarded as concealing the possibility for sudden violent eruptions; this is deemed a carryover from the campesino's essentially premodern, irrational nature. Thus these seemingly disparate images of campesinos were actually two sides of the same ideological coin on which rural people were depicted as a "determinate and virtually unchanging social group" (Boyer 2003, 2). Post-Revolutionary agrarian questions were articulated through the notion of a unified "campesino problem," which tied together debates over citizenship rights and representation with the role of private property in the economic development of the nation. Land reform was first posed as a method of incorporating the rural population into the imagined community and then later, under Cárdenas, of developing a participatory yet authoritarian system of political representation. Within post-Revolutionary political discourse and ideology, the campesino represented a social (rather than class) category that lumped together the rural masses regardless of their ethnicity, religion, relationship to the land, or locality. Boyer asserts that this category only came to have meaning for rural people themselves (as opposed to politicians and pundits) through regionally uneven and often protracted processes of agrarian mobilization in pursuit of land reform. Their cultural transformation into *campesinato* was the "outgrowth of popular militancy as interpreted through localized versions of post-Revolutionary ideology" (Boyer 2003, 3). Through struggles over land reform in the 1920s and 1930s, rural people in different regions of Mexico took up some of those post-Revolutionary ideals as their own while rejecting others. "Eventually, they began to represent themselves as belonging to a social category known as campesinos, that is, as a distinct social group united by a shared set of political and economic interests as well as by a collective history of oppression" (3). A campesino cultural identity developed that intersected with and overlapped other forms of allegiance. While rural people in most regions rejected the secularism of official state ideology and the insistence on national rather than local primacy, they often found it useful to appeal to the sense of class solidarity and rights to the land that it afforded. While the cultural revolution through which the post-Revolutionary state was constituted failed to create a unified, solidary peasant class, it did provide a political grammar through which rural people could make claims on the state. To the extent that the state claimed to rule in the name of the Revolution, it could not openly flout those ideals (Knight 1994b).

Wolf (1959) agreed that land reform and indigenism provided the economic and ideological cement that bound together the newly reconstituted state by transforming the existing political, economic, and social structure and providing the new imagined community with an origin story rooted in the so-called maize culture of the ancient Mesoamerican civilizations. However, he warned that land reform could only stave off the coming crisis over what development path Mexico would take. With the continuation of Mexico's import substituting development plan, which created a consumer society that could never be satisfied domestically, Wolf foresaw the emergence of a new cultural path brought about by dependency on the United States. The result would be lowered self-esteem and the devaluation of Mexican society (symbolized by devaluation of the figure of the campesino), leading politicians to perform an exaggerated nationalism in order to preserve a sovereign national identity in the face of growing cultural similarity with the North.

The Politics of Rural Development

In the 1970s Mexico rediscovered its countryside as a series of intertwined economic, political, and social trends put the agrarian question back on the national agenda in a dramatic way. This began under the administration of Luis Echeverría (1970–1976), who faced serious challenges to the post-Revolutionary developmental state. The faltering of the import substitution industrialization (ISI) model that had guided Mexico's economic planning since World War II was accompanied by a loss of government legitimacy after the infamous Tlatelolco massacre of 1968. Since the 1950s, ISI had focused national resources on the industrial development of several key cities to the neglect of most rural areas. The role of the agricultural segment had been to provide the raw materials for industrialization as well as to generate some foreign exchange in order to finance the "backward linkages" to complete the chain of industrial production. Limited amounts of state investment in agriculture had been concentrated in northwest Mexico and were intended to boost the productivity of export-oriented commercial agriculture through a coordinated package of subsidies, credits, infrastructure, and research and development. But while the Mexican economy as a whole had grown steadily since the 1940s, agricultural production had experienced a steady decline. Annual growth in the agricultural sector fell from a high point of 5 percent in the first half of the 1960s to 1 percent by the second half of the decade, a figure that was far outstripped by a population growth rate of 4 percent (Hewitt de Alcántara 1976, 103). By 1965, in fact, Mexico began importing basic foodstuffs (which it had formerly produced in surplus) from the United States in order to feed its urban workers. This development not only created a balance-of-payments problem but also threatened to turn into a full-blown crisis with the international grain shortages in 1970.

Despite government rhetoric advocating class solidarity in the service of national development, it was becoming increasingly plain that the economic benefits of ISI had not trickled down to most of the rural population and that in fact the country was facing the growth of an unprecedented income gap between classes. Over twenty-five million campesinos—about 40 percent of the population—had been left out of the "Mexican miracle" and seemed to provide fertile soil for the seeds of social unrest that had been sown in the cities in the late 1960s. Much of this disparity can be blamed on what Grindle (1981) has labeled the bifurcation of Mexican agriculture. While large-scale, capital-intensive commercial agriculture received the lion's share of government investment after World War II, the traditional sector, consisting mainly of *ejiditarios* and other smallholders, was largely neglected. It was this sector that produced the basic food crops meant to feed the developing nation. The campesino sector suffered from lack of access to land and water as well as capital and technology. As rural populations grew, more and more campesinos were being forced to migrate out of the countryside in order to find employment, causing runaway growth in major metropolitan areas, especially Mexico City. In rural areas, violent land invasions were becoming more frequent as traditional corporate institutions failed to adequately address campesinos' demands for more land and water. This political tension was especially troubling for the PRI, as it had traditionally relied on the campesino sector (as organized through the CNC) to provide its major support bases.

Echeverría's agrarian policy focused more attention and resources on the plight of the Mexican campesino than at any time since the Cárdenas administration. His strategy was based on an innovative interpretation of the source of rural "backwardness," which located the root cause in the structural relationship of the campesino sector to the rest of the economy and exploitation by intermediaries. Trapped by rising production costs and costs of living, as well as low crop prices, many campesinos retreated into subsistence production rather than participate in disadvantageous markets (Grindle 1981, 10).

In fact, by the mid-1970s, UN statistics showed that the *ejido* sector was suffering from *neolatifundismo*. While large land owners were prevented by law from taking over *ejidal* lands (which could not be sold or mortgaged), lack of government support (including infrastructure and credit shortages) had forced over 80 percent of *ejiditarios* to illegally rent out their parcels to nearby commercial farmers, who then paid them a pittance to work the land. The campesinos had effectively become *peones* on their own land, and large landowners had gained de facto control over most of Mexico's farmland (Hellman 1988, 99).[12]

Echeverría set his planners to the task of creating a comprehensive strategy to aid campesinos in retaining the profits of their labor and reinvesting them in ways that would increase agricultural productivity. The state's new role would be to liberate the campesinos from parasitical intermediaries by offering them more efficient services—credit, direct purchase of crops, infrastructure such as roads, irrigation, and storage facilities, and access to subsidized goods like food, clothing, agricultural inputs and implements, medical care, and education. The *ejido*, long neglected by government programs, figured into the strategy as the primary organizational unit that would allow campesinos to pool their newly accumulated capital and thus avoid exploitation. A new Agrarian Code even sought to strengthen the *ejido* institutionally, requiring for the first time secret ballots in the election of *ejidal* authorities[13] in an attempt to break the political power of the caciques. Oversight of *ejidal* affairs was removed from the hands of state governments and invested in the presidency itself (Hellman 1988, 193). By banding together with the aid of the government, those previously excluded from the benefits of the Mexican miracle would, it was hoped, achieve integration.

The cornerstone of Echeverría's rural development program was the Program for Integrated Rural Development, or PIDER. Funded by loans from the World Bank, PIDER was supplemented by state marketing institutions for key crops, the National Company for People's Sustenance (CONASUPO) program to warehouse the crops of small producers, and credit and crop insurance provided through Banrural, the rural development bank. This represented a considerable increase in public sector investment in the countryside, which by the mid-1970s would amount to 15 percent of the federal budget (Grindle 1981, 13). PIDER attempted to address rural underdevelopment by dividing the country up into a series of rain-fed microregions, each of which would be analyzed and engaged as a unit with individually tailored programs in infrastructure, agricultural extension, health, and education. Implemented through fourteen separate federal agencies, PIDER was designed to bring the Green Revolution to campesinos, thereby increasing basic food production and bringing ISI back on track (Hellman 1988, 96).

In a more controversial move, Echeverría pushed for the collectivization of *ejidos*. Unlike socialist collectivization schemes that relied on unified production, the Mexican system meant "the collective administration of credit, use of agricultural machinery, purchase of inputs, and marketing" (Barry 1995, 37). He also sped up land redistribution schemes, opening up irrigated territories for *ejidal* claims. He was attempting to revamp the Cárdenas administration's populist rhetoric of class solidarity in a way that balanced the interests of commercial and campesino agriculture—a task that in the end proved too difficult. Echeverría attempted to shift agricultural policy away from land reform and toward an emphasis on productivity and social welfare, but land reform was too much a part of the post-Revolutionary government's "constitutive agenda" to simply be discarded without a fight. A series of violent revolts took place across rural Mexico, including in the Hidalgan Huasteca (Foley 1991, 42). Moreover, Echeverría's willingness to honor even limited campesino claims on valuable irrigated land provoked the ire of commercial farmers in the north. His plan backfired. Business leaders were angered, local political bosses on whom the party relied felt cut out of the loop, and campesino groups remained dissatisfied with the reforms, complaining that they did not go far enough to correct the bifurcated system responsible for low productivity.

Reframing the Peasant Problem

Echeverría's successor, José López Portillo, made use of his predecessor's populist rhetoric of class solidarity and social justice for the campesinos but put forth a different vision for the future of the Mexican countryside. While his analysis of the agrarian question also focused on the importance of the agricultural sector in the country's overall development, he assessed the source and solution of the productivity problem very differently. He was deeply troubled by the agrarian unrest that had accompanied Echeverría's attempts at land reform, as it both intimated the breakdown of the PRI's system of corporate political control in the countryside and turned the private commercial sector against the government. Faced with these political tensions in addition to the acute national security and foreign exchange problems posed by Mexico's food dependency on the United States, López Portillo designed his program to increase agricultural productivity in a more business-friendly way. By reworking notions of class solidarity and nationalism, he was able to reorient agricultural policy toward active commercialization in a way that broke with many of the sacred tenets constitutive of the revolutionary state. His Alliance for Production between the state, private sector, and labor, a rejection of his predecessor's populist policies, was based on the premise that significant economic growth must precede any attempts at redistribution. His policies and rhetoric also laid the groundwork for an eventual relocation of the agrarian problem in the subject of the campesino, a move that has had consequences not only for how development is imagined and implemented but also for how rural citizens are governed.

Abandoning Echeverría's structural hypothesis, López Portillo placed the blame for perceived campesino backwardness on the lack of social and productive infrastructure as well as on the underuse of technology. Although advanced agricultural technology was available in Mexico and had contributed to the comparatively high productivity of commercial farmers, the risk factors involved in small-scale farming discouraged campesinos from adopting this new technology. Government analysts contrasted campesinos, whom they characterized as "risk-minimizers," with commercial producers, whom they saw as "maximizing gains." Hence the problem as they saw it was not overinvestment in commercial agriculture or even structural disadvantage; rather, the government needed to "bring campesinos more fully into participation in the national economy" by investing in infrastructure useful to all sectors of agriculture and by helping campesinos to acquire new productive technology (Grindle 1981, 19).

In March 1980, the Mexican Food System (SAM) was launched with the purpose of promoting the nation's agricultural self-sufficiency by increasing agricultural productivity and increasing cultivation in regions formerly dedicated to livestock grazing. SAM was a comprehensive planning and policy strategy aimed at integrating and streamlining the entire chain of food production, distribution, and consumption while improving rural living standards. It was not intended to replace earlier programs; instead, SAM was to be implemented through preexisting programs and institutions. Whereas PIDER had attempted to cut intermediaries out of the food production and distribution network, effectively establishing separate schemes for *ejidal* and commercial agriculture, SAM sought to work together with agribusiness, intermediaries, merchants, consumers, and campesinos in both rain-fed and irrigation districts. It was a strategy of "shared risk," where the Mexican government would subsidize new technology, inputs, research and development, and extension services to all agricultural producers (Grindle 1981, 20–22). Indeed, the López Portillo administration worked to actively support private (domestic and foreign) agricultural industry, encouraging transnational corporations already active in Mexico such as Nestlé and Ralston Purina to expand their operations (Hellman 1988, 100). He called this "betting on the strong."

The rationale of betting on the strong was carried out in other areas as well. The most dramatic shift was in land reform policy. Whereas Echeverría, the old-style PRI politician, took the constitutive agenda of land reform as a political given (and a useful political tool), as a technocrat, López Portillo was far less committed to redistributive policies. In order to restore investor confidence, he actually began to dismantle the *ejido* as a legal and economic unit of rural solidarity. While he did not revoke Echeverría's expropriations, López Portillo compensated northern commercial landholders generously and promised publicly to end land reform during his term. Arguing that there was now no land left to distribute, he admonished campesinos to work harder to increase productivity rather than agitating for more land. Although he was cautious of the political costs of becoming known as the postagrarian president, he set into motion the ideological, political, and administrative conditions that would allow his successor to openly declare an end to agrarian reform.

One of the most significant legacies of López Portillo's agricultural policy was that it started an incremental change in the way the crisis in the countryside was to be framed. All hope of addressing the structural roots of rural poverty—either through a comprehensive agricultural extension service or through redistributive schemes—was abandoned as a waste of resources. Rather, the government posed the marginalization of campesinos as more of a problem of social welfare and political legitimation than one of agricultural productivity in the service of national development. Increasingly, the campesino no longer figured in national debates as a participant in or resource for Mexican modernity but rather as a social problem, an intractable source of backwardness.

Liberalism's Second Coming: Neoliberalism and the Reform of the Agrarian Reform

One hundred twenty years after Benito Juárez's Liberal forces declared victory over the Conservatives in the Reform wars, Mexico experienced "the second coming of liberalism" as a result of an economic and political crisis. Like nineteenth-century liberalism, the neoliberal turn represented a search for new political and economic models from abroad. The crisis that brought about this reworking of Mexican liberalism was an economic collapse, which resulted in the lost decade of the 1980s and unleashed a struggle within the top leadership of the PRI.

> In the 1980s, young technocrats within the ruling party regime, led by Carlos Salinas de Gortari, seized power from the inside and proposed a radical transformation of economy and society based on principles they labeled "social liberalism." They proposed to dismantle the corporatist apparatus that had dominated Mexico throughout the twentieth century and to rebuild it following the ideological tenets of neoliberalism, already prevalent in the international arena. In the second coming, the model again came from North America, as did key international support. (Meyer 2007, 272)

By the time Miguel de la Madrid became president in 1982, the most important decisions in government, namely the management of the economy, were increasingly being decided by technocrats rather than through the traditional sectoral channels of political negotiation. These appointed experts had a strikingly different vision of national progress from their political predecessors; in place of an institutionalized Revolution, they espoused the idea of a "Revolution you can invest in."[14] They critiqued the regime's traditional approach as statist and populist, arguing that the bureaucratic apparatus had grown too labyrinthine and corrupt to govern efficiently. Indeed, they argued that the Revolutionary social pact bred paternalism and dependency, hampering the freedom and creativity of individual citizens. In 1983, de la Madrid implemented Mexico's first Global Development Plan, drawn up by the cabinet Secretariat of Planning and Budget, which was headed by a young Harvard-trained economist named Carlos Salinas de Gortari. The plan contained the ideological seeds of the neoliberal path Mexico was about to embark on, a restructuring program that would eventually come to be known in international circles as Salinastroika. Under Salinas's guidance, first as a member of de la Madrid's cabinet and then as president, Mexico was to become a model debtor and the global poster child for neoliberal reform. Salinastroika was a wide-ranging program to move Mexico away from state-led development and a corporatist system of political representation and entailed the dismantling of the social welfare apparatus, privatization of state-owned enterprises, labor market flexibilization, and the opening of national borders and financial markets to outside goods and investments. It was a bid to catapult Mexico into the ranks of the first world by leaving behind the legacy of Cárdenas. Ideologically, this meant abandoning the path to modernity that emerged from the Mexican Revolution in favor of that outlined by the Washington Consensus.

The social impacts of the debt crisis and the policy changes instituted to deal with it were so grave that the PRI regime, already suffering from a crisis of legitimacy, was destabilized irrevocably. This opened the way for the language of citizenship to become an important part of public discourse once more at the turn of the twenty-first century. The original intent of Mexico's technocrats was to isolate the drastic economic restructuring from the political arena and leave political power concentrated in traditional institutions. Like nineteenth-century liberalism, neoliberalism was presented as a modernization scheme, intended to help Mexico catch up with the first world. However, there were to be political consequences, as the economic dislocations provoked by neoliberal policies aided in the consolidation of an opposition from both left and right, mutually focused on political liberalization—the prodemocracy movement that spanned the presidencies of both Salinas and Ernesto Zedillo (1994–2000). The crisis of the 1980s made citizenship a major issue once again and led to a broadening of its meanings and horizons.

Rural Crisis and Political Fragmentation

In Hidalgo, independent peasant organizations began to emerge in the late 1970s and early 1980s as the pace of land reform slowed, rural populations grew, and small-scale agriculture became less profitable. The growing dairy and textile mill industries absorbed some of the surplus labor from rural areas, but at very low wages. By the 1970s, rural labor migration to Puebla and Mexico City had begun. Increased competition for land and water, combined with erosion, deforestation, and agrochemical pollution associated with the Green Revolution, led to land invasions and sporadic uprisings in the Huasteca and Valle del Mezquital regions of Hidalgo, then under the thumb of PRI cacique José Guadarrama Márquez, who was as notorious for ordering the assassination of opposition figures as he was for embezzlement. In the late twentieth century, military tactics were once again deployed against Hidalgan peasants defending claims to land and water.[15] Official responses to the political unrest and land invasions occasioned by deepening rural poverty also included strategic investment in development programs targeted to highly marginalized regions and the organization of small producer cooperatives to generate rural entrepreneurialism. Some of these programs were administered directly by state agencies, but in other cases, as we shall see in Chapter 2, rural development projects were also undertaken in partnership with NGOs.

The political problems prompted by the growing rural crisis came under greater scrutiny during the administration of president Carlos Salinas (1988–1994) as a potential obstacle to North American economic integration. The Reform of the Agrarian Reform, initiated under Salinas, entailed a massive public divestment from rural development at the same time as it privatized collective landholdings, ended price supports, and opened Mexican markets to highly subsidized agricultural imports from the United States. Salinas's policies were premised on the "liberalization of the market, generalized deregulation, and drastic cuts in subsidies," policies that were intended to foment "flows of productive investment toward the countryside, as well as a shift in the pattern of crops, aimed at the efficient exploitation of our comparative advantages" as well as to reduce the size of the peasant population, which the government saw as "overgrown" (Bartra 1996, 179). This population was intended to be absorbed by an increase in industry and services that never happened. By the end of Salinas's term, the economy was in ruins and political violence was widespread. Political cost analyses trumped all.

A New Model of Active Citizenship for Rural Mexico

The PRI relied on neocorporatist social programs to reconsolidate control in rural areas. The Program of Direct Rural Support (PROCAMPO), for example, was designed as a subsidy that would comply with NAFTA while allowing price guarantees and government brokerage of the maize market to be phased out. But in the context of the 1994 election it was converted into a ten- to fifteen-year extendable redistribution program that benefited the vast majority of small- to medium-scale producers. These programs were never intended to produce structural changes, only political ones. According to Bartra (1996), they created "a vast reservation for the marginalized rural population . . . a subsidy for mass rural unemployment, the swan song of charitable populism" (180). Despite downsizing agricultural programs directed at supporting small-scale agricultural production, the federal government actually expanded its political presence in the countryside. Salinas secured additional World Bank loans in order to institute a new spate of social programs overseen directly by his office and aimed at distributing token support to the most destitute and vocal critics of the regime. This National Solidarity Program (PRONASOL) papered over the cracks in the government's legitimacy, bypassing the PRI and attaching all claims of loyalty to the president himself (Dresser 1994; Knight 1994a). PRONASOL is noteworthy not only because of the positive attention it garnered from the World Bank and foreign governments as an antipoverty program but also for the way it attempted to remake the relationships between the state and rural society. PRONASOL was a specific social program (SSP) aimed at replacing the core institutions of the welfare state through targeted projects. SSPs were intended to liquidate the government's commitment to social justice by focusing on standards of living rather than relations of production. With a five-year budget (1988–1993) of over $12 billion, PRONASOL funded social development projects and infrastructure like schools and hospitals in over 95 percent of Mexican municipalities, directing the lion's share of resources toward hot spots of political dissent (Cornelius, Craig, and Fox 1994). Unlike previous programs, however, it demanded the participation of recipients, appealing to the solidary traditions of the pueblo such as the faena to achieve more with less. Recipients were required to organize themselves into committees charged with coresponsibility in a proposed program, which amounted to raising a portion of the funds or liquidating this quota through labor and assuming all responsibility for maintenance and follow-through. They were assisted by a new set of intermediaries, Solidarity technicians who acted as consultants in the planning and execution of projects by local groups (Braig 1997).

Linking fund distribution to party loyalty allowed the government to co-opt grassroots organizations already involved in attempting to soften the blow of economic restructuring on marginalized communities while simultaneously "redefining the members of the old corporate coalitions (that had tied the PRI to its constituent bases) as consumers of PRONASOL" (Dresser 1994, 144). In fact, this was one of the prime ideological thrusts of the program; through PRONASOL, citizenship began to be individualized as Mexicans were encouraged to identify as consumers, residents of specific territorial units, and members of fragmented political interest groups rather than members of a social class or corporate group (Dresser 1994). The emphasis on transparency and accountability as cornerstones of democratic freedom also contributed to this ideological shift, helping liberal rights to trump collective rights in the struggle to redefine Mexican democracy. With the ascendancy of SSPs like PRONASOL, the developmentalist state gave way to the enabling state. Under Salinas's successor, Ernesto Zedillo (1994–2000), PRONASOL was reborn in 1997 as PROGRESA (Program for Education, Health, and Nutrition), combining cash transfers, health and nutritional supplements, and scholarships for rural students into a single integrated program aimed at "creating human capital to improve the labor market insertion of future generations" (Hevia de la Jara 2009, 44). As he did with his predecessor's economic policies, National Action Party (PAN) president Vicente Fox (2000–2006) continued this program for the first two years of his term. However, in 2002, PROGRESA (Progress) was replaced by Oportunidades (Opportunities), which expanded its reach into urban areas and emphasized coresponsibility, seeking to enhance the capacity of marginalized citizens to find solutions to their own problems. In rural communities of the Tulancingo Valley, all of these programs seemed more or less the same to participants, who referred to them as *las ayudas del gobierno* (help or aid from the government). They understood this support to be framed in terms of charity or reciprocity rather than rights, and it was clear that not only the government but also the local officials in charge of distributing the support expected something in return.

Crisis of the Campesino as Political Subject

During the Fox administration, rural people appeared in official political discourse as impoverished or marginalized figures dependent on state aid rather than as producers of the nation's sustenance or historical protagonists. If actual campesinos were a political resource for Fox, it was primarily due to the over $8 billion in remittances they sent home every year as immigrants to the United States, an amount equal to two-thirds of Mexico's annual oil revenues and over one and a half times its agricultural exports (Brazil 2001; Fidler 2001). These remittances helped rural families to survive in an era of negligible support for small-scale production, rising consumer prices, and falling crop values due to NAFTA. As the state abandoned agricultural development in the countryside in favor of SSPs, and as rural development NGOs both supplemented and contested neoliberal restructuring, social and political fractures deepened in rural society. Rural areas once again posed a problem for civic order, this time as cartels moved into regions abandoned by the central state, where a single party no longer had the power to broker territorial disputes. Heriberto Lazcano, a Hidalgo native, was the leader of the Zetas, a group of former Mexican special forces operatives who first hired themselves out to the Gulf Cartel as enforcers and later unleashed a war when they broke off relations with them to undertake their own trafficking operations. "El Lazco" is widely credited with pioneering the torture methods and other forms of publicized violence (such as the display of mutilated corpses) that have now become the signature of a new school of drug kingpins. Beginning in 2008, the Huasteca and Valle del Mezquital regions were once again militarized by then-president Felipe Calderon in an attempt to quell the Zetas' influence and their diversification into kidnapping and petroleum theft. The highways linking the coast to Mexico City, which move through Tulancingo, came under constant military surveillance. Several of my informants, campesinos who grew up in *ejidal* communities in the Tulancingo Valley and who are now engaged in a variety of farm-related small businesses such as cheese making and trucking, told me that they faced regular intimidation and extortion from Zeta affiliates during this period. From 2012 to 2013, a struggle over leadership within the Zetas erupted into a wave of violence in the region, already hard hit by decades of economic crisis. The Hidalgan countryside once again appeared on the national scene as a site of abject unruliness, with its denizens portrayed as dependent victims or violent aggressors rather than modern citizens.

Lomnitz (2001, xxi) asserts that neoliberalism in the last three decades has brought about not only chronic economic crises but also "chronic crisis concerning the relationship between nationalism and modernization." With the collapse of import substitution, the countryside was reframed in official state discourse from the productive engine of modern industrialization to a vast reservation for the backward poor that consumed precious state resources. Rural institutions were defunded, destroyed, and denigrated as politically corrupt, but little was put forward to replace them. The opposition victory in 2000, while marking the first peaceful change of power in Mexican history, did not spell an end to neoliberalism but rather lent these policies an air of political legitimacy not enjoyed by their original authors. Campesinos were left without the ability to impugn state legitimacy or appeal to revolutionary nationalism in their quest for political traction or even a bit of help. As in the nineteenth century, dependency once again became the chief marker of exclusion from political life. It was precisely this condition of economic and political dependency that NGOs sought to correct when they first began to intervene in the lives of campesinos in the Tulancingo Valley.

CHAPTER 2

The Birth of Tulancingo's Third Sector

On May 4, 2003, Hidalgo Development celebrated its twenty-fifth anniversary with a feast and outdoor Catholic mass on the site of one of its integral development projects in the tiny village of El Ocote. The celebration was attended by hundreds of campesinos from nearby settlements, local political figures, and visitors from as far away as Spain and New York. Seven HD staff members began planning the event nearly eight months in advance, contacting the organization's international partners and old allies in the Christian base communities (CEBs), visiting rural communities that had participated in past HD development projects to drum up support, and calling on contacts in the business community for donations. El Ocote was chosen as the site for the celebration because it represented the culmination of HD's development vision and its long-term impact. Community *faenas* were organized to prepare the site. The well and irrigation pond built in the 1980s with aid from the Inter-American Foundation and Mexican government and loans from Banco Mexicano SOMEX (SOMEX) were cleaned. Nearby, irrigation ditches dug by a youth group from New York fed a community vegetable garden, a recent project undertaken by HD's new generation of staff, which joined the NGO in the late 1990s. The large outdoor stage and meeting area built by community labor was repainted, and the surrounding trees planted by international volunteers were pruned to promote new growth and create more shade in time for the spring celebration. The small abandoned building built by Spanish volunteers, which first housed a co-operative preschool and later served as feed storage for a poultry production project, was cleaned and rehabbed for use as a temporary kitchen. Each HD community contributed to the feast days in advance, sending sheep for *barbacoa*, a pig for *carnitas*, tortillas, rice, vegetables, beans, limes. The men of El Ocote took charge of slaughtering and preparing the meat, while the women prepared rice, soup, and beans, and organized the meal service. HD staff and the resident anthropologist took charge of logistics, setting up rented tables and chairs, an outdoor altar for the mass, a DJ area and dance floor for the *baile* to follow, and trash collection. Several hundred guests, including campesinos, clergy, representatives from international and national partner NGOs, and local government functionaries ate, drank, danced, and reminisced together in El Ocote that day.

The theme of the celebration was the Parable of the Sower from the New Testament. The sermon preached at Mass, the testimonials of campesino leaders about how HD had modernized their communities and transformed their commitments to them, and stories from foreign activists about how visiting HD communities changed their perspectives on global poverty all gestured toward the role of the NGO in propagating change. The event served as a reflection on the accomplishments and failures of HD's rural development work, especially in cultivating solidarity among its members and allies. It was particularly poignant in light of recent changes in the Mexican countryside, as small-scale agriculture succumbed to free trade, structural adjustment, and recurring droughts. Cooperative forms of land tenure and agricultural production were now actively being erased under neoliberal policies that administrated resources on an individual basis to encourage entrepreneurship. Young campesinos, faced with infertile land and fertile families, were moving north in droves to work the soil of the United States—and fragmenting rural communities in the process.

Over the course of recent Mexican history, pastoral projects aimed at converting rural denizens into citizens of the modern nation have been proposed as a means of resolving agrarian questions. Such efforts have always sought to reforge the links between public and private, remaking communitarian and domestic relationships thought to undergird the public order. In the late twentieth century, nongovernmental organizations emerged as important new actors, comprising a third sector dedicated to the promotion of new forms of civic engagement. The NGO form facilitated new kinds of public–private partnerships in rural development, but its deployment also generated new democratic dilemmas. This chapter examines the growth of Tulancingo's third sector from its origins in the 1970s until the end of the Fox administration.

Hidalgo Development is one of the oldest development NGOs in Mexico and the oldest independent NGO in the Tulancingo region. The organization's history is representative of the far-reaching changes that the country has experienced during the last three decades of neoliberal reforms. In the 1970s, a series of intertwined economic, political, and social tensions put the agrarian question back on the national agenda in a dramatic way. HD's founders, two young men from prominent Tulancingo families, began contemplating a joint project that would combine youth service, poverty alleviation, and rural development over the entire Tulancingo River Valley. They were inspired both by older models of civic Catholicism and by newer strains of liberation theology and third world solidarity. HD was initially allowed to carry out select development projects that were seen by some factions of the PRI and officials in the national and state governments to be in their own interests, as those projects were aimed at ameliorating the rural poverty that had led to violent land invasions in other regions of Hidalgo. Later the group participated in the human rights and prodemocracy movements, shifting focus from production-based projects to popular education. The political and social role NGOs like HD have constructed for themselves over the last three decades has been profoundly shaped by their ongoing negotiations with political elites, state agencies, and funding sources over the extent of their organizational autonomy. The historical development of Tulancingo's NGO sector reveals important insights into the relationships between NGOs and the political class with whom they are intimately, if sometimes uncomfortably, engaged. It also demonstrates how the work of NGOs is performed at the intersection of multiple, sometimes contradictory projects of rule, avoidance, and resistance. Consequently, the kinds of change it is possible for NGOs to produce depends on the conditions under which these interventions are cultivated and what participation in them comes to mean for the various actors involved.

La Mano Solidaria: Civic Catholicism and Rural Development in the Tulancingo Valley

During the 1970s, most Mexican NGOs were influenced by the values of civic Catholicism if not directly affiliated with the Church (see Forment 2002). The dominant form of organization was the *patronato*, or charitable foundation, with roots in the Spanish colonial period. The *patronato real*, or royal patronage, was a treaty agreement between the Spanish monarch and the papal government in Rome. It afforded the crown control over the appointment of high-ranking religious officials and oversight of Church revenue in its colonial territories. In the Americas, this resulted in a union of the authority of the Church and the ruling class. Over time, *patronato* came to denote a charitable society or foundation, organized separately from religious orders and confraternities and governed by a board of trustees, usually appointed by its main patron. These organizations engaged mostly in projects of civic improvement sponsored by economic elites. In the 1930s, in the wake of the destruction and deprivation caused by the Revolution, merchants, factory owners, and ranchers in the Tulancingo Valley founded several such organizations. They included a home for the destitute elderly, an orphanage, a hospital, and a local branch of the Red Cross. Their efforts focused mainly on providing basic social and safety services inside the city of Tulancingo. In the 1940s, local branches of international service organizations such as the Soroptomists, Lions' Club, Boy Scouts, and Rotary Club were imported from the United States under the "Good Neighbor" policy. The later emergence of rural development organizations like HD was a result of these combined influences, as well as the spread of liberation theology in central Mexico during the 1960s and 1970s.

In the 1960s, the aftermath of the Cuban revolution inspired the United States to launch the Alliance for Progress, an aid program to Latin American countries that sought to prevent the spread of communism by combating poverty through development and counterinsurgency assistance. The era of developmentalism that ensued was complemented by the Vatican's own anticommunism efforts, summed up in the *Populorum Progressio* (1967). Pope Paul VI appealed to lay Catholics to take the initiative in "improving the temporal order" by "offering their skills and earnest assistance to public and private organizations, both civil and religious, working to solve the problems of developing nations." By end of the 1960s, organizations independent from both the Mexican government and the Catholic Church began to emerge, but they remained influenced by developmental nationalism and the religious mandate to minister to the poor.

In the late 1960s and early 1970s, central Mexico served as the backdrop for a growing movement among progressive bishops committed to the tenets of liberation theology. Bishop Sergio Méndez Arceo of Cuernavaca encouraged the development of Christian-based communities among the rural and urban poor. Mendez, who served as bishop of Cuernavaca from 1953 until his retirement in 1983, hailed from a wealthy and powerful family. Before his appointment to Cuernavaca, he had studied in Rome. He was influenced both by the principles of Vatican II and by the work of radical Austrian priest and philosopher Ivan Illich. He promoted the formation of ecclesiastical base communities (CEBs) in rural areas and poor urban neighborhoods. These CEBs refocused religious life around the everyday struggles of parishioners, promoting popular participation in the liturgy, dialogue between clergy and parishioners, and collective analysis of important social issues. Mendez insisted that Church should not remain impassive in the face of injustice (Burdick and Hewitt 2000). He became known as the Red Bishop for his open support of socialism as a solution to Mexico's social problems, and he went against the position of the Church hierarchy in supporting the student protestors after the 1968 Tlatelolco massacre as well as striking workers and rural rebels.

Although the idea of enacting a "preferential option for the poor" proved quite influential in many quarters, as the 1970s wore on, various forces sought to tame the radical tendencies of the liberation theology movement. Pope Paul's death and the appointment of the more conservative Pope John Paul II (along with a cadre of new, right-leaning bishops) meant an end to official support for liberation theology. In Mexico itself, President Echeverría's populist authoritarian administration sought to relegitimize the government after the public outcry over Tlatelolco and to foreclose spaces of rebellion through a campaign of co-optation and persecution of independent NGOs (Aguilar Valenzuela 1997b). During the Dirty War of the 1970s, government forces infiltrated universities and independent unions, the largest civil society groups that lay outside the official corporatist structure. The forced disappearance, arbitrary imprisonment, and extrajudicial execution of activists became common, producing a chilling effect. In most cases, the Mexican government used a combination of co-optation and repression to contain social movements and independent organizations (CNDH 2001; Bizberg 2010). The NGOs that managed to survive under Echeverría and his successor, Lopez Portillo, were mostly Church-related charities and service organizations or local branches of international organizations like Lions' Club and Boy Scouts.

During this period, the two young men from Tulancingo began contemplating a joint project that would combine youth service, poverty alleviation, and rural development throughout the Tulancingo River Valley. In 1977, the pair began meeting in Mexico City with representatives of the Fundación Mexicana para el Desarrollo Rural (Mexican Foundation for Rural Development, FMDR). The FMDR, sponsored by Don Lorenzo Servitje (owner of industrial food conglomerate Grupo Bimbo), had evolved from the Union of Catholic Businessmen (UDEC) in the mid-1960s. A reformist group inspired by both the Alliance for Progress and the *Populorum Progressivo*, the FMDR was dedicated to combating poverty in the countryside in order to prevent popular insurgent movements. They were worried about the possible consequences of *ejido* collectivization and land redistribution for large commercial farms in the north. As an alternative to the government's efforts at rural development, which they considered to be antibusiness, the FMDR organized a national network of regional development centers dedicated to reducing poverty in the countryside by increasing campesinos' productivity (Gordon 1998).

According to HD's cofounder, the early FMDR espoused a philosophy of entrepreneurial solidarity whereby Christian businessmen would use their socioeconomic position and political contacts to give a hand up to poor campesinos and set them on the path toward entrepreneurship. The FMDR saw lack of access to credit as the primary obstacle to entrepreneurship; given that *ejidal* lands could not serve as collateral for commercial bank loans, and because government development loans were inefficiently managed and often politically motivated, most campesinos had little hope of obtaining credit. The key to their strategy was the *aval*, a countersigning practice whereby wealthy and respected members of the FMDR would vouch for the creditworthiness of campesino cooperatives, thus enabling them to secure commercial loans. After a series of meetings with officials in the head office, HD was founded as a regional center in the FMDR network. They began by naming a board of directors composed of prominent businessmen from Tulancingo and Mexico City.[1]

The local context into which HD was born was a product both of the way the agrarian question was framed in the national agenda of the late 1970s and how those policy debates and programs were articulated to the particular conditions of rural Hidalgo. With a population that was more than 80 percent rural and mostly engaged in subsistence agriculture, along with its proximity to the capital, Hidalgo appeared on the national political radar as a potential hot spot of insurgency. Agrarian violence had already erupted in the Huasteca, a region to the northeast of Tulancingo with a ranching economy and a large indigenous population. The expansion and intensification of cattle ranching by large landowners, often in disputed territory claimed by indigenous *ejidos*, provoked a series of bloody skirmishes between independent campesino organizations (organized outside the CNC/PRI) and the ranchers' private militias, the *guardias blancas*. The conflict in the Huasteca brought to the surface a whole series of class tensions that had intensified as growing population density had resulted in elevated levels of rural unemployment, leading both to outmigration and to new demands for land redistribution. Though ranching occupied a large amount of arable land, it provided relatively few local jobs. As the ranches expanded, the region became a fertile ground for insurgency (Gutiérrez 1990; Schryer 1990; Vargas González 1998).

If the danger of rural rebellion caught the attention of PRI politicians and planners in the capital, then the close social ties connecting major Hidalgan officials to key national political figures and institutions facilitated the flow of federal resources to the formerly neglected province. In the late 1970s and early 1980s, two key figures, Jorge Rojo Lugo and Guillermo Rossell de la Lama, were able to convince the national government to invest in the development of rural Hidalgo. Rojo Lugo, who hailed from a powerful Huastecan political family, was elected governor in 1975. He was later appointed Secretary of Agrarian Reform by his old school friend, José López Portillo, then Mexico's president, which enabled him to direct substantial federal funds toward the resolution of the Huastecan conflict (Gutiérrez 1990; Valdespino Castillo 1992). Rojo Lugo's successor was Guillermo Rossell de la Lama, a member of the earliest generation of PRI technocrats who had occupied important planning posts in the national government and the PRI before attaining the governorship (Valdespino Castillo 1992, 87–90). Both Rojo Lugo and Rossell sought to stem the spread of agrarian revolt to other parts of the state, but the post-1968 political climate forced them to consider strategies other than indiscriminate repression.[2]

The conflict in the Huasteca would enable HD's founders to launch their project in the infamously conservative Tulancingo Valley with a modicum of official support, a factor crucial to their success. The PRI establishment viewed the growth of independent campesino organizations as a threat to the social and political order, but Rojo Lugo saw a clear advantage in allowing HD to attempt the development of rural communities in the valley. The governor hoped to harness the helping hand of this new branch of the FMDR to weed out unrest before it reached the southern part of the state. In fact, Rojo Lugo took a personal role in drumming up political and financial support for the project among the local elites. He helped HD's founders to plan a benefit banquet at a local hacienda, to which he personally invited the region's most prominent businessmen and ranchers. Arriving fashionably late, Rojo Lugo addressed the guests with a message of Christian charity and national progress, inviting those assembled to join their civic-minded neighbors in the modernization of the valley by financially underwriting HD's projects. At his signal, a bevy of attractive young hostesses wheeled a large blackboard onto the patio where the guests were seated, and the pledge drive began. Slips of paper were circulated among the guests, who were asked to write down their names and the amount of their pledges. The hostesses collected them, announcing each pledge before the group and recording it on the blackboard for all to see. One of the organizers recalled that Rojo Lugo set the example by making the first pledge. After that, she told me, the other important men of Tulancingo attempted to outdo one another; while none of them was loose with his money (especially where campesinos were concerned), no one wanted to risk being seen as cheap or uncharitable by his peers. By the end of the evening, the organizers had solicited enough pledges to provide a comfortable endowment for their new organization.

Given that these pledges of solidarity were exacted from a conservative provincial elite whose closest personal relationship to campesinos had been that of rancher to peon, mill owner to worker, master to servant, the motivational power of the articulation between the image of the Good Samaritan and the latent threat of rural rebellion was significant. Although Rojo Lugo's endorsement of HD went a long way toward securing the political opening necessary for the success of the project, many who had pledged their support in public would later privately attempt to distance themselves from their obligations. HD staff discovered the depth of their reluctance when they attempted to collect on the public pledges.

One of HD's early organizers told me the story of his visit to the offices of Guillermo Palomar, a local landowner and commercial dairy farmer who had pledged a sizable donation at the aforementioned banquet. Palomar initially tried to wriggle his way out of the pledge, now that he was past the scrutiny of his elite peers, by painting himself as a beleaguered patron of the campesinos. "I'm ashamed to say so, but just between the two of us, I cannot donate such an exorbitant sum. I am already responsible for the well-being of the many campesinos in my employ. If I pay you this money, then how will I pay their salaries?" When the HD staff member protested, Palomar rebuffed him. "Who looks out for the campesinos more than I do? I give them work at my dairy. I have a thousand head of cattle, and they are milked twice a day. I keep their hands busy." After a long pause, the staff member replied, "A thousand cows is a large number. It must take a lot of fodder to feed a herd that size." "Why yes," replied Palomar. "Still," continued the HD staff member, "I am impressed with an operation the size of yours. How many men does it take to do your milking?" "There are about 150 of them," answered Palomar. "How many hands is that?" asked the visitor. "Three hundred," Palomar said, "but why do you ask?" "It's just that I'm baffled," said the HD staff member, "that someone in your position would renege on his pledge toward our project when he has so much to lose." Palomar, agitated, ordered him to leave, but not before the HD representative declared loudly for all to hear, "I think it is time you reconsidered who really supports whom in this valley, and whether you'd prefer those 300 hands to be busy milking your cows or wringing your neck!" In the end the organizers managed to collect only about half the amount of the original pledges, but in May 1978, HD rented an office, hired a staff, and commenced their first slate of development projects.

Their initial efforts were directed at subsistence producers (both *ejiditarios* and small-property owners) spread out over the entire Tulancingo Valley. HD's early strategy, copied directly from the FMDR, was to increase the productivity of these small farmers through credit injections and technology transfer. Concretely, this meant working to identify and organize groups of campesinos who, with access to credit and the proper training, would be able to increase the productivity of their current endeavors and undertake new ones (for example, growing commercial instead of subsistence crops or raising livestock), thereby lifting their families out of poverty and isolation. HD promoters visited feed stores and roadside refreshment stands and even set up a booth at Tulancingo's annual fair in hopes of recruiting campesinos for their projects.

The NGO quickly identified access to water as the key to boosting productivity in this semiarid region. Most smallholder parcels were rain fed rather than irrigated and were prone to wind erosion in the dry season and flash flooding in the rainy season. Both of these processes depleted the precious topsoil of the plain while limiting the types of crops that could be grown and the number of potential growing cycles per year. Moreover, campesinos were forced to travel for miles to procure water for drinking, cooking, washing, and watering their livestock at rivers controlled by powerful ranchers. As HD staff members discovered through their recruiting chats with campesinos, many dreamed of owning a cow whose milk could be sold for cash. Access to water sources and irrigation technology would enable them not only to increase their production of basic crops such as corn and beans but also to sow pasturage with which to support livestock, in addition to redirecting female labor power from water procurement to other productive tasks. With this in mind, HD soon settled on a development strategy that hinged on the drilling of cooperatively managed wells in rural communities.

Through their affiliation with the FMDR, HD formed working relationships with government agencies, international aid organizations, and private banks to finance its projects. The Programa de Inversiones para el Desar-

Figure 4. Campesino family receiving plants through an HD reforestation and community garden project.

rollo Rural (Investment Program for Rural Development, PIDER) was typical of the semiclientelism that characterized the relationships between state agencies and rural development organizations. Funded in part by the World Bank, PIDER aimed to preserve the social peace in regions of growing tension by funding infrastructure and farm-credit projects involving community participation (Fox 1994, 162–163). HD promoters would identify and organize development groups in rural communities, provide technical and planning assistance for their projects, and guide them through the official paperwork necessary to secure funding. Environmental studies and drilling/access permits were arranged through PIDER, while commercial credit was procured through the SOMEX Bank, with *avales* and backing from FMDR. Once a well had been drilled, irrigation systems built, and pasturage cultivation demonstrated, HD would inaugurate a local project with Heifer International. This US-based international aid organization, founded by Christian relief workers, provides livestock to families in impoverished communities who agree to pass on the gift by donating future female offspring

Figure 5. Prayer during dedication ceremony for HD reforestation and community garden project.

to others. The Ford Foundation sponsored educational projects in six of HD's project sites, and the Inter-American Foundation awarded grants for heavy equipment. Through HD's efforts, twenty-two wells were drilled in rural communities over four municipalities, converting 1,700 hectares of land to irrigation and transforming the valley into a small-scale dairy region. By the mid-1980s, a dairy cooperative organized by HD was producing an average of 90,746 liters of milk per month and running three distribution centers within the city of Tulancingo. In addition to the FMDR's standard spate of projects, HD initiated a cooperative microcredit program to resolve household financial emergencies for which bank credits could not be obtained. To address topsoil erosion and water table depletion, they initiated a reforestation and soil conservation program rooted in their experience with scouting using state forestry funds obtained through contacts in Pachuca.

In spite of HD's success in increasing the economic productivity of local campesinos, its organizers thought that their development program had hit a cultural roadblock. Although the irrigation had brought about greater individual financial returns to campesino household heads, those economic benefits had not translated directly into increased cooperation and community solidarity. The cooperatives that HD organized to apply for loans and carry out projects tended to fall apart once their material goals were achieved. But the HD team was even more disturbed to realize, as they became better acquainted with the campesinos through promotion work in the communities, that the economic benefits obtained through these development projects were not being used in ways they considered true to the notion of solidarity. HD, along with planners in the central office of the FMDR, had assumed that campesino household heads would direct their increased income toward providing their families with better health care, clothing, education, and modern housing—in short, that they would reinvest this new income in a way that reflected both entrepreneurial logic and middle-class values. Instead, much of this cash was used instead to finance traditional saints' fiestas and ritual kinship obligations or articles of conspicuous consumption such as television sets.[3] Because this income was channeled through household heads, it also provided men with another source of authoritarian power over the family. Those with irrigation rights might charge outsiders for access to water, or members of a tractor cooperative might rent out the group's machinery to nonmembers. This new wealth, paltry though it might have been, was deepening the rift between the haves and have-nots in the countryside, creating *envidia* (envy) and division in rural communities.[4] This realization cast doubt on the capacity of entrepreneurial philanthropy to produce egalitarianism and community spirit in the countryside. This was a common ongoing complaint among Tulancingo NGO workers in general. Even those I interviewed during my 2002–2003 fieldwork period expressed frustration with what they viewed as inefficient or even immoral spending by campesinos involved in development projects. One development NGO staffer told me, "With regard to fiestas, they are perfectly happy to give their money to buy tequila or act as a godparent, but when I show up and ask for each cooperative member to chip in for equipment or the next round of artificial insemination [of dairy cattle], suddenly no one has any money to cooperate." Campesinos in turn complained to me that NGO workers failed to recognize the importance of obligations to participate in ritual kinship relationships and the religious cargo systems in their communities. These social networks, cemented via fiestas, were essential to the long-term socioeconomic stability of campesino families, and they took on even greater importance in the context of unreliable external ties with government agencies and NGOs alike. Likewise, the purchase of consumer goods like televisions represented a means of connection to the life of the modern nation. As one project participant put it, "Why am I not allowed to have a TV when he [an NGO worker] has one in his house?"

Indeed, as Wolf (1956, 1959; Mintz and Wolf [1950] 1977) has pointed out, equality in rural Mexican communities has often been maintained through a combination of leveling mechanisms and social sanctions for deviance, not mere voluntarism. Nevertheless, when development workers of the 1980s failed to find the sort of communal relationships they had imagined, they began to question the campesinos' worthiness as an instrument of national development. Before, the countryside had seemed the bastion of national folklore and history, with the campesinos downtrodden but Revolutionary subjects. Now they saw them as petty children who complained of oppression yet seized the chance to lord it over one another when an opportunity presented itself. HD promoters framed the problem in terms of a Mexican proverb, "*Los peces gordos siempre comen a los pequeños*" (the big fish always eat the smaller ones). It was a dilemma faced by many contemporary Mexican development practitioners and as such provided fodder for a good many debates over what to do. For HD, the debate was put into sharp focus in 1982 when FMDR hired a team of outside consultants to assess the efficacy of its development program and Tulancingo was chosen as a field site for the study (see González Graf and Camacho Alfaro 1983).

After completing field surveys of the organization's rural project sites, the consultants agreed that the FMDR's capitalization program, rather than integrating campesinos as a whole into Mexican modernity, as intended, was actually creating a rural elite. However, the researchers went farther than HD promoters in their critique, locating the failure in the FMDR's conception of its relationship to the regional centers and, through them, to the campesinos. The original idea of the foundation had been to create the regional centers as conduits for transferring capital and technical assistance to the countryside. The centers would begin by organizing campesinos into cooperatives that could then become subjects of credit, setting them on the path to entrepreneurship and hence full citizenship in a modern Mexico. Once this stage was complete, the centers could be turned over to the campesinos to manage autonomously while the foundation invested its resources in creating more centers in new regions. The funds for the continued operation of said centers could be raised by charging the new rural entrepreneurs for the technical assistance that had previously been subsidized by the foundation. This was becoming standard international practice in many NGOs. It was intended not just to shift responsibility onto campesino participants but also to create long-term financial sustainability for the NGOs themselves, both by reducing donor dependency and by increasing the reach of their signature development models. In the opinion of the consultants, however, this model could never work in rural Mexico. The first reason was that the campesinos' poverty was not merely the result of a lack of appropriate government policy, competently applied. Rather, it was the result of the entire productive system, which promoted industrial over agricultural development by transferring resources from the countryside to the city, coupled to a political system based on the marginalization of campesinos as a class as well as a social system where rules of land tenure (that is, the *ejido*) prevented modernity (in the form of private property, the basis of entrepreneurship) from easily penetrating the countryside. Without drastic changes to the political, economic, and social *structures* within which campesinos were embedded, campesinos as a class would never overcome their marginal position on their own. Although the centers might become relatively more independent of the foundation, with campesinos taking a greater role in governing and planning processes, they would still need to draw on the foundation's financial resources in order to carry out projects.[5]

The consultants recommended that regional centers take advantage of extant cooperative labor mechanisms such as the *ejidal faena* in planning their projects, especially those directed toward the procurement of resources that could presumably benefit an entire community, such as water. They observed that while attitudes of solidarity and cooperation tended to prevail during the initial stages of cooperative organization by FMDR promoters, as greater agricultural productivity was achieved, these attitudes were increasingly threatened by urban values of consumption. The FMDR's strategy of organizing cooperatives at the individual (or household) level rather than the community level was in direct contrast to government schemes that were attempting to organize on the level of the *ejido* or the village. Although it produced its own set of problems, including *caciquismo*, the government

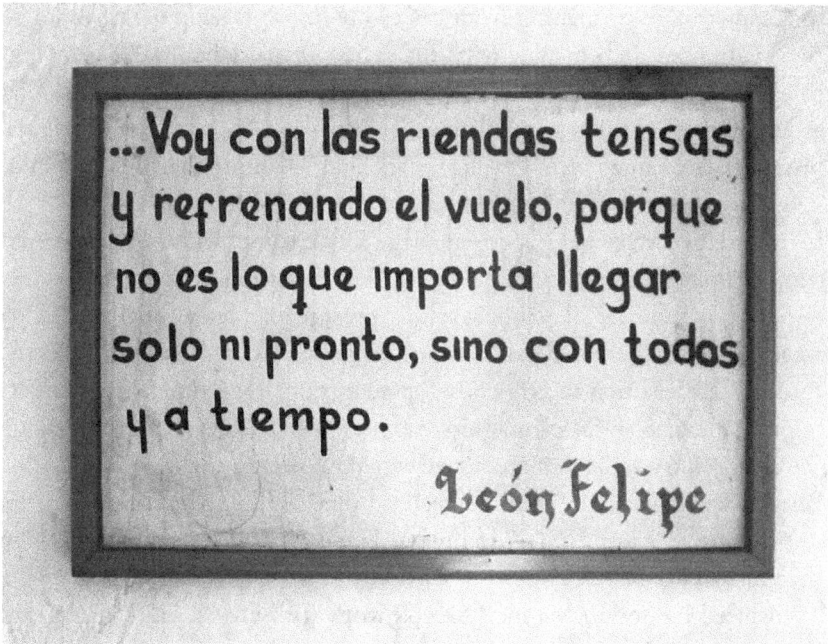

...Voy con las riendas tensas
y refrenando el vuelo, porque
no es lo que importa llegar
solo ni pronto, sino con todos
y a tiempo.

León Felipe

Figure 6. Sign in HD headquarters, dating from the early 1980s. "I hold the reins tight and restrain my gait, because it is not important to arrive alone or with haste, but rather all together and on time."

model had placed a premium on communitarian values and internal hegemony because of the representative structure of the corporatist system (see Nader 1990). In essence, the FMDR's cultivation of entrepreneurial campesinos, intended to ameliorate rural poverty and integrate campesinos into the space of Mexican modernity, was in fact destroying the very (admittedly mythologized) principles and practices of solidarity that represented (for the developers) the cultural value of campesinos to the nation's historical project. It could be said that the subtext of the report was a deep questioning of just what modernization meant in this context and how NGOs, as new institutional forms, should participate in its cultivation.

What was needed in order for the cooperatives to eventually function autonomously, in the opinion of the consultants, was a rural education campaign directed at the reformation of campesino community culture. There was a sense among both the FMDR consultants and HD's own promoters that something was missing from the campesinos' development. Although they had raised their productivity, the fruits of their labors were being put to uses the developers considered less than worthy. "Everyone knows that a rich campesino is far worse than a *rico de abolengo*,"[6] one of HD's original promoters explained to me twenty years later, claiming that the difference between the two was culture, which provided more affluent citizens with the values necessary to properly manage money, both with respect to consumption and the role money plays in one's relations with others. While upper-class families like the Servitjes presumably knew how to deploy their wealth in the pursuit of national progress, the new affluence created through participation in HD's development programs led to "envy, infighting, and discord" in the campesino communities. "I believed that by making the campesino a subject of credit, we would make him a human subject," he lamented. "But little by little we realized that cultural education was what was lacking, not just capital" to prepare the campesino to take his place in the modern nation.

Inspired by Sergio Mendez Arceo's work with CEBs, HD's promoters began constructing their own approach to rural development based on Christian brotherhood rather than Christian charity. Through their experiences with governmental and philanthropic power structures, the organization's leaders developed a further distaste for hierarchy and bureaucracy as well as a more structural understanding of agrarian questions. They seized on the culture of paternalism—instantiated in daily life from the level of the state and the Church hierarchy down to the relationships among family members—as responsible for the failure of economically developing campesinos to become more solidary members of their communities. Furthermore, it was this paternalism and the structures that embodied it that prevented campesinos from becoming integrated into the nation as citizens on equal terms. In order to counter it, HD promoters reasoned, they would have to find a way to make campesinos recognize and unite around their common economic and political interests. This would involve broadening local conceptions of community and solidarity beyond kinship networks and ties to the same *ejidal* land. It also involved attacking what they viewed as ideological dependency through popular education programs (rural communities had very low literacy rates, no access to education beyond poorly staffed and funded primary schools, and almost no access to books or newspapers). Against paternalism, HD organizers sought to promote an ethic of brotherhood among campesinos as a class, a more democratic *fuerza campesina*. Their strategy involved a combination of consciousness raising (*conscientización*) and informal education (*capacitación*), coupled with a complex of development practices designed to expand and reinforce communitarian relationships. These practices built on their previous experiences in cooperative projects but also integrated others such as regional retreats, workshops, and exchanges, as well as campesino participation in the organization's decision-making structures and processes. While credit was imagined as the magic bullet of rural development during HD's inaugural era, by the mid-1980s, the focus shifted to the search for the "human factor," the *factor aglutinante* that would be the key to reinvention of campesino community. The shift toward an educational mission was also propelled by HD's dwindling financial resources and the difficult economic climate caused by the debt crisis and ensuing austerity policies. Just as HD was undertaking a campaign to rehabilitate and recreate forms of campesino solidarity, the technocratic revolution was incrementally erasing the political, economic, and legal bases of reciprocity and cooperation in the countryside.

Cooperatives and Integral Development

In 1983, three key rural development programs—PIDER, SAM, and the Office of Nacional Plan for Depressed Zones and Marginalized Groups (COPLAMAR)—were eliminated. All three had been directed at combating poverty while stimulating staple food production and had served as an important institutional support during HD's early years. By the late 1980s, small-scale agriculture no longer played a part in the economic plans of the neoliberal technocrats, but in Hidalgo, it remained the primary means of livelihood. In addition to changes precipitated by the successive national economic crises, in the 1990s, the local dairy industry underwent structural adjustments of its own. Under President Echeverría (1970–1976), a government project intended to augment and streamline the supply of milk to the capital led to the development of an enormous system of industrial stables and processing plants in the area surrounding the city of Tizayuca. The project, amounting to what one former government extension agent described as a "city of cows," greatly increased the production of milk. This had two effects: by the 1980s, it drove the price down drastically and shifted the supply center for the capital from Tulancingo to Tizayuca. Having already been decapitalized by the devaluation of the peso, the large family-run stables that had been the staple of the Tulancingo dairy industry since colonial times went into decline. Falling milk prices and rising labor costs (exacerbated by the threat of unionization) encouraged the closure of many of these enterprises.

In the *ejidos* surrounding Tulancingo, a new system of dairy production was coalescing. With the arrival of irrigation and other development projects, more campesinos acquired dairy cattle. While the traditional stables had to pay for feed and labor, campesino families invested the extra unremunerated labor power (usually female) available to them into animal husbandry in hopes of a cash return. But getting the milk to market presented campesinos with a new problem, especially given the lack of roads and transportation and the perishable nature of their product. A new system sprang up in the breach; a few families with access to trucks became *boteros*, or intermediaries, collecting their neighbors' milk once a day for transport to processing centers for a fee. Soon campesino families were at the mercy of these intermediaries, who paid them twelve pesos a liter, only to sell the milk to processors and stores in Tulancingo at thirty pesos. Thus, although the campesino cooperatives associated with HD now for the most part had access to water and the use of a tractor, as well as owning cattle, they could not convert that into capital as the price of milk fell. The poor of Tulancingo were also at a disadvantage as the debt crisis and subsequent devaluation had placed basic food items such as milk beyond the reach of many families.

The problem was put to HD staff by a group of campesinos from the municipality of Acatlán at a meeting in October 1982. It was agreed that the solution would be for HD to help the campesinos to form a cooperative to market their milk directly to consumers in Tulancingo. They would eliminate both the *boteros* and the processing centers from the equation, offering milk to consumers directly at an affordable price. For HD's organizers, this seemed a prime opportunity to put into practice their new ideas about how to combine educational and productive projects to promote and expand campesino solidarity. After a month of planning and organization, the operation commenced in November 1982 and involved sixteen household heads.

The municipal government of Tulancingo lent HD a long abandoned police substation in a working-class neighborhood for use as a distribution point. Using HD's pickup truck, members of the group took turns collecting their neighbors' fresh milk in large metal cans (*botes*) and transporting it to the distribution point, where it was sold to the urban public from the hours of 7 to 10 AM and in the evening from 6 to 8 PM. They sold the milk at twenty-eight pesos per liter—lower than the wholesale price—returning twenty-five pesos of the price to the producer and using the remaining three pesos to cover the costs of transportation. The associates named their cooperative the Campesinos' Union (UC) and adopted the slogan invented for them by the HD promoters: "Milk from the poor people of the countryside, for the poor people of the city" (*Leche del pobre del campo, para el pobre de la ciudad*). This strategy and its accompanying slogan represented a new evaluation of the agrarian question as well as of the dynamics of solidarity necessary for rural development. It embodied a clear understanding of the structural roots of rural poverty—symbolized by the figure of the corrupt *botero*—and a surprising reversal of the dynamics of solidarity. Whereas HD's initial forays into rural development had been predicated on a philanthropic model whereby an urban elite sought to lend a helping hand to their impoverished countrymen out of a sense of Catholic charity and nationalist boosterism, this new turn sought to produce a different, more popularly based sense of solidarity between the city and the countryside. The unified *fuerza campesina* that HD hoped to promote through the UC project would not only help campesino cooperatives overcome their internal conflicts but would also be a first step toward reorganizing structural relationships between the city and the countryside on more democratic terms. Campesinos would thus once again become historical protagonists of modernization.

The UC project was an immediate economic success. Initially the co-operative sold only three to four *botes* of milk per day, but within a matter of weeks the operation had attracted the interest of a number of other campesinos in the region who were eager to take part in the project. HD soon focused most of its resources and energy toward developing and expanding the project, which became the new cornerstone of their strategy for regional development. Within a year, the number of UC associates (*socios*) had grown from six different families to seventy-two in the municipalities of Tulancingo and Acatlán. HD procured credits for the genetic improve-

Figure 7. HD store in Tulancingo, offering products from campesino cooperatives.

ment of the associates' livestock and stables from the Rural Development Bank (BANRURAL), the payments for which were subtracted directly from associates' weekly profits. It also provided the associates with courses in animal husbandry, construction of silos for the storage of fodder, and various feeding techniques. Additionally, it arranged another donation of 120 calves from Heifer International and instituted a partnership with a local veterinary school, which sent its recent graduates to complete their professional practicum as volunteers for the UC. HD envisioned the UC as the *factor aglutinante* that would unite the campesinos of the region and invested significant energy and resources into the cooperative's growth.

In order to equip the associates to eventually take over the management of UC on their own, HD solicited a grant from the Ford Foundation to launch an educational project in the six communities. The project, which was funded from 1982 to 1985, sought to educate UC members for entrepreneurship as well as to "transform [their] mentality, motivations, and attitudes toward solidarity, commitment, service, and love" for one another as brothers and sisters.[7] This *capacitación* was carried out through three interconnected sets of practices. In weekly meetings of the association's officers, HD promoters sought to instill financial and management skills through technical workshops and group analyses of the cooperative's problems, in which the associates discussed operational procedures and attempted to solve internal conflicts. These meetings were supplemented by monthly assemblies involving all the associates, where business matters were discussed, leaders were chosen, and films were shown on new scientific advances in animal husbandry. Finally, HD arranged retreats and exchanges between the UC and campesino cooperatives from other regions to compare experiences and techniques. The capstone of the *capacitación* project took place in 1984, when posts for four campesino representatives were added to the board of directors. The intention was to slowly turn HD over to the campesinos, whose numbers on the board would increase relative to those of the distinguished businessmen, until eventually HD would be governed entirely by the campesinos it had "developed."

Even as the UC continued to grow, the next few years found it beset on all sides by a variety of challenges. To begin with, Mexico's debt crisis and currency devaluation decapitalized the cooperative. Dreams of opening a large stable and milk processing facility were put on hold. Although they eventually received a grant from the Konrad Adenauer Foundation of Germany in support of the construction of a milk processing plant on the outskirts of Tulancingo, and the residency of a German expert who spent five months teaching the UC associates to make and age cheese in the spare rooms of HD's office building, internal conflicts erupted that proved difficult to solve. An external manager was brought in with the backing of the Konrad Adenauer Foundation to professionalize the administrative structure and practices of the UC. According to HD's promoters, although he carried out his duties well, the manager's presence was viewed as an imposition from above by the campesino associates of the UC. His authority contrasted with the idea of the UC as an egalitarian brotherhood of campesinos.[8] It also was a perceived affront to the authority of the UC's campesino leaders, who were not formally educated but were highly respected within their communities and among the associates. While the UC associates perceived the manager's presence as indicating a lack of trust on the part of HD, it also indicated a paradox inherent in the NGO form itself. As an organization, HD was accountable to the Konrad Adenauer Foundation, the Ford Foundation,

Heifer International, and commercial banks for the funds to underwrite the project. Because HD was so heavily invested in the UC, those actors' perceptions of the UC's success or failure could make or break the NGO. This upward accountability was in tension with HD's intent of turning the reigns of the UC over to its associates.

Other conflicts emerged between HD and the associates of the UC over the future scope of the cooperative. HD staff envisioned expanding the UC into a regional cooperative that would unite campesinos and the urban poor throughout the entire Tulancingo Valley in a diversified, integrated, and self-sufficient food system. The founding members of the UC, however, were reluctant to allow the admission of new associates to the cooperative. HD staff attributed this refusal to *envidia* and closed-mindedness. The associates, however, worried that the expansion of the cooperative might mean losing the very control and autonomy that was one of the greatest advantages of becoming organized. The conflict produced a growing breach between the UC and HD, leading to the eventual dissolution of the relationship. It was clear that the cooperative model—derived from German examples—could not simply be transplanted to Mexican soil without modification. The NGO form itself also presented challenges to enacting the sorts of horizontal relationships between campesinos and NGO workers that were inspired by the model of the CEB.

Solidarity and the NGO Form

By the late 1980s, some of the tensions inherent in the NGO form were becoming apparent. The form itself, however, would soon take on new social and economic importance in Mexico. In 1985, the human suffering caused by the debt crisis and structural adjustment was exacerbated by a natural disaster of epic proportions. On September 19, a massive earthquake, measuring 8.1 on the Richter scale, took place in Mexico City and was followed by a 7.6 aftershock the next day. The shaking was felt as far away as Texas and Colorado, and the destruction was extensive. Seven thousand buildings were leveled, with total damages estimated at $5 billion. Out of a population of eighteen million, an estimated ten thousand people died, fifty thousand were injured, and 250,000 instantly became homeless. Tens of thousands of them joined the growing population of Tulancingo, expanded from 70,782 in 1980 to around 335,000 by 1990 (Gobierno del Estado [de] Hidalgo 1993, 1). The ensuing social crisis provoked a focus on survival and fulfilling the basic needs of the population, but it also created spaces for new forms of solidarity outside the state as means to achieve those goals.

While the Echeverría and Lopez Portillo administrations had attempted to monopolize social organizing by co-opting and persecuting independent NGOs and bolstering social programs channeled through the PRI's sectoral structure, the government's failure to respond adequately in the aftermath of the earthquake both led to a change in social consciousness and enabled independent organizations to exploit the growing cracks in government control. In the days and weeks after the quake, ordinary citizens banded together to deal with the destruction in a variety of ways—forming rescue crews to dig their neighbors out from under the wreckage, for example.[9] The earthquake became a historical watershed of the same proportions as Tlatelolco; it is cited by academics and activists alike as a foundational moment in the life of the Mexican NGO sector (Aguilar Valenzuela 1997a). In addition to the neighborly response of the city's residents in the face of government indecision, indifference, and ineptitude, an outpouring of international aid was mobilized in record time. While a good deal of this assistance came in the form of state-to-state aid packages[10] and recovery loans from international agencies such as the World Bank, many private international donors, concerned with the Mexican government's reputation for corruption and inefficiency, sought out grassroots groups through which to channel their contributions to the victims. These nascent partnerships helped to open up a new paradigm of international cooperation in Mexico and bolstered the bargaining power of the new organizations springing up around a variety of issues related to the crisis (Miraftab 1997, 43). The loss of state legitimacy further provided an opening for social movements and NGOs to assert rights to associational autonomy, beginning an iterative cycle of negotiations with political officials and reformist or technocratic state managers (Fox and Hernández 1992).

At the same time Mexicans were contending with the ongoing economic crisis and the aftermath of the tragedy in the capital, a series of civil wars in Central America unleashed a flood of refugees whose flight northward would also profoundly affect the shape of changes then taking place in the

NGO world. In these waning years of the Cold War, the United States was less concerned with the debt crisis than with a Sandinista victory in Nicaragua and civil wars that threatened to spread communism in El Salvador, Guatemala, and Honduras. Aguayo[11] asserts that Mexico opened to human rights from the South rather than the North, as NGOs on the ground in southern Mexico teamed up with international aid workers to address the refugee crisis. In 1983, Mexico took the lead in the peace process. The Diocese of San Cristóbal, headed by Bishop Samuel Ruiz, supported the asylum rights of Central American refugees by referring to their universal human rights, a concept disseminated through the combined efforts of Mexican and international activists. With time, domestic and international focus shifted to human rights violations within Mexico itself, especially in Chiapas. As a consequence of these dynamics, the language of individual human rights gained legitimacy within Mexico, as well as helping to foster communication and cooperation between domestic NGOs and new social movements and international agencies and NGOs like the United Nations Human Rights Council (UNHRC) and Amnesty International.

The human toll of the proxy wars in Central America served to widen a split among Church-influenced NGOs that had been developing since the late 1960s. By the mid-1980s, the lines of conflict between those organizations that followed the tenets of liberation theology and those whose outlook more closely resembled the Christian Democrats (like FMDR) were becoming more pronounced. Members of HD, whose promoters felt more closely drawn to the vision of solidarity laid out by the former contingent, were caught in the middle and forced to choose sides. The organization undertook a series of exchange visits between campesino participants in its own projects and those of other small provincial NGOs from other parts of Mexico. The purpose of these visits was to provide an opportunity for campesinos to learn from one another's development experiences while cultivating a shared sense of identity and interests.[12]

As a result of its search for new approaches to popular education, in 1986, HD joined a network of local liberation theology and development groups organized by the Secretariat for New Experiences in Community Education (SENEC). Based in a working-class neighborhood of Mexico City, SENEC was the brainchild of Francesc Botey, a Piarist missionary priest from Barcelona. Twice yearly, the members of SENEC communities sent delegates to participate in popular *encuentros* (meetings). Each community took turns hosting a weeklong retreat in which participants conducted workshops on current events and social issues, performed popular theater, sang songs, prayed, and worked on development projects together. The SENEC *encuentros* were organized thematically and were designed not only to provide a group-building experience but also to disseminate information and analysis. One of the *encuentros* focused on democracy and human rights, with performance pieces on the different Mexican political parties and a mock election designed to prepare delegates to participate actively in the ill-fated 1988 presidential election.

Although the FMDR was pleased with the results of HD's development projects, the leadership of the foundation became increasingly uncomfortable with the organization's popular education program. To promote economic self-reliance and democratic political participation, HD's personnel had begun promoting integral development projects in poor farming villages, combining infrastructure projects with popular education. Members of HD were encouraged to participate in regional assemblies of popular organizations, and some HD staff promoted the founding of a sister organization dedicated to protecting human rights. The distinction the PRI made between political and social organizing placed limits on the strategy of NGOs like HD:

> The classical political bargain required official incorporation of social groups under state tutelage in exchange for access to social programs. Mass protests that were strictly "social" were sometimes tolerated, but if it was perceived as "political" (that is, challenging the hegemony of the ruling party), the usual mix of partial concessions with repression shifted toward the latter. (Fox 1994, 159–160)

Hence HD's shift from a primarily philanthropic orientation to an approach aimed at fostering rural civic engagement, particularly one framed in terms of claiming political and social rights, brought about tension both with the FMDR and with key figures in the PRI, whose tacit support had enabled the organization's early inroads. A rift emerged between FMDR's national directorate and HD during this era as FMDR began to accuse HD of drifting toward political rather than social aims.

Decades later, HD staff members recounted to me the moment they regarded as the straw that broke the camel's back. The incident took place during the Christmas season, when a representative from the FMDR headquarters in Mexico City made an unannounced visit to the Tulancingo office. The United Nations had declared 1986 the International Year of Peace, and in anticipation, participants in a HD/SENEC retreat had constructed a *periodico mural* on the state of world peace. The work was exhibited in the entrance to the main office, alongside a display of Christmas cards from HD's supporters and partner organizations put together by the secretary and office assistant. Alongside doves and olive branches, however, the installation featured newspaper images of the wars in Central America, including pictures of Nicaraguan refugees and a memorial to slain Archbishop Oscar Romero of El Salvador. There were excerpts from critiques of the Reagan Peace Plan for Central America by leading liberation theologists. The title, handwritten in thick black marker across the top, read "La Paz de Reagan No Es La Paz de Jesus."[13] "Of course," one HD staff member remarked to me two decades later, "they were not pleased." That displeasure, shared by local authorities from the conservative diocese of Tulancingo who accused the group of promoting communism in the countryside, would ultimately result in the dissolution of the relationship between the FMDR and HD.

At the same time the FMDR stopped funding the Tulancingo group, problems erupted in the relationship between HD and SOMEX. Refusing to confine its role to the recruitment and organization of credit applicants for the bank, HD directed its efforts instead toward developing integral projects in more communities. The bank responded by withdrawing its partnership, claiming that HD's failure to recruit new groups at its previous pace meant that their joint venture was no longer financially worthwhile. Soon afterward, Mexico suffered a new series of major currency devaluations, which effectively decapitalized HD by drastically shrinking the real value of its endowment. In 1988, HD was forced to raffle off a pickup truck in order to continue its development work; this was but the first of many small-scale fund-raisers that (along with support from international partners) would sustain the organization over the next decade. By the 1990s, FMDR had founded a new regional affiliate in Tulancingo, the Hidalgan Foundation for Rural Service (FHAR). The FHAR continued the FMDR's long-standing focus on rural development projects aimed at increasing agricultural productivity and commercialization; as its name suggests, it frames its intervention in the idiom of charitable service. In contrast, HD redirected its program toward rural popular education, human rights, and fair trade initiatives. In 1990, the board elected its first campesino president. As the new decade dawned, changes were taking place in Mexico that would profoundly alter the fields in which HD worked. HD began taking steps toward a new vision that placed its program of rural development firmly at the center of national struggles for democracy. It was becoming part of a democratic civil rights movement that would help to change the form and content of Mexican citizenship and the possibilities for rural development in unexpected ways.

Although social and economic demands formed the primary agendas of Mexican social movements in the 1970s and 1980s, the focus had begun to shift by the 1990s toward calls for human rights and democratization. This shift, which accompanied crises of state legitimacy and accountability, was characterized in part by demands from NGOs for official recognition and the beginning of a long struggle to institutionalize their role in policymaking. Thus NGOs came to serve as institutional links between grassroots movements and intellectuals and "in the process, a new sense of citizenship . . . emerged, combining community-based self-organization for socioeconomic development with a political push for accountable government" (Fox and Hernández 1992, 168). This new framework encouraged many more NGOs and movements to become involved in electoral politics, but often from the side of voter education and poll monitoring rather than direct engagement with political parties or candidates. Horizontal alliances among civil society groups later enabled the successful growth of the prodemocracy movement of the 1990s. Umbrella groups like Civic Alliance (Alianza Cívica) skillfully leveraged international media attention and human rights discourse in order to pressure their government into a series of important reforms.

Nodes in the Network: Coalitions for Change, 1994–2006

On January 1, 1994, the day NAFTA took effect, indigenous rebels calling themselves the Zapatista Army of National Liberation (EZLN) occupied several towns in the impoverished southern state of Chiapas. Denouncing the Mexican government's capitulation to the Washington Consensus, they demanded indigenous rights, land reform, and democracy. Chiapas became the site of a low-intensity war in which the Mexican government attempted to wear down Zapatista support bases, invading civilian areas and unleashing a refugee crisis. Mexican NGOs in the conflict zone responded by calling for international observers to monitor the human rights situation. Hundreds of international delegations have traveled to Chiapas in the last two decades, linking Mexican NGOs into a variety of transnational networks. For HD, as for other Mexican NGOs, the Zapatista challenge served as a catalyst in the search for political solutions to the social costs of the neoliberal transition. Through their organizing practices, however, HD and other Mexican NGOs were beginning to work out and promote a new ideal of solidarity based on flexible relationships among autonomous units. As the twentieth century drew to a close, solidarity began to take on the aesthetic form of the network.

Throughout the decade after the Zapatista uprising, HD sent delegations to Chiapas to acts as human rights observers in the conflict zones. They worked with the Fray Bartolomé de las Casas Human Rights Center (founded by Bishop Ruiz), Servicio Internacional para la Paz (SIPAZ), and the Mexico Solidarity Network (MSN) to document human rights abuses by the Mexican military and regional paramilitaries in civilian zones and to serve as witnesses and human shields. Campesino participants in HD project sites and members of a HD youth group also traveled to Chiapas to participate in international assemblies of civil society organizations convened by the EZLN. HD hosted multiple Zapatista delegations at their headquarters in Tulancingo during the ensuing decade, including a stop in 2006 for *La Otra Campaña*, a nationwide political tour in advance of the controversial presidential elections. HD also participated in numerous other NGO networks aimed at cultivating democratic change in Mexico.

In the late 1990s, the proliferation of Mexican NGO networks like Civic Alliance, Citizens' Movement for Democracy (Movimiento Ciudadaño por la Democracía, MCD), and the "All Rights for Everyone" National Human Rights Network (Red Nacional de Organismos Civiles de Derechos Humanos "Todos los Derechos para Todos," known as Red TDPT) was hailed internationally as a positive indicator of Mexico's progress toward democracy. HD participated in the work of all three of these umbrella networks to shape a national agenda for the prodemocracy movement. In addition to attending national conferences, workshops, and marches, HD staff coordinated a series of voter education workshops in the organization's rural project sites. It also trained campesino observation teams to monitor their local polling places and encouraged young people from rural communities to become involved in local municipal government. Working with partner organizations within these networks contributed to a sense of camaraderie and common purpose, HD staffers told me in 2002 and 2003. Many of them still kept their name badges and T-shirts from national conventions as mementos in their homes or offices. The wide range of attendees at HD's twenty-fifth anniversary celebration was also a testament to the lasting impact of networks forged during this crucial period.

In the 1990s and early 2000s, the changing political economic landscape of rural Mexico and the structural and ideological shifts in the NGO world eventually forced HD to reconstruct its development strategy using those same networks. Ongoing financial hardships compelled the organization to abandon most of the capital-intensive infrastructure and productive projects in campesino communities in favor of projects focused on education and outreach, and to join forces with other grassroots Mexican and foreign NGOs. In 1998, HD joined with four other independent rural development organizations to launch Raiz, a holistic development project that sought to revive the production and consumption of amaranth in impoverished regions of Central Mexico. Amaranth, a nutrient-rich and highly drought-resistant grain, had made up an important part of the region's pre-Conquest diet, but Spanish missionaries outlawed its cultivation because of the plant's use in indigenous rituals. The mission of Raiz was twofold: to combat malnutrition and environmental degradation through promoting the cultivation of amaranth in rural communities and to generate cash income by processing part of the harvest into packaged foods that could then be sold in urban areas. Since its inception, the project has won numerous national and international awards and has spawned a fascination with amaranth among the local development community.

HD staff simultaneously promoted the production of amaranth in rural communities and launched an education campaign in Tulancingo and Pachuca aimed at "rescuing the amaranth culture" as a part of Mexican heri-

Figure 8. HD staff members visit a Tulancingo elementary school to educate the students about amaranth cultivation and the Raiz project.

tage.[14] They held demonstrations and tastings at health food stores and designed and delivered educational programming to local public and private schools. They also featured Raiz products prominently at HD's campesino store in Tulancingo, which serves as an outlet for campesinos to sell food and other products to urban residents. Both of these enterprises are run according to fair trade principles.

The commercial success of the Raiz project in Tulancingo has been limited by the expense of these social enterprise products—they were popular among residents who knew about and could afford natural foods, but in a working-class city like Tulancingo, this was a small market niche. It was difficult for Raiz to compete with Frito-Lay, Coca-Cola, and Bimbo, whose industrialized food products are both cheap and familiar to Mexican consumers. Nonetheless, the integral nature of the Raiz project, its low start-up costs, and its indigenous cachet all made amaranth attractive to PRI staff in Hidalgo's state development ministry (Integral Family Development [Desarrollo Integral de la Familia, DIF], Hidalgo) looking for a magic bullet with which to quickly boost statistical indicators of rural well-being. Work-

Figure 9. Elementary students sow amaranth seeds to take home with them.

ing through personal social contacts, the PRI first moved to recruit the local manager of Raiz away from HD with promises of a large operating budget and a post in the state government. When she refused this initial offer, they proposed a "partnership" between HD and the state government, whereby she and her staff would provide information and training for state employees in the organization and maintenance of community amaranth projects in exchange for funding. Although HD staff debated this tempting option, they soon concluded that the risks of political co-optation outweighed any potential financial gains. Eventually, several state agencies in Hidalgo launched their own amaranth-related projects with the help of outside consultants. Recent years have seen a rapid increase in the use of the NGO form as a means of organizing public–private partnerships, especially in the areas of service delivery and the management of public space and patrimony in Mexico. As we will see in Chapter 5, these arrangements position NGOs as a new category of intermediary, with its own structural dynamics and political limitations.

Conclusion

For nearly four decades, HD has attempted to cultivate new forms of social and productive relations in the Tulancingo Valley. The history of this work reveals the way the NGO form enables the fusion of public and private in efforts to reconfigure such relations. The results of these labors have been uneven, but many projects have borne unexpected fruit. During earlier epochs of the organization's history, HD's leaders sought to nurture and harness what they imagined to be existing forms of social solidarity in the countryside as a means of furthering their development goals. At times, as in the case of the UC, they were disappointed to find that cooperation among campesinos did not work as they thought it might. Although the *ejido* had been envisioned as an egalitarian collectivity by post-Revolutionary ideologues and as a base community by social reformers inspired by liberation theology, in practice, this ideal was intertwined with and interpenetrated by other forms of loyalty and cooperation like ritual kinship. As HD staff learned, communitarian forms transplanted from elsewhere might fail to thrive in such soil. Since the mid-1990s, however, individualizing discourses of democratic rights have been accompanied by the erasure of the institutional underpinnings of campesino cooperation, such as the *ejido*. In turn, HD's capacity to address these problems has been influenced by important shifts in the Mexican NGO world, which will be discussed in more detail in Chapter 4.

   The history of HD and organizations like it demonstrates the difficulty of sorting NGOs into normative categories; they change over time in response to the relationships, challenges, opportunities, and political and policy shifts that shape the environments in which they operate. Their aims are never neutral but rather reflect regional and class-based worldviews and the dispositions of their organizers and supporters, which also alter as they are brought into dialogue with funders, collaborators, and participants in project sites. Nor are the outcomes of their projects guaranteed, as they are produced through practices of negotiation among actors in relationships of dynamic tension.

Public discourses concerning the erosion of traditional forms of community have accompanied periods of rapid social change throughout modern Western history (Deakin 2001; Yar 2004). Over the last several decades, the political and economic restructuring undertaken by states in the name of free markets has spawned new assemblages of human needs without explicitly creating new institutions of social reproduction (Ong 2003). The privatization of service provision and the education of new citizens have instead engaged the leadership of a growing NGO sector funded largely through private philanthropy and, more recently, social enterprise. While the 1980s and early 1990s saw a wave of rights-based social movements aimed at obtaining state recognition, the global ascendancy of the NGO heralds the construction of a new mode of citizen inclusion and participation on the margins of traditional political processes. NGOs are increasingly tasked with bringing together public and private actors and resources to repair or rework the social ties perceived to undergird the public order.

CHAPTER 3

Withered Milpas

Rural Development after Neoliberalism

The founders of HD and other Tulancingo organizations that followed it created local development projects with a nationalist aim: to organize rural communities for increased production, citizen engagement, and mutual aid. They looked for ways to create a new *fuerza campesina*, independent from the corporatist party structure as well as the Church hierarchy.[1] However, by the 1990s, poor Mexican peasants came to be regarded as iconic victims of structural adjustment and free trade policies under the Washington Consensus. The Zapatista rebellion helped to draw attention to the human costs of neoliberal reform, but institutional and demographic shifts also meant that the countryside was losing its traditional political importance as both a source of votes and a symbol of national identity. In Hidalgo, the synergistic effects of North American economic integration, the privatization and corporatization of Mexican agriculture, and global climate change created new forms of political, economic, and social risk for participants in the rural development project sites described above. This chapter examines the way climatic anomalies and anthropogenic hazards have intersected with newly generated forms of social vulnerability to create a governmental disaster that served to foreclose traditional collective forms of political agency. The disaster was interpreted locally through discourses of desiccation, which diagnosed the premature death of the countryside as a result of human failures to maintain systems of reciprocity. Although they resisted government attempts to naturalize this disaster by pointing out its origins in changing strategies of rule, the erosion of collective rural institutions ultimately created new challenges for NGOs seeking to cultivate rural citizenship.

I explore the links between material, metaphysical, and metaphorical disasters in the contemporary experience of Hidalgan campesinos in order to analyze how a particular consciousness of catastrophe is produced that works to circumvent established forms of collective agency. I trace these dynamics through two moments of national crisis: the campesino protests against NAFTA that resulted in the 2003 National Accord for the Countryside and the 2006–2007 tortilla crisis in which the relationships between democracy and neoliberalism were hotly contested. What some might pose as the unintended effects of human practices these campesinos interpreted as a form of willful neglect that endangers not only rural livelihoods but also the nation itself.

In the winter of 2006, the new president, Felipe Calderón, faced a major crisis as angry crowds throughout Mexico protested the skyrocketing price of tortillas. The price for a kilo of tortillas, the country's staple food, had more than doubled in the past year to reach eleven pesos. This was four times the rate of salary increases and triple the rate of inflation (Becerra-Acosta 2007). Since the advent of NAFTA, commercial maize processors like Cargill had increasingly substituted homegrown white maize with highly subsidized US exports dumped onto the Mexican market. However, the ongoing US war in Iraq and public outcry over global warming had prompted widespread speculation on ethanol production, rapidly inflating the price of maize futures on the global market.[2] Suddenly many of the people whose ancestors had originally domesticated maize could no longer afford to consume it. The tortilla crisis unleashed widespread accusations of government betrayal from Mexicans who felt trapped into dependency on the United States for their very sustenance. Following on the heels of a highly contentious presidential election, this latest crisis was widely acknowledged as a test of Calderón's leadership and a harbinger of future economic policy. Protest slogans like "sin maíz no hay país" (without maize there is no country) reflected the material and ideological significance of maize to historically sedimented notions of Mexican nationhood.

Four years earlier, Calderón's predecessor, Vicente Fox, had confronted a closely related debacle. On January 1, 2003, a farmer's movement called El Campo No Aguanta Más (The Countryside Can Endure No More) blocked the Cordova International Bridge linking Ciudad Juárez to El Paso, Texas. Marking the anniversary of Mexico's entry into NAFTA and of the Zapatista rebellion, they seized ports of entry for US agricultural products on the site where campesino armies had struck a blow against the dictatorship of Porfirio Díaz in 1911. Five days later, over a hundred thousand protestors marched to the Zócalo, Mexico City's main square, to demand a renegotiation of the agricultural chapter of NAFTA and an end to illegal dumping. The protestors argued that neoliberal policies and environmental degradation from earlier rounds of development had turned the countryside into a disaster area. That New Year's Day, I was in the municipality of Acatlán, just outside of Tulancingo. On top of the policy-induced crises described above, the region had also been experiencing droughts and dramatic flash flooding over the past several years. The protests in Juárez featured prominently in conversations among the campesinos and return migrants who gathered to celebrate in the *ejidos* where I had been working. Many of them expressed strong support for the El Campo No Aguanta Más movement. However, when I asked why there had been no such marches in Hidalgo, I received the same answer time after time. "Ya se acabó todo" (it's all finished now), "el campo ya se secó" (the countryside has withered). In order to diagnose the meaning of this seemingly contradictory response, I begin by considering the cultural categories of crisis generated by the dynamics discussed above.

Governmental Disasters

The notion of governmental disasters, which emerges from contemporary Mexican debates over the changing relationships between society and the state, is particularly useful for exploring the crisis in the Mexican countryside. It highlights how changing forms of rule create differentiated structures of vulnerability, but it also enables us to discern how hazards themselves may be the products of human actions. In the Tulancingo River Valley, climatic anomalies and anthropogenic hazards have intersected with newly generated forms of social vulnerability to create a governmental disaster that serves to foreclose traditional collective forms of political agency. The disaster is interpreted locally through a discourse of desiccation, which diagnoses the premature death of the countryside as a result of human failures to maintain systems of reciprocity. This perceived rupture of a total system has produced a cataclysmic consciousness among many campesinos. Although they resist government attempts to naturalize the disaster by pointing out its origins in changing strategies of rule, the erosion of collective rural institutions leaves them to confront an uncertain future as individuals all the same.

It has become commonplace for Mexican journalists, political commentators, and activists to refer to the countryside as a disaster area. Some have even christened a new category of crisis: the governmental disaster. This term has been used to highlight the social and political implications of recent natural disasters, as well as to provoke discussion around the role of national and local governments in precipitating them. Contrasting governmental disasters to natural ones, Carlos Montemayor of *La Jornada* emphasizes the increasing use of public power to secure private profit in ways that cause harm to citizens and violate national laws. He suggests that "the disasters occurring within Mexican territory continue to stem not only from natural forces, but from the irresponsibility of the authorities" (Montemayor 2005).[3] Hence misuse of political power and public authority is categorized as a hazard, alongside natural forces like hurricanes and droughts. Rural society is constantly referred to as suffering catastrophic crisis, but the popular mobilizations in 2003 and 2006 demonstrate that many Mexicans reject the notion that the demise of the countryside is simply the result of backwardness or inefficiency on the part of campesinos (Richard 2013). The Mexican food sovereignty movement, for example, defends maize as national patrimony and promotes the traditional milpa intercropping system as guarantor of sustainable agrobiodiversity.

Because food is both sustenance and symbol, agricultural crises may be experiences through which social actors gain new perspectives on the intersections of ecological, political, economic, and social changes (Davis 2001;

Figure 10. Milpa with mature maguey in the foreground.

Díaz and Stahle 2007; Endfield and Fernández-Tejedo 2006; Endfield and O'Hara 1997, 1999; Escobar Ohmstede 2004; Florescano and Swan 1995; García Acosta, Pérez Zevallos, and Molina del Villar 2003). To label disasters governmental is to reject the customary implication that they are spontaneous or serendipitous. It situates them as punctuating moments in much larger patterns of demolition and reengineering of social, political, and economic infrastructures, which Harvey has referred to as the rerouting of the "sclerotic arteries" of capitalism (1995, 3). Governmental disasters serve to finish off those earlier material and human infrastructures, paving the way for a new order of things. The naturalization of those processes as inevitable and inexorable—or, worse, as an unavoidable consequence of the imagined backwardness of milpa agriculture—consequently needs to be critically examined.

Far beyond a failure of state agencies to prevent or manage natural catastrophe, governmental disaster entails an active reordering of subjectivities and forms of rule. The concept of governmental disaster foregrounds questions of power and agency, situating environmental risk in the context of the expansion of global capitalism and highlighting links between rural and urban dynamics often neglected in ethnographies of globalization. As used by Montemayor and other journalists, the term "governmental disaster" connotes a catastrophe brought about by a government's refusal to protect citizens from impending harm. Indeed, use of the term often implies a willful disregard for the well-being of the nation on the part of state authorities. This understanding articulates well with Hidalgan campesinos' sense that the demise of the Mexican countryside is a direct result of the national government's betrayal of its earlier corporatist social pact and the overexploitation of rural people as second-class citizens. I suggest that these disasters may also be understood as governmental in the Foucauldian sense, in that they function to produce subjects who may be governed at a distance through shaping the fields in which they act (Foucault 1991). Hence the experience of disaster as a foreclosure of collective forms of political agency serves to reinforce neoliberalizing projects that work to individualize practices of citizenship in Mexico. Ongoing shifts in the political and economic status of campesinos in neoliberal Mexico influence a sense of lost agency, which is articulated through a discourse of desiccation. In characterizing the countryside and their futures as withered, Hidalgan campesinos explicitly link disastrous droughts in their political and natural environments.

Central Mexico has served as the region's "tortilla basket" since the ancient domestication of teosinte. In recent decades, however, the combined effects of the Green Revolution, privatization and free trade, and global warming have rendered campesinos more vulnerable to ruin by intensifying cycles of extended drought and extreme flash flooding while simultaneously introducing newly individualized forms of economic and political risk. Recent natural disasters and climatic anomalies have therefore been closely linked in the minds of many campesinos to ongoing crises in rural society. Their experience underlines that most "natural" disasters are in fact socially elicited, experienced, and interpreted.

Nonetheless, it would be a mistake to categorize their predicament as solely a rural crisis. As the large-scale mobilizations of 2003 and 2006 demonstrated, what is at stake is not only the status of campesinos but also the cultural politics of large-scale change in Mexico generally. Distinctions between rural and urban are discursively produced, with the rural standing in for an idealized authentic local past and the urban an industrialized global future. Williams (1973) notes that these notions about the city and the country in fact serve as "partial interpreters" of experiences of capitalist transformations (293). They are "forms of response to a social system as a whole," a system that constantly remakes country and city alike (294). "The industrial–agricultural balance, in all its physical forms of town-and-country relations, is the product, however mediated, of a set of decisions about capital investment made by the minority which controls capital and which determines its use by calculations of profit" (294–295). Governmental disasters, then, are one means by which subjects become conscious of these systemic shifts. That is, they serve as critical events around which cultural knowledge can be brought to bear, to rework cultural categories in ways that orient new forms of practice (Das 1996). This is especially important in the case of Mexico, where contestation over democratic forms of citizenship practice is ongoing.

According to Douglas (1975), discourses around environments at risk may be understood as techniques of social control in that they are predicated on shared notions of a natural order. Cultural notions of the laws and limits of a particular environment, conceived as a total system that includes both human societies and the natural world, lend credence to warnings of endangerment via pollution or human imprudence. Many Hidalgan campesinos I worked with interpreted and articulated their experiences via a discourse of desiccation, in which political and hydrological droughts combine to bring about the premature death of rural communities and the foreclosure of collective forms of political agency. This helps to explain their seeming fatalism in the face of crisis, despite expert claims that ethanol speculation means a more secure future for small farmers. In their view, the "countryside can endure no longer" not because campesinos lack the will to adapt and survive but because the land and those who work it have been exploited beyond their natural limits, pushed past the point of recovery, and subsequently abandoned. This folk analysis is based on a shared understanding of the web of reciprocal relationships that formed the historical and material basis for collective political agency and social reproduction in the countryside. Many of these relationships are deeply rooted, but their renovation was enabled in recent history by other links that emerged from the Mexican revolution. According to an older generation of Hidalgan campesinos, decades of human greed have destroyed these reciprocal ties, leaving rural communities high and dry. They view the contemporary crisis as the end of an epochal cycle, an historical erasure of the struggle undertaken by Emiliano Zapata, which is returning Mexico to the days of the Porfiriato.

Drought and Deluge in the Tulancingo River Valley

Renewed efforts to chronicle the history of natural disasters in Mexico have revealed the social character of catastrophes such as droughts and floods in the Meseta Central (Escobar Ohmstede 2004; Florescano 1969; Florescano and Swan 1995; García Acosta, Pérez Zevallos, and Molina del Villar 2003; Gill 2006). The Tulancingo River Valley is part of the Río Panuco watershed, situated on the edge of the Meseta Central at the mouth of the eastern Sierra Madre. It lies in a temperate semiarid zone where control of water resources has traditionally been closely guarded by elites (Endfield and O'Hara 1997). Access to rivers and aqueducts was controlled by hacendados until well into the mid-twentieth century, even after portions of their estates were appropriated in the post-Revolutionary land reform. As we saw in Chapter 2, *ejido* lands were almost exclusively rain fed until the late 1970s, when a series of development partnerships between local NGOs like HD, international funding agencies, and the state enabled campesino cooperatives to secure credits for drilling wells and purchasing Green Revolution technology. This democratization of access to water represented a challenge to the power of wealthy landowners and a symbolic reaffirmation of the importance of campesino agriculture to national development.

In recent years, however, synergy between global warming and the El Niño phenomenon has led to intensified cycles of drought and deluge in the Tulancingo Valley.[4] Throughout the 1990s, strong El Niño conditions prompted summer droughts between May and August, a crucial period in the growth cycle of rain-fed maize. In 1998, for example, the Meseta Central did not receive its first spring rains (usually expected in March or April) until halfway through May, reducing crop yields by 15 percent (Magaña 1999, 112). In addition to climate effects driven by El Niño and La Niña, rising temperatures associated with the greenhouse effect have also led to drought in Central Mexico. Mexico's National Ecological Institute (INE) has predicted that if global temperatures continue to rise at the present rate, the region's rainfall will decrease by at least 7 percent. By the end of this century, that could mean that 75 percent of Mexico's land would no longer be suitable for agriculture, a 50 percent reduction in overall arable land. Researchers at the INE and the Center for Atmospheric Science of the National University estimate that Hidalgo will be among the states most dramatically affected by this trend (Flores et al. 1996). This growing tendency toward drought is exacerbated by the exhaustion of regional aquifers; the Río Panuco watershed is among the most vulnerable to overexploitation as a result of population growth, increased irrigation, and lack of recharge (Jiménez Román and Maderey Rascón 2004).

Increasingly volatile storms in the nearby Gulf of Mexico associated with global warming have meant that these extended dry periods are frequently punctuated by violent flash floods that destroy crops, erode farmland, and severely damage transportation and urban infrastructures.[5] Tulancingo has historically been subject to seasonal floods, especially in the zone of confluence between the Río Chico and the Río Tulancingo. Often flooding is caused by heavy rain associated with tropical storms and hurricanes, such as the 1955 flood that engulfed the entire downtown area and destroyed four major bridges. However, recent inundations have occurred on a larger scale and with much greater frequency. Severe floods took place in the Tulancingo River Valley in 1998, 1999, 2002, 2005, 2006, 2007, 2010, and 2011. In 1999, one-third of the average yearly rainfall fell in a twenty-four-hour period, devastating the entire region. High-water marks from the 1999 floods are still visible on walls of local buildings. The year 2007 proved to be another record breaker. Unprecedented summer heat waves were followed in late August by flash flooding caused by Hurricane Dean. Heavy rains fell for more than eighteen hours straight, bursting dams and causing the Tulancingo River to overflow its banks. This emergency was followed by further floods one month later caused by Hurricane Lorenzo. While human fatalities were minimal, the loss of crops, livestock, and homes was dramatic.

On October 23, just a few weeks later, Tulancingo experienced its first freeze of the year. The National Meteorological Service reported it as a record low temperature, noting that the arrival of freezing temperatures had occurred far earlier than usual for the past three years (Padilla 2007). According to Hidalgo's State Department of Agriculture, over 9,000 hectares of crops were lost during fall 2007 as a result of weather anomalies (http://www.hidalgo.gob.mx). The social impacts of these recent catastrophes are magnified by other changes related both to earlier agricultural development schemes and to the restructuring of local and global markets.

Innovations associated with the rural development programs of the 1970s and 1980s helped to pull some campesino communities out of grinding poverty by increasing their access to irrigation and by facilitating technology transfers that led to increased use of tractors, pesticides, herbicides, and chemical fertilizers. Over the short term, these changes increased agricultural productivity and converted the Tulancingo River Valley into a center of artisan dairy production. However, the long-term implications of this period of rapid changes are only now becoming apparent (see Sonnenfeld 1992). Chemical runoff from agricultural fields and improper disposal of dairy industry by-products has polluted the Tulancingo River and its tributaries, rendering the water unfit for irrigation or human consumption. Population growth and industrialization in nearby towns have also contributed to water contamination and intensified water consumption. Droughts lead to increased use of irrigation by campesinos with access to wells and pumps. Others who are unable to survive on their rain-fed plots clear cut hillside timber stands to sell the lumber, creating erosion and possibly altering the water cycle.[6] Together, these factors lead to further environmental degradation and intensifying resource struggles. Moreover, they render the valley increasingly vulnerable to cycles of drought and deluge.

In recent decades, the restructuring of markets in maize and agricultural credits and the creation of new markets in land have further contributed to campesinos' vulnerability. A new spate of research into the long-term impacts of free trade and neoliberal restructuring on the Mexican countryside has yielded a stark portrait. The "reform of the agrarian reform," initiated under Carlos Salinas, entailed a massive public divestment from rural development at the same time as it privatized communal landholdings and opened Mexican markets to highly subsidized agricultural imports from the United States. Although the *ejido* retains significance as a social and cultural institution in rural Hidalgo, its economic role is greatly reduced.

Flooded Markets, Dried-up Futures

The neoliberal policy framework implemented by Salinas was continued and deepened by his successors, Zedillo and Fox. Calderón seemed to be reading from the same playbook as he confronted the tortilla crisis in 2006. He responded to the protests by importing more yellow maize from the United States, claiming that increased imports were necessitated by the failure of Mexican campesinos to meet the nation's subsistence demands. However, Mexican and international scholars have repeatedly contested these claims on the grounds that the tortilla crisis did not result from domestic lack of productivity but in fact came about as a result of corporate monopolization of food markets enabled by NAFTA (Barkin 2006; de la Tejera, Santos, and García 2007; Vargas et al. 2006). Nor was the tortilla crisis driven by increased demand: consumption is down as the basic market basket of products has increased steadily while real wages continue to drop in value (de la Tejera, Santos, and García 2007, 7). The demise of campesino agriculture has not merely been a natural withering away of outdated modes of production but rather a clear case of planned obsolescence. The introduction of new forms of financial risk, far beyond the control or even scrutiny of local farmers, helps to govern rural subjects at a distance.

For the past two decades, maize prices in Mexico have fluctuated on the basis not of the internal dynamics of supply and demand but on global corporate strategies. NAFTA originally provided for the liberalization of agricultural trade between the United States, Mexico, and Canada in stages over a period of fifteen years, with a series of protections on sensitive products to be phased out one by one. Tariffs on imported maize were phased out in 2008. Originally the removal of tariffs was intended to promote fair competition between Canadian, Mexican, and US producers by developing the comparative advantage of each over a decade and a half. However, the drastic disparity in government support for agricultural production between Mexico and the United States prevented level competition. In 2000, US maize producers received $10 billion in subsidies, an amount equal to ten times the Mexican government's entire agricultural budget (Amat et al. 2003). While austerity policies encouraged the Mexican government to cut agricultural extension and credit programs to small farmers, the US government steadily increased funding to its own counterparts. The 2002 Farm

Bill raised subsidies to US farmers by an unprecedented 80 percent, to the tune of $18 billion per year by 2010.[7] Enacted mere months before the lifting of tariffs on key agricultural products, the Farm Bill was denounced by campesino organizations as a strategic act of aggression intended to cement US domination of Mexico. Many of these groups swelled the ranks of protestors in Juárez and Mexico City in January 2003.

Traditional tortillas are made with fresh dough derived from white maize. However, as Mexico urbanized in the latter half of the twentieth century, a commercial tortilla industry arose based increasingly on dehydrated maize flour. Two companies, Maseca and MINSA,[8] controlled production, buying most of their supply from the government broker, CONASUPO. CONASUPO was eliminated in 1999 as part of neoliberal reforms, and MINSA was privatized. Now the Mexican tortilla industry is controlled by a transnational agribusiness oligopoly that includes players like Arthur Daniels Midland, Cargill, and ConAgra (de la Tejera, Santos, and García 2007; Vargas et al. 2006). US subsidies make imported yellow maize cheaper for large commercial buyers (de la Tejera, Santos, and García 2007, 18–19). Arroyo Picard (2003) estimated that agricultural products dumped by US producers into the Mexican market were priced at an average of 46 percent below the cost of production on the world market. Purchasing dumped maize is easier for major tortilla producers than purchasing homegrown white maize not only because it is facilitated by high-volume brokers but also because doing so affords them access to cheap credit. US exporters and government export-financing organisms, particularly the Commodity Credit Corporation (CCC), offer low-cost loans to Mexican importers buying US grains. Although rates have decreased in recent years, prevailing credit rates in Mexico in the mid-1990s were over 30 percent, while the CCC offered between 7 and 8 percent. For Mexico-based import companies, the CCC's sweetheart rates were like rain in a drought (Carlsen 2007, 3).

In the 1990s, large Mexico-based corporations like Bimbo, Maseca, and Lala were routinely allowed to import three times the legal quota of maize and other basic agricultural products established under NAFTA, and successive Mexican administrations failed to cite these violations or to levy the prescribed fines (Ortega Pizarro 2001). Researchers estimate that had the fines actually been collected, several billion dollars could have been invested in agricultural development programs to increase access to credit, crop insurance, and markets, which most small farmers lack (de la Tejera, Santos, and García 2007; Galarza et al. 2004; Henriques and Patel 2004). Yet the Mexican government slashed the agricultural ministry's budget, closed the rural development bank, and placed most of the remaining agricultural funding into cash-based assistance programs like Salinas's PRONASOL, which were often strategically disbursed to influence rural voters (Dresser 1994).

In the decade after NAFTA's implementation, maize prices fell 70 percent, and Mexico became the world's largest importer of maize in 2006 (de la Tejera, Santos, and García 2007, 3). Nonetheless, the dramatic boost in imports was not induced by domestic shortages. Maize production remained relatively constant after NAFTA, however little the corporate processors purchased. Lacking other options, small farmers responded to lower prices by intensifying cultivation, expanding into marginal areas, and investing remittances into agricultural inputs (Henriques and Patel 2004, 5). Although agriculture accounted for only 4 percent of the Mexican GNP, it employed 25 percent of the economically active population (Henriques and Patel 2004, 4). Even when small-scale producers managed to contract their crops to processors, the price fluctuated between planting and harvest on the basis of the global futures market. In 2006, for example, the price per ton fell from 3,500 pesos to 1,800 pesos by the end of the season. The Mexican tortilla industry speculated that the global price would continue to fall and opted not to buy from campesinos (Becerril 2007). The result of their bad bet was skyrocketing tortilla prices and deepening rural poverty.

These government policies and corporate strategies introduced new forms of risk into rural life that were compounded by the other forms of ecological, political, and social insecurity discussed above. Like spiraling cycles of drought and deluge, wild market fluctuations are precipitated by human agents, yet they rob campesinos of the ability to adapt by eroding traditional collective forms of political agency. Whereas earlier generations of Hidalgan campesinos were able to adapt to structural change by banding together with other members of their *ejidos* to create cooperatives and make claims on the state for development projects, the privatization and breakup of those collective landholdings has meant that families are often left to weather such storms alone. Village assemblies have disappeared, along with the *ejidos* they were responsible for managing. Villages themselves are fragmented by immigration. Small farms are increasingly subsidized not by government programs but by remittances earned through low-wage migrant labor. The NGOs that labored to organize those cooperatives now find that one of the primary goals of such projects—to render campesino agriculture more productive—has become meaningless as both maize and milk have fallen in value with the increase in US dumping. Productive projects that require investment in rural infrastructure or technology transfer are unlikely to find funders or achieve long-term success. As we saw in Chapter 2, even fair trade projects encounter obstacles in marketing and selling their products to a shrinking middle class in a crowded food industry monopolized by large multinational corporations. Individuals and families may find ways to make ends meet, but the collective *fuerza campesina* that HD hoped to build in the 1980s has become a distant dream.

Many interpret the current state of extreme instability as a sign that the limits of the natural system have been breached. They complain that even *las cabañuelas*, a traditional method of weather prediction based on a count of precipitation incidents in the month of January, no longer functions as it once did. The signs and cycles by which people lived their lives and upon which they staked their survival are fast disappearing. In their view, the source of disaster is not external to society but rather the result of failures of reciprocity. Earlier rounds of development had fueled human greed, campesinos said, causing people to neglect their obligation to maintain the environment and their ties to one another. As a result, they said "the land no longer gives" as freely as it once did; plants that grew wild and sustained campesino families in times of hunger no longer appear with the same abundance. The land seems exhausted, its energies sapped. In contrast to statements by politicians and free market advocates, which naturalize the social disaster in the Mexican countryside, the discourse of desiccation deployed by many Hidalgan campesinos firmly locates the catastrophe within the realm of human agency. The only thing natural about its origins, according to them, is the inherent tendency of the powerful to consume the poor.[9]

Political Droughts and Campesino Subjectivity

When campesinos in the Tulancingo Valley complain that "la milpa ya no rinde como antes" (the milpa no longer produces as it once did) or that "el campo ya se secó" (the countryside has withered), they are referring not only to changes in agricultural yields but also to the end of an era in which national politics was firmly grounded in the fate of the countryside. Since the founding of the *ejidos* in the 1930s, land had been the primary patrimony of campesino communities. Maintaining the milpa and teaching one's children to farm ensured the future of both family and rural society. Now with rising production costs, rock-bottom maize prices, and unpredictable rainfall, the milpa could no longer be counted on to sustain families, much less turn a profit. "El campo ya no es negocio" (the countryside is no longer a [profitable] business) was a phrase I heard repeated in village after village during my research visit in summer 2006. Now that the *ejidos* had been privatized, many reasoned, it might be better to sell their land and to send their children to school or to the United States. "If the milpa no longer yields anything of value," mused one campesino who had recently received the deed to his plot, "then perhaps we'll plant bricks and see what comes up."[10]

Knight (1994b) points out that in the past, Mexican citizens could make collective claims on the state by exposing the gap between Revolutionary rhetoric and actual state practices. But beginning with the presidency of Carlos Salinas, many revolutionary precepts (like the right to land) have themselves been dropped. According to Lomnitz (2001), the 1988 presidential campaign was the first time a discourse of individualized citizenship had emerged in Mexico since the inception of the corporatist model under Cárdenas. When Salinas launched PRONASOL, the revolutionary state that had protected and cajoled campesinos gave way to an "enabling state" that attempted to "empower" them as "entrepreneurial subjects of choice" engaged in a "quest for self-realization" (Rose 1999, 147). Salinas de Gortari (n.d.) blamed bureaucratic ineptitude and classical *cacicazgo* (political brokerage) for the countryside's inability to develop civil society. The PRONASOL program has been recycled and renamed by each of Salinas's presidential successors. This shift from state support of campesino production toward cash-based social programs targeted at individuals has been accompanied by the changes to land tenure schemes aimed at replacing collective holdings with individual ownership. This reform of the agrarian reform began in the 1990s with the often contentious process of surveying collectively held lands and awarding individual title and inheritance rights to specific plots. At the close of the Program of Certification of *Ejidal* Rights (PROCEDE) program in 2006, 90 percent of the lands formerly awarded to Hidalgan *ejidos* and indigenous communities in the post-Revolutionary land reform had been deeded to individuals (Secretaría de la Reforma Agraria [SRA] 2006).[11]

Although Mexico's new presidents have continued to acknowledge the countryside as central to Mexican heritage, they have increasingly treated campesinos as museum pieces rather than constituents or serious interlocutors. The saying "el campo ya no es negocio" pertains to politicians as well as to campesinos. Although the revolutionary pact between the PRI state and the peasant sector had been dismantled incrementally since the 1980s when the debt crisis marked a watershed and technocrats took over macroeconomic planning to administer structural adjustment policies, the government's refusal to negotiate with the movement over the conditions of NAFTA's final implementation indicated a definitive end to the political bargaining power of rural smallholders. This was an outright rejection of collective forms of political representation by an administration that no longer depended on a rural power base for legitimacy and no longer wished to engage citizens as mass sectors but rather as individual voters.

One of the chief demands of the El Campo No Aguanta Más movement was the renegotiation of NAFTA to protect small family farms from the dumping of highly subsidized US maize, beans, and milk. Fox's minister of agriculture, Javier Usabiaga, ridiculed the movement's plan as "a hare-brained scheme" in the national press (Cabildo 2003). In Hidalgo, the last thirty years of neoliberal reforms have meant a concomitant devaluation of rural people in public discourse. The more rural families are forced to diversify their economic activities to survive, the less they seem to resemble the idealized figure of the revolutionary campesino. The comments of a retired loan officer from the (now defunct) Tulancingo branch of Mexico's rural credit bank exemplified this attitude. As we sat chatting in the plaza one Thursday afternoon, he gestured with disgust toward a passing group of young campesino return migrants wearing baseball caps and T-shirts marked with English advertising slogans. "We had a chance to save the countryside twenty years ago and we failed," he said. "Now look at them. These are not campesinos. They have lost their identity. Now they are just like any other *desclasado*. They are not folkloric, just tacky."[12] His comments placed the value of the campesino to the nation firmly in the past, despite the substantial contribution rural migrant remittances make toward sustaining Mexico's economy.

In the Tulancingo River Valley, campesino subjectivity is deeply informed both by the legacy of revolutionary nationalism and by the experience of governmental disaster. Many people I interviewed described their communities as *remolidas*, ground down into dust by the rural crisis of the past decades. A powerful sense of finality surrounded the privatization of *ejidos* and the opening of NAFTA. These policies threaten campesino livelihoods, but they also erode the historical and material bases for collective organizing and social reproduction. For the most part, collective political action and protests by and on behalf of campesinos—like the marches carried out by the El Campo No Aguanta Más movement and demonstrations against the maize monopolies held during the tortilla crisis—have garnered substantial popular support. Yet they have not been successful in producing policy shifts. Young people who see no future for themselves in the countryside, and no way to change the political climate from a polling booth, often vote with their feet. Salinas, California, is one of the most popular labor migration destinations from the Tulancingo region. The ironic connection between the name of that town and the name of the ex-president whose policies helped to populate it with a highly vulnerable migrant labor pool is not lost on homesick young Hidalgans I visited there. In the summer of 2006, I visited La Esperanza, a neighboring community to El Ocote where I had conducted fieldwork in 2002–2003. I brought with me video messages recorded by young undocumented workers from the community who were living in Salinas, a few hours away from my home in California. In the days before inexpensive smartphones made Facebook and WhatsApp into essential links between migrants and their families back home, I often carried videos, letters, and photos back and forth with me on my trips. During that visit to La Esperanza, I stayed overnight in the home of my friends Doña Angela and Don Ramiro. Four of their six grown children were living in Salinas, and their three-year-old granddaughter had just joined her parents there, after living for a few months with her grandparents until her parents were settled enough to send for her. The next morning, after the cow was milked and Don Ramiro left home to begin his daily rounds as a *botero*, collecting his neighbors' milk to deliver to the processing plant in the municipal center of Acatlan, Doña Angela and I went out to pasture the couple's sheep. This had been a familiar ritual during my earlier fieldwork. Herding sheep with women in rural communities yielded lessons in cultural cartography, history, and kinship. As we navigated through the fields surrounding their villages, I learned the boundaries of private and collective properties and the stories of their stewards. They taught me to read the condition of the soil, the state of the weather, and the potential yields of particular milpas. They shared stories of how their families claimed the land and how political parties and NGOs had intervened in the lives of their communities, and they gossiped about births, deaths, and romantic liaisons. The hours-long daily round of taking out the sheep and cutting pasturage for the cows from now-irrigated fields took on the same social function for them that the long trek to the river to wash clothes, bathe, and carry back water had served in earlier generations.

That morning, Doña Angela took with her a small portable radio and her knitting, and she told me to bring my video camera. Accompanied by three dogs and an odd goat, we set out across the plain, stopping to let the dozen or so sheep strip the tender young grass from the irrigation ditches along the way, careful not to let them cross over into the fields themselves, where the neighbors' maize and pasturage for dairy cows sorely tempted them. Eventually we arrived at Doña Angela and Don Ramiro's milpa, planted on private land inherited from her father, one of the founders of the *ejido*. Once the sheep were situated, with the dogs to keep them in line, Doña Angela turned to me and said, "Take out your camera. I have something to show to my granddaughter." Earlier that spring, she had brought her granddaughter, Esther, with her to clear the field and plant it. Together they had visited the plot to look for new sprouts, to give them water, and to pull out the tenacious weeds that threatened the young plants. We started filming from a distance, then zoomed in to show the plants, the wildflowers growing at the edges of rows, the dogs romping through them. "*Mira, mijita, como esta de chula tu milpita, mira que va creciendo como tu* (Look, my little daughter, see how nicely the milpa is growing, it's growing up like you)," she declared to the camera, snapping an ear of maize off the stalk and pulling back the dark green husk to reveal the small white grains beneath. "I wanted her to have a milpa, to see it grow and change, to defend it, to work and care for it," she told me. "This might be her only milpa." Later, she said, "You show her this so that she remembers who she is." I suggested that perhaps when Esther returned she would be old enough to truly help her grandmother in the milpa and with the sheep. But Doña Angela shook her head. "They won't be back," she said. "And when we die there will be no more campesinos."

Sherry Ortner's (2006) work on agency and subjectivity is particularly helpful in clarifying how the interlocking crises described above have produced a cataclysmic consciousness in rural Hidalgo. Ortner emphasizes the social embeddedness of agents, whose action is constrained both by ties of solidarity and by relations of power and social inequality. She argues that agency is best viewed as a process entailing two modes of enactment: intentionality and power. Intentionality is concerned with the pursuit of culturally defined projects, whereas power refers to action taken within relations of social inequality, asymmetry, and force (Ortner 2006, 136–139). Ties of solidarity like those forged in the post-Revolutionary struggle to claim land, or reinforced in the day-to-day conduct of *ejidal* business and ritual cycles of the community, may form the basis for collective projects "on the margins of power" (142). However, when livelihood and social reproduction are rendered impossible, when social ties are ripped asunder by migration—in short, when the withered milpa can no longer sustain rural society—the "agency of projects" becomes increasingly difficult to maintain (144). Neoliberal discourses promoting the rights and responsibilities of the individual have encouraged rural people to accept these changes as natural and inevitable, to confront the crisis in which they find themselves alone, rather than as collectives or communities. Meanwhile, the reform of the agrarian reform has badly weakened the ability of the *ejido* to serve as a material basis for collective organizing in the countryside, either by NGOs or by social movements. This is apparent in the lack of political traction encountered by recent popular mobilizations. According to Ortner, the agency of projects is precisely the mode of agency denied, disrupted, or disallowed in subordinates by powerful actors in the enactment of their own projects (146). Hidalgan campesinos interpret this planned obsolescence of their communities as interconnected with the increasingly dramatic cycles of drought and deluge that point to an irreversible end of an era.

Desiccation and Desertion: Campesino Experiences
of Governmental Disaster

Campesinos in the Tulancingo River Valley repeatedly described the countryside as withered. The term they used, *secarse*, denotes two related forms
of desiccation: the withering of plants as a result of drought, neglect, or
improper cultivation and the progressive maturation and death of humans
and maize. Campesinos deployed a discourse of desiccation to articulate
their experience of simultaneous and related shifts in the natural and social
climates of their homeland. Many interpreted recent anomalies as indicators of a fundamental rupture in the web of reciprocal relationships among
human communities, flora and fauna, and the earth itself, which contributed to their sense of the future as rapidly evaporating. The countryside can
endure no longer, they argued, not because campesinos have given up but
because they and the land they work have been exploited beyond the point
of recovery.

This discourse of desiccation draws on an understanding of the human
and natural worlds as connected through interlocking reciprocal ties. Proper
maintenance of these relationships is achieved by cultivating a dynamic balance between four key categories of life: hot, cold, wet, and dry. The material and symbolic significance of these precepts and practices has been well
documented for Mesoamerican maize cultures both past and present. Chevalier and Sánchez Bain (2003) place particular emphasis on the parallel life
courses of humans and maize, a concept that is central to the significance of
the discourse of desiccation deployed by Hidalgan campesinos. According
to the authors, three underlying principles govern these cultures' complex
and varied humoral worldviews: balance, periodicity, and heliotropic movement. Humans, like maize, move through dynamic cycles of hot and cold
states over the life course. Both are germinated and born into cold, wet
states and, under the influence of the sun's heat, warm up through a process
of maturation and reproduction before eventually drying out completely
and dying. Indeed, in rural Hidalgo, healthy, chubby babies and water-
fat young ears of maize are both described as *chulo*, while withered maize
plants and elderly persons are labeled *seco*.[13] Chevalier and Sánchez Bain
assert that pathology results from threats to the balance between the above
states, or to the orderly progression of the nested cycles of warming and

drying that repeat throughout the life course. My research revealed multiple terms used to designate unnatural states of dehydration in both maize and humans leading to overall pathology and eventually death. Withered plants and undernourished or disease-weakened people were both referred to as *chupado* (sucked dry), for example. Chemical fertilizers and whey (a by-product of the local cheese-making industry commonly leaked into local waterways) are both said to "heat" and "dry" the earth, and if present in sufficient quantities may "burn up" plants or people they come in to contact with. If addressed promptly and at the correct point in the growth cycle, such pathologies could be remedied, thus restoring the natural progression. Drought-damaged maize plants may be revived and their ears "refilled" if sufficiently irrigated; damaged human communities might be renewed and produce new growth (*retoñar*) if properly cared for in times of crisis. However, a campesino who is unable to irrigate or who waits too long to do so faces a total crop loss. By the same token, rural society, like the milpas on which it is based, can be induced to wither and die before its time via human neglect and overexploitation.

When campesinos refer to their milpas as *secas*, they are remarking on both a physical state of dehydration leading to decreased production and a metaphorical state of "overheating" due to overexploitation. They say the milpa appears permanently *acabada* (finished), no longer capable of sustaining life. After the privatization of *ejidos*, more and more rural Hidalgans confront such disasters as individuals or families rather than as collectivities. The result is often increased emigration, which interrupts the processes of social reproduction responsible for the enculturation of new generations of campesinos. Many fear that the milpa can no longer endure as the material grounds for rural society.

Many campesinos in the Tulancingo Valley who supported Vicente Fox in 2000 had hoped the new president would renew the historical relationship between rural society and the state, ending the long political drought. In retrospect, however, Fox is now remembered by many as "the ranchero president who turned the countryside into a disaster area" (Pérez 2006). The prolonged drop in maize prices under NAFTA was attributed to a series of failures on the part of government leaders to maintain their historical relationship with the countryside. The government, it was said, had abandoned the countryside, like a field left uncultivated in the absence of its owner. It was not the case that they had preferred the old corporatist PRI system but rather that it was no longer clear how exactly campesinos might effectively press their claims on the state. In the words of one *ejidal* official,

> Before [Fox's victory], the PRI politicians and caciques gave everything to their friends, to those who supported them, with votes. In a democracy we suppose that everyone should be treated equally. But now, instead of spreading support around, or supporting those who need it most, to those who have the most, they [the Fox government] give more. And to those who do not even have enough to eat, they give them nothing.[14]

Doña Valentina, quoted in the Introduction, offered a similar analysis of recent changes to the relationship between the Mexican government and rural society. "Before," she said, "*the government spoon-fed the campesinos. Now they neither give us anything nor allow us to do things for ourselves.*" While PRI governments neglected campesino agriculture for decades, many viewed Vicente Fox's refusal to enforce tariff rate quotas and the government's collusion with the commercial maize monopolies as outright sabotage. Fox was not the first president to neglect his rhetorical obligations to the countryside, but when presented with the opportunity to save it by renegotiating NAFTA or resurrecting agricultural development programs, he chose instead to accelerate its demise. "Now they are just sucking the Valley dry," the same *ejidal* official commented, "wringing out the very last drop."[15] Many Hidalgan campesinos anticipated a future in which maize, the nation's gift to the world, would disappear in its own homeland and be replaced by genetically modified imports. While optimistic economists expect ethanol futures to continue elevating maize prices, thereby stimulating Mexican agriculture, experts on the ground aver that this increase in production is likely to come from corporate agribusiness rather than small family farms. In 2004, Senator Jorge Martínez warned the Mexican Congress that the countryside might never recover from this governmental disaster:

> If we analyze on the one hand the implications of the agricultural crisis (an important decrease in the number of hectares under cultivation, the migration of small farmers and campesinos, changes in land use, unemployment, etc.), and on the other hand we consider the variety of resources and actions that would have to be put into play to reverse these effects, we discover that

it will take so much time, and that the magnitude of the damage done is so great, that even if we cannot (or will not) call these effects irreversible, they remain, for all intents and purposes, irreversible. (Camera de Diputados 2004; author's translation)

If campesino futures have already evaporated, then NAFTA's primary political accomplishment has been to secure the neoliberal economic model against possible democratic challenges. Flooded markets and political desertion, much like the intensified cycles of drought and deluge brought about by global warming, have often been presented as external forces beyond the control of human agents. However, groups like El Campo No Aguanta Más have consistently resisted government attempts to naturalize the ongoing disaster in the Mexican countryside by drawing attention to the ways in which the neoliberalizing projects pursued by PRI and PAN leaders alike have precipitated successive crises. Even so, the governmental effects of disaster are clear to Hidalgan campesinos. Neoliberalizing measures have increasingly disabled the agency of projects for rural Mexicans by eroding the material bases of collective organization, rerouting channels of political participation, and relegating campesino protagonism to the country's premodern past.

Conclusion: Uncertain Futures

Raymond Williams (1973) holds that scholars tend to frame the decline of the countryside primarily as a problem of settlement. That is to say, rural crises are constructed as provocations to rescue old ways of life because they capture something about how our present identities are rooted in a distinct rural past. Governmental disasters, however, are dramatic manifestations of the mutual constitution of country and city via larger dynamics of capitalist transformation. Such disasters punctuate national histories, functioning as critical events through which a variety of links are revealed: between local and global power structures, ideological and material culture, and human societies and natural environments. The combined effects of North American economic integration, the privatization and corporatization of Mexican agriculture, and the local effects of global climate change have rendered

Hidalgan campesinos increasingly vulnerable to ruin in recent decades. The premature demise of the Mexican countryside may be characterized as a governmental disaster, generated by incremental policy decisions and the willful neglect of authorities. However, governmental disaster does not merely threaten campesino livelihoods; it also works to foreclose collective forms of political agency, reinforcing neoliberalizing projects aimed at individuating the practice and limiting the purview of democratic citizenship.

The discourse of desiccation through which Hidalgan campesinos articulate their experience of disaster refutes government attempts to naturalize the demise of the countryside as a result of impartial market rationalities, the presumed backward nature of campesinos themselves, or even a capricious environment. This disaster is interpreted against the backdrop of cultural notions concerning the laws and limits of a natural order dependent on those relationships. Cycles of drought and deluge are experienced not as chance occurrences but rather as ecological evidence of a dangerous social rupture that heralds the premature end of an era and the permanent foreclosure of the prospect of equality promised by the Revolution.

When campesinos declare that "it's all finished now," that "the countryside has withered up," they are mourning the end of a way of life that holds deep meaning for them. Perhaps most importantly, they are mourning the demise of a form of subjectivity born of earlier struggles to adapt to capitalist transformations and to stake a claim within them for their children's futures. The governmental disaster they refer to is not merely the passing of a form of settlement or an infrastructure of mastery over nature. It is also a shift in the infrastructures of human exploitation that disables established collective forms of political agency. It also portends a shift in rural development NGOs' strategies of intermediation. Traditional development projects require participants to invest a considerable amount of time, effort, and capital in ventures that were slow to return significant profits and vulnerable to market fluctuations, among other factors. For poor campesinos struggling for survival, it is often difficult to hold out for deferred gratification, especially after suffering previous disappointments. As one cooperative member put it, "We're not businessmen. For them, if things go badly on one side, they can take from another side to cover it until things go better. We can't do that. We're poor people who barely manage to eat, and the countryside is no longer a (viable) business. We cannot be businessmen."[16] NGOs are cautious about "wasting" scarce resources on risky ventures and hence have come to practice a sort of developmental triage in which those potential co-operatives most likely to produce quick, quantifiable results receive support. Chapter 4 examines how NGO workers themselves confront these dilemmas, negotiating conflicting demands and alternative models of mediation.

CHAPTER 4

Mediating Dilemmas

Compromising NGO Work

One warm spring night in Tulancingo in 2003, I sat chatting with a group of middle-class professionals at the birthday party of Marco Urrútia, a local section chief of the Federal Elections Institute (Instituto Federal Electoral, IFE).[1] The party was hosted by a group of friends, men and a few women who had, at various points in their careers, all worked in the IFE, National Institute of Statistics and Geography (Instituto Nacional de Estadística y Geografía, INEGI), and various local rural development NGOs. Although these institutions were officially independent from one another, all drew from a relatively small pool of educated *licenciados* and *ingenieros*. The conversation turned toward partygoers' collective disillusionment with new president Vicente Fox and their anxieties over the future of their own careers. Urrútia's best friend, Hector Salazar, a loan officer at a nonprofit microcredit program, spoke with great nostalgia about his work in the IFE in the 1990s. He told us how he traveled with his team to remote rural communities to update voter registration rolls and distribute photo credentials in hopes of preventing electoral fraud. Maria Ramos, an HD staff member, told of organizing voter education workshops in local *ejidos* to teach campesinos about the political platforms of the various parties and to facilitate community discussions about democracy. Everyone, it seemed, remembered the period as one of intense camaraderie and unity of purpose among rural NGO workers. With the "candidate of change" finally in office, however, their work had lost its former sense of urgency and importance. By the spring of 2003, many NGO workers were struggling to redefine their role in the countryside, but with limited success. Their political projects as well as their personal lives were threatened by the course of change.

"If there ever was a *cambio*, it never made it here to Tulancingo," Marco Urrútia complained bitterly. "Really?" I asked. "So then what happened to the famous *cambio* here?" Urrútia merely shrugged in response. "Don't pay him any mind, *güerita*, he's gotten bitter in his old age," Salazar interjected with a wry grin. "Besides, soon you'll see how everything here has changed because of Fox." Intrigued, I asked what he meant. "Don't tell me you haven't noticed, as much time as you spend out in the communities, that now it is we [the NGO workers] who work the milpa? "¿A poco sí?" I ventured. "¡Pos' sí, mijita, mil pa'alla . . . mil pa'aca!"[2] Salazar chuckled. His friends and colleagues toasted him, in stitches.

Salazar's joke indexes the deep anxieties rural NGO workers feel concerning their precarious futures in neoliberal Mexico. Although perhaps not in the ways they had initially anticipated, the fields they work in and the types of work they do have undergone a profound transformation that intensified after Fox's victory. Salazar's jest is a play on words that references the increasing flexibilization of their work, as they are forced to look "here and there" for ever more elusive sources of political and financial support. With the slow decay of the democratization movement and the disintegration of the grand NGO networks like Civic Alliance, MCD, and the Red TDPT that were its backbone, rural NGOs were forced to rethink their relationships to the state as well as to the campesinos they purport to serve.

Although neoliberal ideologues advocate the elimination of intermediaries in order to free individuals to interact in the marketplace, in practice, neoliberalizing projects have relied on the cultural knowledge and practices of a variety of actors, including NGOs (Brenner and Theodore 2002; Harvey 2005; Tsing 2005). This chapter examines the relationship of Tulancingo NGOs to more traditional Mexican cultural models of mediation, highlighting the categories of social action through which NGO workers make sense of their own interventions. It explores how they reworked cultural idioms of mediation to position themselves as legitimate intermediaries linking rural cooperatives, state officials, international donors, and global activist networks. Tulancingo NGO workers struggle to reconcile external pressures to act as self-interested entrepreneurs with an older moral order based on solidarity and reciprocity. Examining this complex relationship to past cultural forms reveals the limits that civil society institutions face in the neoliberal era, as well as the ways in which NGOs, and not just their project participants, are rendered vulnerable by large-scale transformations.

The NGO form is powerful in part because it produces legibility at a distance, "moving across what is included and excluded by the state," while simultaneously conjuring a distinction between public and private (Bernal and Grewal 2014, 8). NGO workers' need to cultivate moral legitimacy through cultural idioms of solidarity and reciprocity is bound up in the symbolic maintenance of this distinction, even as the dilemmas they confront as intermediaries highlight the ways their work helps to produce a continuity between those fields of power. In order to contextualize the dilemmas Tulancingo NGOs face, I begin by discussing the classical anthropological literature on mediation. This earlier work attempted to theorize the modes and models of mediation that enabled large-scale structural change but was ultimately limited by a narrow focus on nation-state politics and a static spatial imaginary. Ironically, the very dynamics of globalization that revealed the limitations of these earlier models, such as transnational issues networks and economic integration policies, also depend on the cultural work of intermediaries. The next section demonstrates how the emergence of the NGO sector in Mexico was both a response to and a catalyst for such changes. In particular, I examine how the role played by NGOs in the Mexican transition to multiparty democracy and their proliferating links to government agencies and international donors after the 2000 elections yielded unexpected changes. The contradictory outcome of the Mexican transition confronted these NGOs with a crucial dilemma. In order to survive in a new funding climate and to be taken into account by the state, they were pressured to act in ways that risked damaging their local legitimacy. Their strategies for confronting this dilemma were rooted in long-standing Mexican cultural modes of mediation, which I analyze in the following section. The dilemmas faced by Tulancingo NGOs and their strategies for positioning themselves as legitimate mediators in processes of structural change reveal the importance of intermediaries to the instantiation of neoliberalizing projects.

Anthropological Theories of Mediation

During the post–World War II community studies boom, anthropologists examined culture brokers and other intermediaries as an entry point into the power-laden processes through which local communities became linked into postcolonial nation-building projects (Geertz 1960; Press 1969; Wolf 2001). Eschewing prior models that represented the modern nation-state as an aggregate of hermetically sealed local communities, Wolf (2001) proposed a number of "supplementary sets" that enabled the functioning of formal institutions in complex societies by bridging gaps among social groups or types and between institutional levels (182). Patron–client relations, for example, constituted a type of "instrumental friendship" encountered where "the formal institutional structure of society is weak and unable to deliver a sufficient steady supply of goods and services, especially to the terminal levels of the social order" (180). According to Wolf ([1966] 2004), new groups of intermediaries tend to emerge during processes of recentralization of power after major upheavals. Studying them would yield insight into the configuration of particular power structures: "Complex societies in the modern world differ less in the formal organization of their economic or legal or political systems than in the character of their supplementary interpersonal sets . . . [which] make possible the functioning of the great institutions" (19). In post-Revolutionary Mexico, the pursuit of power by groups and individuals eventually came to be mediated through the state party, the PRI. According to de la Peña (1981), post-Revolutionary Mexican society was organized as

> a pyramid of patron–client relationships which permit concentration of power at the top. The complexity of this fabric determined a dual phenomenon: individual maneuvering is quite possible because it is impossible to

achieve structural change. . . . A man can use his relationships of trust to obtain individual power as long as such relationships do not become horizontal alliances which lead to the emergence of an independent faction, and as long as his political network includes external patrons. (246–247)

This hierarchical and holistic structure enabled collective demands to be manipulated or silenced in exchange for personal favors.

Fox (1994) notes that the number of studies on the role of intermediaries in national politics diminished significantly after the 1970s and that such studies were largely absent from the later literature on regime change and democratization. Although the burgeoning NGO sector has received a great deal of attention from scholars in regard to its potential role in democratic transformations, comparatively little emphasis has been placed on investigating how NGOs might be related to older organizational forms in the societies in which they have taken hold. Normative theories of civil society tend to presume a system in which individual rights-based liberalism is well institutionalized, but these conditions were not evident in Mexico during the 1980s and 1990s (Olvera Rivera 1999b). Like many civil society theorists, Fox (1994, 153) framed the problem of political change in Mexico as a transition from a political system based on authoritarian clientelism[3] to one based on citizenship, where negotiations or bargaining between state and citizens over material benefits is not predicated on forfeiture of their associational autonomy. The presence of NGOs was regarded as an indication of the strength and autonomy of civil society in overcoming corporatism and forging new forms of political collectivity (Olvera Rivera 1999a; Verduzco, List, and Salamon 2002). However, the erosion of established patterns of political deference can lead as easily to the use of force as it may to democratic pluralism (Fox 1994). As Olvera Rivera (1999b) points out, Mexican NGOs and social movements have always coexisted alongside enduring patterns of clientelism and corporatism. Moreover, de la Peña (2007) argues that the social movements and NGOs that pushed for democratization in Mexico have not promoted a vision of individuated political rights. Instead, "this struggle to broaden human rights is tied to a new definition of citizenship—not a given, but a goal to achieve, a constructive process that demands the constant participation of dynamic and heterogeneous social sectors" (307). The concept of citizenship as a participatory process implies both the emergence of new collectivities and a change in modes of mediation.

Analyzing the role NGOs play in these processes requires rethinking the two-dimensional topography that animated classic models of mediation (de Vries 2002; Ferguson and Gupta 2002). Indeed, the spatial imaginary deployed by Wolf and his contemporaries was predicated on the state's metaphorical "vertical encompassment" of society, which fails to attend to "the social and imaginative processes through which state verticality is made effective and authoritative" (Ferguson and Gupta 2002, 983). As discussed in Chapters 1 to 3, there is a continuity in fields of power between state practices and those of NGOs, which cuts across public/private distinctions. Further, Lomnitz (2001) points out that the centers and peripheries bridged by Mexican intermediaries are relative and mutually dependent rather than fixed. Thus, intermediaries arise to represent "authentic" local collectivities in the national space via specific cultural idioms and in fulfillment of particular values. De la Peña (1981) further calls attention to the situational nature of such collectivities and their constitution in relation to external forces. In his view, local communities represented by intermediaries (be they political bosses or NGOs) may be more akin to political domains than they are to durable, internally coherent groups. Acting as an intermediary, then, necessarily entails constructing (or reconstructing) a collectivity to represent.

In place of the classic schema that represented the state as composed of stacked levels (sometimes linked via the work of intermediaries), Ferguson and Gupta (2002) propose the concept of "transnational governmentality" (990) to capture how new nonstate actors like NGOs are implicated in neoliberal modalities of government. During the waning years of the corporatist political system that informed Wolf's classic theory of the culture broker, Mexican NGOs challenged the state-oriented system of mediation by appealing to ideals of universal human rights and leveraging connections to transnational issues networks. According to anthropologist Anna Tsing (2005), universalist aspirations, like those embodied by appeals to universal human rights, "can only be charged and enacted in the sticky materiality of practical encounters" between disparate and unequal groups, encounters that may produce unanticipated "new arrangements of culture and power" (1, 5). The practical encounters through which Mexican NGOs succeeded in embedding these universalist ideals into the political discourse have, however, yielded some unexpected results. In recent years, NGOs have found themselves repositioned by political reforms aimed at institutionalizing multiparty democracy. No longer easily categorized as opposition activists, they are struggling to redefine their role as legitimate intermediaries. Moreover, traditional arenas of mediation, like state development agencies, have been transformed as decentralization schemes diffused political power and development resources to multiple centers (Rodriguez 1997).

Whereas the role of the intermediary in classical theory was to act as a buffer, translating between social groups and administrative levels, this new multipolar configuration presents a novel set of challenges for NGOs. Unlike political intermediaries under the corporatist state, NGOs do not hold a monopoly on the flow of resources from elsewhere into their local project sites. Sources of material support are not at all secure, as Marco Urrutia's "mil-pa" joke insinuates. In fact, many Tulancingo NGOs compete with one another for access to funding sources. In order to survive, they must aggressively market themselves to donors, seek out advantageous public–private partnerships, and strategically manage their investments in local project sites. While this entrepreneurial behavior is viewed favorably by foreign donors, it may be interpreted in an entirely different light in the rural villages where development programs are carried out. Hence NGOs do not fit in smoothly between state and society; rather, they must negotiate an uneasy set of connections and constraints. Some of these are brought about by the structures to which NGOs are articulated as supplementary sets, but others derive from the systems of public symbols through which their actions are constructed and interpreted.

Caught in the Middle: NGOs in the Mexican Transition

The debt crisis of the 1980s and the structural reforms that it precipitated severely weakened the PRI's capacity to maintain the corporatist model through patron–client relationships. The ability of NGOs to negotiate with the state on behalf of particular groups, like poor farmers, was not the result of a unified state strategy (as the earlier pyramid of brokers employed by the PRI had been) but came about as a result of the reduction of authoritarian capacity and disagreements within the political class between hardliners and reformists. As we saw in Chapter 2, the distinction the PRI made between political and social organizing and protest had a lasting effect on the environment in which Tulancingo NGOs operated, thereby influencing the way they configure their role as intermediaries. After the opposition electoral victory in 2000, NGOs across Mexico began to lobby for official recognition, launching a decade-long struggle to institutionalize their role in policy making. Given the important role NGOs had played in the prodemocracy movement, they expected to wield greater influence in policy discussions at the local and national levels and to receive public support.

Ironically, in the years immediately after Fox's victory, the Mexican NGO sector slid into a period of disenchantment. After championing free elections as the instrument of democratic change, many found themselves shut out of decision-making processes dominated by appointed technocrats. When the outcomes of those decisions led to further economic hardship, the NGOs were called on to fill in for shrinking social services. In the 1970s and 1980s HD had been accused of spreading communism, and in the 1990s it was celebrated locally as a champion of democracy, but by the date of its twenty-fifth anniversary, in 2003, the organization's cofounder complained that it was largely ignored by politicians. "It is better to be thought dangerous," he said, "than not to be thought of at all."[4] His concern that the federal government sought to domesticate the activist agendas of NGOs after Fox's election was shared by many of his Tulancingo colleagues.

The Struggle to Be Taken into Account: Hidalgan NGOs after the Alternancia

In the period immediately after the 2000 election, many of the NGO coalitions that had helped to organize the prodemocracy and human rights movements began to fall apart, leaving their former members isolated from one another. In their place, a series of major NGOs like Marta Sahagún de Fox's foundation, called Vamos México (Let's Go, Mexico), organized on the North American nonprofit model, have risen to national prominence. The number of grant-maker and pass-through foundations in Mexico has grown rapidly, opening Mexican NGOs up to corporate and international sponsorship (Natal, Greaves, and García 2002; Verduzco, List, and Salamon 2002). Whereas many older organizations founded during the 1970s and 1980s pursued deprofessionalization and popular education as models for social solidarity, the newcomers promote professionalism and technical assessment, relating to their constituents more as consultants than as companions on the road to national progress.

These changes have prompted reflection on the shifting composition of the so-called third sector and its relationships to the state. In social science and activist circles during the late 1990s, this tension manifested itself in a series of debates on public–private partnerships. A heavily cited article by development scholar Faranak Miraftab, republished in *Sociedad civil: Analisis y debates* (the journal of Mexico City's Fundación DEMOS), asked whether it was possible for NGOs to use state funds or partner with state agencies without compromising their organizational autonomy. To what extent must NGOs engage in "flirting with the enemy" (Miraftab 1997)? What were the available means by which NGOs might participate in policy-making processes without becoming co-opted? Although the normative tone of these debates often obscured the complex political and social compromises that had enabled the emergence of Mexican NGOs in the first place, they indexed a growing anxiety over the increasingly difficult institutional position of NGOs.

In Mexico, NGOs established for public benefit are officially designated as *asociaciones civiles* (civic associations). In order to operate legally, they must apply both to the Public Registry of Property and to the Federal Taxpayers Registry. The formal paperwork entailed by this process is infamously burdensome. According to the NGO Law Monitor, published by the International Center for Not-for-Profit Law (ICNL),

> A number of reports have to be filed such as government funding reports, fiscal reports to the federal government, as well as the local government: monthly, annual, transparency, social security reports, audits, information for the Transparency web page . . . reports to the government where an organization receives public funds, reports to the ministry of the field of activities, like the Education Ministry, reports to the Labor Ministry, reports to the Ministry of Social Development where an organization is registered with the Registry of Social Development, and reports to federal and state tax authorities. (ICNL 2012)

At HD, for example, this official documentation customarily required the labor of one full-time employee and periodic assistance from a local accounting firm. Hence, although no legal barriers prevented any Mexican citizen from founding an NGO, the resources and level of education required for official inclusion within this "space of participation" effectively barred all but the small middle and upper classes. In this sense, the ability to deploy the NGO form as a form of "agency of projects" (as discussed in Chapter 3) was restricted.

From the 1980s on, the federal Finance Ministry treated NGOs and cooperatives as if they were large businesses or tax shelters by taxing them at high rates. In fact, it was not until 2007 that the Mexican legislature approved a bill that exempted private donations to nonprofits from federal taxes. The NGOs interpreted this treatment as an attempt to broaden the federal tax base and impose greater control on their operations (Fox and Hernández 1992, 185–186). Taxation has served as a rallying point for NGOs during the last two decades as they have sought to institutionalize their social and political role vis-à-vis both state and society. One common goal has been to establish clear legal distinctions between NGOs, corporations, and political parties so that the former may legitimately enter into partnerships with state agencies without casting aspersion on their motives. In 1994, a coalition of NGOs called the Civil Society Council (Consejo de la Sociedad Civil, or CSC), led by the Mexican Center for Philanthropy (Centro Mexicano para la Filantropía, or CEMEFI), began to lobby the Mexican Congress in favor of the creation of a law of promotion for civil society organizations. The purpose of the legislation was to publicly recognize their role in Mexican society, provide an official legal framework for partnerships with state agencies, and enable NGOs to participate in official policy-making processes.[5] The number of NGOs had exploded in the late 1990s, and many began to look for new sources of support and ways of participating in public decision-making processes. The quest for public legal recognition became especially urgent after the 2000 elections, as the large prodemocracy coalitions lost their common focus and consequently their political clout.

While the leaders of some Tulancingo NGOs began to support candidates from particular political parties, others quietly cultivated relationships with multiple groups of political elites simultaneously. Still other organizations, particularly newcomers affiliated with prominent international NGOs, or INGOs, had not yet developed strong political reputations. Yet to publicly ally with one particular political position was to endanger the organization's legitimacy as a social rather than political actor, authorized to represent the interests of civil society in general rather than those of a particular class or faction. These implicit rules of the game linked contemporary NGO practices to both the ethic of civic Catholicism as well as the earlier organizing categories deployed by the PRI. They were also related to an emergent phenomenon in Tulancingo politics: a growing number of politicians, seeking to secure the nomination of their parties to candidacy for high office but prevented by new electoral rules from engaging in some of the more blatant methods of vote buying, had taken to founding charities or assistential development NGOs whose sole purpose was to purchase goodwill and name recognition through "good works."[6] The best-known example is that of the Fundación Hidalguense, which was used to promote the political career of infamous Hidalgan PRI politician Gerardo Sosa Castelán. Sosa founded the organization in 1997, during his long career as rector of the Autonomous University of Hidalgo. Starting in his days as a student there in the 1970s, Sosa led a violent group of *porros* that eventually came to control not only the Federation of Students but the entire university itself.[7] From his base at the university, Sosa launched a political career, serving in the Chamber of Deputies and in several appointed posts in the state government and the PRI. His goal was to become governor of Hidalgo. He initially used the foundation as a means of siphoning university and other funds toward his cronies and appointees while making a name for himself by doing "good works" in rural areas. However, by the early 2000s, internal power struggles within the PRI and increased public scrutiny brought by the prodemocracy movement made his bloody, authoritarian reputation a detriment to the party. Sosa attempted through the foundation to buy a new political identity for himself as a benevolent philanthropist concerned with Hidalgo's deep poverty (Rivera Flores 2004). The foundation spent vast sums on publicity and massive public events, but Sosa ultimately failed to win the party's nomination for the governorship, which instead went to Miguel Ángel Osorio Chong. When an unauthorized political biography detailing his history of corruption and collusion was published in 2004, Sosa sued the author for defamation. Likewise, it is possible to interpret the growth of NGOs during this period as a response in part to new political opportunities rather than a transparent upwelling of civic engagement. This dynamic heightened the tension that had already been developing between NGOs focused primarily on social assistance and those motivated to transform social, political, and economic structures.

In December 2003, the CSC sponsored the Hidalgo State NGO Forum in the capital city of Pachuca as part of a national organizing drive in support of its legislative efforts. In the library of the Arturo Herrera Cabañas Foundation, representatives of more than a dozen NGOs from the region gathered to discuss the common problems they faced after the 2000 elections. The organizations ranged from indigenous media groups to development organizations, education and health care service groups, and artists' collectives. What emerged from their discussions was a clear understanding of NGOs as legitimate representatives of civil society with a moral imperative to respond to social needs. They demanded to be "taken into account" (*ser tomados en cuenta*) by the politicians and technocrats who had shifted so much responsibility onto their shoulders.

While most of the participants in the forum agreed on the importance of presenting a united front, there was little consensus on what sorts of organizations should be included under the law and how a unified agenda might be articulated. Much of the disagreement took place over whether merely assistential organizations (viewed by the forum participants as paternalistic charities) should be included in the definition of an NGO. Magazine (2003) describes the circulation of a similar discourse among NGOs working with street children in Mexico City during that same period, noting that the critique of *asistencialismo* there rested on the potential of charitable giving to foster dependency on the part of recipients. Likewise, conversations at the Hidalgo State NGO Forum centered on the perceived tendency of this mode of philanthropy to reinforce patron–client relationships rather than fostering rights-based democratic citizenship. Some participants also questioned whether NGOs, which represented diverse sets of issues and constituents, could reasonably be expected to support a single social or political agenda; this also seemed to them reminiscent of patronage politics rather than pluralistic democracy. They feared that the third sector might be transformed into yet another interest group grafted onto old pyramidal political models.

Despite these disagreements, however, the participants were consistent in their characterizations of NGOs as both representatives of and mentors for civil society. Participants agreed that the services they provided were by all rights owed by the state to its citizens, but NGOs had taken on the responsibility for their delivery, as the state was either ineffective or unresponsive. As one participant put it, "All civic organizations are for the public benefit. Therefore, they ought to be supported with legal and financial guarantees, and with funds." Thus NGOs were posed as voluntary public advocates for the fulfillment of the social rights of citizens. As advocates of the common good of the nation, they were deserving of government recognition and support, regardless of whether their organizational objective was social transformation or temporary assistance to the needy. While the participants in the event recognized the work of their organizations as supplementary to the state, however, they placed great importance on the legal designation of NGOs as a separate sector with independent motives and practices.

The new Law for the Promotion of Activities Undertaken by Civil Society Organizations, for which the CSC was lobbying, seemed to offer a juridical basis for such a relationship but also presented the forum participants with a threat to their organizational autonomy. Although NGOs had long used personal connections to power brokers and participation in popular demonstrations as means of influencing the public agenda, the proposed law did not concretely specify additional channels for them to participate in policy making. Given the high degree of connectivity between the NGO leaders and the political class, participants in the forum also quickly pointed out the possibility that the proposed law might merely provide a new source of official funds for patronage. One representative of the CSC suggested that self-regulation and transparency in the use of state funds (specifically, setting up a system of reporting that would feed into a public information clearinghouse) might be a partial solution. On the whole, however, participants seemed nervous about the implied shift in their organizations' identities from democratic activists to social service intermediaries. One later complained that she was particularly troubled by the notion that the new law, although it recognized the importance of NGOs' work for Mexican society, would ultimately make them more accountable to the state than to the rest of society.

After a decade of negotiation, the final version of the Law for the Promotion of Activities Undertaken by Civil Society Organizations was signed by President Vicente Fox in 2004. In 2005, an official federal registry of NGOs was created. Registration is required of any NGO that wishes to access federal funds or participate in public-private partnerships created by the Ministry of Social Development or other federal entities. Applicants are required to rewrite their bylaws to conform to a single federal standard and are limited to applying for funds from already existing programs (rather than proposing new ones). The final version of the law not only prohibits NGOs that receive state funding from supporting particular candidates (as expected) but also contains a provision prohibiting them from engaging in any political activity intended to influence legislation. Hence the law encourages the activities of NGOs that are complementary to the state's social development goals, but it does not provide a direct or legitimate means of influencing the formulation of those goals. Moreover, although NGOs are no longer subject to the sort of government harassment many experienced in the 1970s and 1980s, the ICNL found that they "are often not provided adequate protection by the government in the face of threats and violence from others" (ICNL 2012). This has become a grave problem in recent years as NGOs working in rural areas, with indigenous groups, and on environmental and human rights issues have experienced increasing threats from organized crime groups and the politicians connected to them.

During the period of democratic disenchantment that followed Fox's election, the staff of HD, like the members of other Hidalgan NGOs, saw clear advantages to the unified pursuit of official federal recognition and support. By the end of the decade, however, few of their initial concerns about the possible modes by which their work might be taken into account by the state had been resolved. Some of the older NGOs in Tulancingo declined to petition for inclusion in the National Registry of Civil Society Organizations on the grounds that the costs in labor and resources outweighed any potential benefits. Others, like HD, took part in a campaign of nonconformist NGOs, which have rejected the registration process outright as antidemocratic and continue to operate informally. By 2010, most of the Tulancingo NGOs listed in the National Registry were relative newcomers, not in existence during the period leading up to the 2000 elections.

By controlling the way organized civil society is managed, and by excluding groups that are not defined in this way from deep participation and dialogue on policy, the Mexican state is able to define the category of its legitimate interlocutors as well as the scope of any dialogue. The National Prize for Volunteerism and Solidarity (Premio Nacional de Acción Voluntaria y Solidaria), instituted by President Felipe Calderón in 2009, is a symbolic indicator of this strategy. The award was created to "encourage the participation of citizens and NGOs in the monitoring, operation, and evaluation of state policy" and is bestowed annually on two exemplary Mexican citizens and one NGO (http://www.premioaccionvoluntaria.gob.mx). The awarding of the prize was viewed by many NGOs as an attempt by Calderon to co-opt some aspects of the pro–civil society agenda of his leftist electoral rival, Andres Manuel Lopez Obrador. In fact, Calderon's neologism of "organized civil society" precisely highlights a contrast between the perceived orderliness of the NGO form and the more difficult-to-control social activism that filled Mexico City's streets in the days after Calderon's controversial election. The selection committee for the National Prize, composed primarily of representatives from the executive branch of the federal government, has since awarded the prize exclusively to apolitical assistential or charitable organizations enrolled in the National Registry. This practice is widely regarded as an indicator of the state's desire to domesticate the political clout of NGOs by tightly confining their legitimate role. It also enforces the functional continuity of fields of power between the state and NGOs while simultaneously simulating a distinction. It was precisely this distinction between the state and NGOs as representatives of an independent civil society that the attendees of the Hidalgo State NGO Forum had sought to reinforce as they struggled to define their role as a new category of intermediary.

Tulancingo NGOs, like their counterparts elsewhere, faced a paradox of participation brought about by the interwoven processes of economic and political liberalization that have come to characterize modern democratic transitions in Latin America and beyond. In an insightful analysis of the cultural work involved in "marketing democracy" in Chile, Paley (2001) illuminates how understandings of citizenship rights and responsibilities are reworked through official state discourses and practices in order to produce consent for neoliberal restructuring. She argues that Chilean NGOs were "asked to 'participate' by giving of their labor, often to activities previously performed by the welfare state. While framed as a way of bolstering democracy by strengthening civil society, this kind of participation subsidized and fortified neoliberal economic reforms" (6). In Mexico, rural development NGOs were being interpolated to fill in not only for the downsizing of social services but also for the rollback of the political patronage system that had subsidized rural communities for decades. NGOs were being asked to take on more responsibility than ever but with far fewer resources at their disposal.

A split between NGOs closely connected to social movements and increasingly professionalized nonprofits, already discernible in the late 1980s, became exaggerated by changes in NGO roles as mediators between global capital, states, and local populations. Many NGO workers I spoke with complained that they had lost the shared sense of purpose that formerly made their work seem worthwhile and meaningful. In order to understand the ideological and material stakes of their dilemma, we must take into account the cultural framework used to distinguish between legitimate and illegitimate forms of mediation.

Mexican Cultural Modes of Mediation

Two cultural modes of mediation, embodied in the ideal types of the local intellectual and the political boss, or cacique, are of special relevance to the dilemmas of Tulancingo's development NGOs. Both were historically subsidized by the post-Revolutionary state apparatus and became integral to the functioning of modern Mexican society. Because they are firmly anchored in local institutions, these ideal types operate as durable public symbols through which collective identities are constructed and reconstructed, and through which historical events acquire coherence and meaning. As ideal types, caciques insert themselves into structural gaps in an entrepreneurial fashion, seeking to gain personal power by monopolizing resource flows. Local intellectuals also bridge levels and groups, presumably in the service of integrating national society. Both caciques and intellectuals endure as cultural models for mediation, yet only the latter is perceived as acting legitimately. Tulancingo NGOs have traditionally emulated the model of the local intellectual; the increasing pressure to adopt certain entrepreneurial practices thus places them at risk of losing both their legitimacy and their sense of themselves as agents of improvement.

According to classical anthropological theories of mediation, the ability of an individual or group to become an effective intermediary is contingent on managing conflicting roles and expectations. Press (1969) argued that an intermediary's "mandate to innovate" (205) derived from the initial ambiguity of his or her role with respect to a local community. Once a role configuration became fixed, however, deviation from the new expectations attached to that role could quickly damage the intermediary's reputation and imperil any innovations he or she attempted to bring about. Contradictions or conflicts eventually provoked by these changes might also damage the leadership capacity of an intermediary (de la Peña 1981, 236). Furthermore, Geertz (1960) demonstrated how a shift in modes of mediation, even on the part of established brokers, might negate the very cultural foundations of the intermediary role. For example, HD workers' ability to introduce rapid changes in rural life during the 1970s and 1980s was predicated in part on their positioning as altruistic provincial intellectuals. When HD and other NGOs, pressured by competition for funding and international donor protocols, began to behave in more entrepreneurial ways, their reputations were threatened and their motivations questioned. However, their dilemma can only be fully understood by revising the framework above to account for how the structures to which NGOs have become articulated as supplementary sets are being reconfigured by neoliberalizing projects.

When the Mexican Revolution of 1910 destroyed the hacienda along with the social forms that it mediated, new gaps were opened between local communities and nascent national institutions (Wolf 1956). These gaps were filled in part by caciques. Entering into patron–client relationships with powerful regional and national political figures, caciques gained power for themselves by channeling state resources to their local communities (Gledhill 2000, 113). In post-Revolutionary Mexico, the pursuit of power came to be mediated through the sectoral organs of the state party, the PRI. During the presidency of Lázaro Cárdenas, the party launched an unprecedented effort to integrate remote rural and indigenous populations into the new political structure, creating more positions for caciques like those described by Friedrich (1986). The figure of the cacique symbolized both the pleasures and perils of venality and violence in the popular imagination (de Vries 2002). However, this new class of political entrepreneurs eventually posed a threat to centralized power. The organization of the party along sectoral lines and its monopoly on key political and economic resources helped to "check the transformation of power seekers from local communities into individual entrepreneurs" (Wolf 2001, 135). As Mexico underwent successive modernization programs, *caciquismo* (political bossism) contracted and expanded in accordance with the availability of state resources and opportunities for mediation (Zárate Hernández 1997, 9). *Caciquismo* became more ingrained in some regions than in others. Nonetheless, the one-party corporatist system survived for over seventy years, at least in part by reworking this older cultural form of mediation to suit the purposes of Mexican state building. In the state of Hidalgo, it attained the status of a high art. The growth of alternative parties after the 2000 elections in many municipalities, far from signaling a fundamental shift in power, merely enabled lesser members of these powerful families to seize new opportunities for political advancement.

In the Tulancingo region, independent development NGOs challenged the power of the PRI and the caciques' monopoly on resource distribution in the 1970s and 1980s by delivering development projects directly to local communities and by organizing them into producer and consumer cooperatives. This made NGOs a threat to the political status quo and placed them in competition with the more established intermediaries, so they were closely watched, and some were frequently harassed. However, it was not until the 1980s that *caciquismo* was specifically targeted as corrupt and undemocratic by local NGOs connected to the Mexican prodemocracy movement. In particular, groups like El Barzón and HD were active in voter education initiatives in rural villages, where their projects were located and where they trained volunteer teams from those locales to serve as poll monitors. Several of these volunteer teams were successful in preventing incidents of vote buying and denounced voter intimidation by local caciques. Currently members of the Tulancingo NGO sector vocally oppose *caciquismo* as a major roadblock to rural development and democratic citizenship. They model their interventions into rural life on an alternative form of mediation, that of the local intellectual.

The role played by provincial intellectuals, like schoolteachers and priests, as "pious technicians" of social change predates Mexican Independence (Lomnitz 2001, 203). Lomnitz (2001) traces a historical shift in styles of intellectual intermediation that is linked to changing modes of citizenship. He argues that the limited reach of the governmental state during the colonial era and the dependency of the majority of the population after Independence prevented the ideal of liberal citizenship from becoming a reality (208). While all citizens were guaranteed basic constitutional rights, in practice, many were so isolated from the state apparatus or so dependent on patron–client ties that they could not claim them. In addition, many authorities deemed indigenous and rural citizens incapable of participating in national politics by virtue of their perceived backwardness. The provincial intellectual mediated between the national state and local communities by integrating local people into the nation via modernizing projects and by discursively representing the essence of local authenticity back to the state (208–209). The role of such intellectuals was to produce and measure progress, which could then be used to legitimize the state as the guarantor of the public good. After Independence, a second task of interpreting and "somatizing" popular sentiment emerged. Because the poor were assumed to exist in coerced silence in times of peace, intellectuals developed discourses that served to represent the sentiments of local and regional populations in the national arena (208). In contrast to the violent image of the cacique, the figure of the provincial intellectual embodied pastoral benevolence.

This role continued in a modified form after the Revolution, when agrarian reform measures not only redefined the corporate relationships between peasants and the state but also inaugurated a new project aimed at creating a shared national consciousness. According to Zárate Hernández (1997),

> the revolutionary state proposed the creation of a national consciousness among groups that, because they lived in situations of extreme backwardness or marginality, did not have a sense of nationality or Mexicanness. The reasoning was clear as there did not (yet) exist a national consciousness, and moreover there were zones of the country in which the rights of citizens were functionally subordinated to the interests of particular groups. . . . The political reforms that were undertaken hence had this double purpose (or were directed toward the resolution of this double problematic): on the one hand to resolve or mitigate some of the more notable inequalities, and on the other to form or forge citizens with a clear national consciousness, thus strengthening the national state. (259; author's translation)

The creation of these ideal citizens, however, depended on the strength of the state and the development of markets—conditions that were not yet favorable to the formation of a political culture based on autonomous individuals rather than hierarchically organized groups. Here again we see the historical interplay between evolving forms of corporatism and individualism that Reina, Servin, and Tutino (2007) argue informs every major turning point in state–society relations in Mexico. Far from destroying earlier forms of mediation, the Revolution renovated them and reworked them as the basis for incorporating new collectivities into the national state. In fact, nationalism would soon provide a new symbolic resource that could be deployed by competing groups in order to claim legitimacy for projects of social change (Zárate Hernández 1997, 261–262). Whereas the cacique symbolized venality and lust for personal power, the intellectual mode of mediation was predicated on the value of self-sacrifice in service to national progress. Provincial intellectuals in post-Revolutionary Mexico figured as legitimate intermediaries laboring for the common good of the nation rather than for personal gain. The vocation of schoolteachers, development workers, and other civic missionaries was to extend the promises of the Revolution and the rights of citizenship to everyday Mexicans (Foweraker 1993; Vaughan 1997).

The nature of this historical moment helped to shape the future role and mode of mediation used by Tulancingo NGOs in their rural project sites. As was the case with the activist priests of Morelos described by de la Peña (1981), the ability of these NGOs to organize and implement development projects in rural villages was closely tied to their leaders' "access to, and manipulation of, a number of social and economic resources which were completely out of the reach of any local person" (236). For example, HD's early irrigation infrastructure projects depended on the organization's links to Mexican government agencies, like PIDER, and to foreign donors, like the Inter-American Foundation, procured through the organization's affiliation with the FMDR. In addition, as members of two of Tulancingo's most prominent merchant families, HD's cofounders enjoyed access to elite social networks through which large donations could be solicited and a modicum of political support could be procured against the interference of local PRI bosses.

Although Tulancingo NGO workers modeled their work on this intellectual ideal, their development mission was originally rooted in an oppositional logic. Unlike the provincial intellectuals who attempted to integrate campesinos and indigenous people into the corporate state apparatus, they advocated a broader vision of progress, drawing on discourses of universal human rights that sought to liberate everyday Mexicans from that very corporatist system. Like their colleagues elsewhere in Mexico, they sought to expand the rights of individual citizens and educate them for participation in grassroots democracy. Their vision was one of "collective modernity" based in social rights, where inequality was understood to be as antithetical to democracy as authoritarianism (de la Peña 1981, 337). During the 1970s and 1980s, many Mexican NGOs promoted an institutional culture of solidarity and fraternity, both within the organizations and in their relationships with project participants. Concretely, this vision of social change prompted a trend of deprofessionalization and an emphasis on consensus-based planning and decision-making processes (Aguilar Valenzuela 1997b, 299–309). A moral commitment to solidarity, equality, and grassroots democracy became key motivations for employment in Tulancingo NGOs, and their moral mission of national improvement lent legitimacy to their local projects.

In the neoliberal era, however, the problem of the intermediary in Mexican society has taken on renewed significance. The student and labor movements of the 1960s criticized the corporatist system's reliance on political mediation, calling for a more open democracy and independent unions. They were joined by proponents of liberation theology, who accused the Catholic hierarchy of illegitimately profiting by acting as a power broker and spiritual gatekeeper. By the 1980s, many activists in Mexico, including the development sector of Tulancingo, had seized on the language of universal human rights as a means of asserting individual liberty against the authoritarianism of the state. However, deployment of this discourse of individual freedom was not confined to advocates of democracy and social justice. Throughout the 1970s, large business interests had gained new power in Mexican politics and had fortified their ties with foreign capital (Harvey 2005). They too attacked the corporatist state, not in rejection of its authoritarianism (which they relied on to push through unpopular economic reforms) but rather on the grounds that its inefficiency and protectionism hampered economic growth. Salinas co-opted the discourse of individual freedom used by opposition activists but divorced it from the ideals of social justice and equality that had accompanied it (Harvey 2005). The outcome of this unlikely ideological convergence has been a crisis of legitimacy for NGOs, which must now defend their role in a political environment where intermediaries of all stripes have been rendered suspect. In contrast to the much-maligned cacique, NGOs have sought to become the new legitimate intermediaries between rural communities and diffused centers of power. One of the most difficult dilemmas confronting NGO workers in Tulancingo is how to survive in an organizational climate that encourages self-interest and entrepreneurialism without imperiling the ethos of solidarity that they claim makes their work personally meaningful and socially important. Without it, rural development work becomes, in the words of one Tulancingo NGO worker, "business by other means, and a failed business at that."[8]

Vulnerable Intermediaries: Reworking Cultural Idioms of Mediation

The capacity of Tulancingo NGOs to pursue their programs of social change in the countryside depends in large part on their perceived legitimacy as intermediaries. One major challenge they face is that international donors and project participants often have conflicting expectations of how these NGOs should go about their development work. NGO workers must also confront the gap between their earlier expectations of democratic transition and the contradictory path it has taken in practice. Together, these dynamics trap Tulancingo NGOs in a crucial dilemma: operating successfully within an increasingly marketized NGO paradigm threatens to undo the terms of their own local legitimacy as intermediaries.

Tulancingo NGO workers viewed themselves as democratic activists and advocates for the poor, but over the past several years, they have experienced increasing pressure to convert themselves into freelance development consultants. In fact, many NGOs in the Tulancingo area have begun to charge campesinos for the services they provide in order to survive. Several more established organizations have been reconfigured into *despachos técnicos* (technical consulting offices), acting as liaisons to state bureaucracies and commercial creditors on behalf of campesino cooperatives.[9] Even though many campesinos are entitled to apply for government grants or credits to start up small cooperative enterprises, many of them are unaware of these programs or cannot access them because of the large volume of highly technical paperwork involved.[10] Most of these benefits have been monopolized by local caciques with connections in the state government, even when the program guidelines stipulate that the supports must be shared by an entire community or cooperative association. Several local banks also offered project proposal services but charged an average fee equal to about 30 percent of the solicited funds. In Tulancingo, an established NGO that had recently received official certification to apply for such funds on behalf of campesinos reported charging a 5 percent rate per project, enabling them to organize proposed cooperatives and to provide ongoing technical support. The NGO manager justified this new consultative role as an extension of the organization's earlier prodemocracy work. He distinguished between two forms of mediating between campesinos and government agencies: *aprovecharse* (taking advantage) and *facilitar* (facilitating). From his point of view, both the banks and the caciques typically acted in an entrepreneurial fashion by taking advantage of the campesinos' lack of access to information and political clout. By channeling public funds to the poorest peasants rather than those with the strongest political connections, he reasoned, his NGO could instead facilitate citizen access to public resources. The fee they charged for this service, he argued, was intended only to cover the organization's labor costs and not to fill its coffers. However, other NGO workers in Tulancingo pointed out that charging for services often prevented NGOs from reaching the poorest of the poor. The manager of the FHAR complained that this model forced him to perform "development triage"[11] by choosing to invest the organization's limited resources in only those campesino cooperatives (usually those with prior business experience and higher cash incomes) deemed most likely to succeed. For many NGO workers in Tulancingo, the marketization of development work and the rise of the audit culture in international aid represented a drastic paradigm shift that contrasted sharply with their own visions and earlier strategies for producing social change.

Although neoliberal ideology insists that political and economic action must be both direct and individualized, Tulancingo NGO workers justified a continued need for mediation on the ground that their rural constituents lacked access to the rights of full citizenship and needed assistance in claiming them. In doing so, they reworked existing cultural models of mediation to constitute themselves and their organizations as legitimate intermediaries. This required cultivating particular forms of subjectivity that allowed them to balance conflicting expectations and values. They did so by continuing to make sense of their development work in terms of an ongoing struggle for democracy and human rights. Like the US-based educational reformers described by LaShaw (2012), their work became a means of cultivating a particular moral identity. For them, an NGO career was meaningful as a form of middle-class martyrdom whereby they sacrificed financial security and upward mobility in the name of their commitment to Mexico's future.

Lomnitz (2001) argued that provincial intellectuals initially constituted themselves as intermediaries, operating in the governmental breach between isolated local communities and the capital, by claiming to represent marginal citizens who lacked the resources, preparation, or autonomy to represent themselves. Even after the prodemocracy movement culminated in the 2000 elections, Tulancingo NGOs continued to represent themselves as the voice of civil society using rhetoric similar to that discussed by Lomnitz. They saw their intermediary role as twofold: to assist disadvantaged Mexicans (primarily campesinos and indigenous people) in claiming the rights and benefits to which they were entitled as citizens and to *capacitar* (train) these same groups to participate fully in Mexico's new democracy. The former goal included helping citizens access government development and assistance programs, as well as advocating for the political, civil, and property rights of citizens who did not have the wherewithal to defend themselves legally. The second role, that of *capacitación* (training), figured as an extension of the voter education campaigns NGOs had carried out in the countryside around Tulancingo during the heyday of the prodemocracy movement. The technical consulting offices discussed above were also a key component of this approach, enabling NGOs not only to help campesinos access government development funds but also to assist groups with follow-up training that would help them succeed in producing and marketing agricultural products and administrating small businesses.

In constituting themselves as legitimate mediators, Tulancingo NGOs sought to distinguish themselves in the public eye from intermediaries who took advantage of campesinos to amass wealth and power for themselves, such as Gerardo Sosa's Fundacion Hidalguense. They also positioned themselves in explicit opposition to the new philanthropic culture exemplified by former first lady Marta Sahagún de Fox. Her *Vamos México* foundation fully embraced the marketized model favored by US nonprofits. Vamos México was founded in the fall of 2001 to combat poverty through targeted programs in education and basic health care. It inaugurated its mission with a charity concert at $10,000 per head featuring British pop star Elton John and managed to raise $40 million in ten months. The press, however, criticized Sahagún's aggressive promotion of Vamos México as shameless politicking, claiming she suffered from "Evita syndrome" (Cansino 2004).[12] Tulancingo NGO workers publicly criticized "Martita's" organization as a paternalistic anachronism out of step with Mexico's new democracy. One Vamos México initiative in particular, a campaign seeking private donations of used bicycles for rural schoolchildren who traveled long distances to attend classes, earned their angry condemnation. Education, they maintained, was the constitutional right of every Mexican citizen. The proper solution to rural students' problems was for the Fox government to deliver on its campaign promises to build and staff more and better schools in the countryside, rather than giving Marta Sahagún de Fox a photo opportunity.

Worse still, congressional investigations into possible financial links between the Fox government and Vamos México fueled existing rumors that represented NGOs in general as parasitical middlemen in the political power game. NGOs faced scrutiny not only from the national press but also from their target communities. For example, some local beneficiaries of NGO programs questioned how helpful these projects really were in their daily struggles. Many campesinos in the Tulancingo region complained that while NGO workers promoting new projects were full of interesting ideas, they seldom had sufficient resources at their disposal to carry them out successfully. It was also plain to them that the success of rural development projects ultimately depended on the vagaries of global market fluctuations and macroeconomic policies—factors neither the NGOs nor the campesinos could control. One woman,[13] a member of a foundering dairy cooperative, alleged that the NGO organizing her group only went around raising false hopes, eager to enlist them in what she saw as a risky venture but less than forthcoming with the hard cash needed to found a real business. The NGO claimed to be helping out the campesinos, she said, but in the end she questioned whether the campesinos, through their work on the cooperative, might instead be helping to guarantee the survival of the NGO. Her viewpoint was shared by others who had come to see the proliferation of NGOs in the countryside not as a radical departure from the old patron–client politics but rather as an impoverished form of its spoils system.

The peril of being perceived as illegitimate intermediaries deeply influenced the way individual NGO workers framed their careers. They struggled to reconcile external pressures to act as self-interested entrepreneurs with closely held notions of the inherent value of solidarity and self-sacrifice for the common good. They responded to emerging forms of vulnerability by highlighting the altruist and humanist motivations behind their work, emphasizing the downward rather than upward accountability of their role. Before the debt crisis of the 1980s, professional development work—especially posts in government agencies—had meant a secure middle-class lifestyle. Those displaced by the crisis, who had found a niche during the NGO boom of the 1990s, while less secure, managed to keep their heads above water. Nevertheless, the new trends in NGO funding left many of these workers without the wherewithal to procure the most basic markers of middle-class status. In 2003, NGO workers in Tulancingo earned between $50 and $150 per week, but because of the per-project basis of their jobs, some might only work for three months at a time and then be out of work for a month or so, or forced to find another source of employment in the interim.[14] During this same period, food for a family of four cost around $40 per week. Tuition for one student at a private secondary school started at $70 per month. According to Mexican government statistics, the average family in an urban area spent around $60 per month on housing and about $120 on transport and communications (INEGI, http://www.inegi.gob.mx). This does not even begin to account for medical care, taxes, or rising utility prices. It is widely acknowledged that the middle class has been hard hit by economic reforms, especially after the peso crisis of the early 1990s that erased many Mexicans' life savings (Gilbert 2007; Moreno 2002; Thompson 2002). Local newspapers routinely covered the plight of the rural and urban poor who fled north to find work, but it was big news in the fall of 2004 when *La Ruta*, Tulancingo's independent biweekly, reported unprecedented levels of unemployment and immigration among educated professionals (*La Ruta* 2004).

Tulancingo NGO workers continually framed their precarious careers as a conscious sacrifice for the greater good. They insisted that although professionals with comparable expertise and job descriptions were well paid and highly respected in the private sector, they preferred to work in NGOs out of solidarity with the campesinos and a commitment to democracy and human rights.[15] One young HD staff member, recounting that organization's abundance of past funding in light of its current austerity, declared that she was glad she had only begun working there in the past five years. Rather than lament her lot, she maintained that she had been privy to the "nicest era" of HD's history, in which staff were motivated by their moral convictions rather than by material gain. For her, NGO work was a meaningful, if underappreciated, pursuit.[16] Among many of her compatriots, self-sacrifice had become grounds for claiming moral authority to speak for Mexico's future on behalf of the marginalized.

The struggle to maintain legitimacy as intermediaries also compelled Tulancingo NGOs to reconsider the value of professionalism as a prerequisite for being taken seriously by politicians, government technocrats, international funders, and their campesino clientele. In this context, professionalization meant attending to two often contradictory sets of values. On the one hand, surviving as an NGO was an exercise in self-entrepreneurship. This entailed establishing one's self as a field expert, not only proficient in technical matters but also in touch with one's campesino constituency and competent at getting things done bureaucratically. It required combining intimate familiarity with local agrarian conditions with technical knowledge of current trends in development solutions. On the other hand, professionalization could be reframed as a new form of solidarity with campesinos. By offering campesinos professional consulting services, NGO workers insisted, they could help them achieve better results with the limited resources available to them. By staying abreast of trends in development solutions, NGOs could reconcile local needs with external funding trends. Professionalism might endear NGO workers to their campesino clients if it rendered them better technical consultants and more effective intermediaries on the campesinos' behalf.

In their relations with campesinos, NGO workers from Tulancingo were at pains to distinguish themselves from other outside intermediaries like caciques. They attempted to legitimate their interest in the survival of campesino villages by demonstrating that they belonged there and that their work was motivated both by ties of affection toward rural people and respect for the innate value of rural culture. They took pride in greeting villagers by name with a firm handshake, and they took special pleasure in sharing meals in the homes of their project participants. Invitations to serve as godparents were prized by NGO workers as indications that they had indeed proven their worthiness as friends and usefulness as intermediaries. By comparison, organizations that failed to maintain these relationships or to deliver successful projects could develop reputations as *quemados* (burned), which might damage their ability to launch future projects in the area.

The way one Tulancingo NGO negotiated requests by the community of San Isidro for assistance in the face of a long-standing drought provides a clear example of how NGOs have tried to strike this delicate balance. It was nearly impossible at the time to procure funding to expand the community's irrigation system, as capital-intensive infrastructural projects had fallen out of favor with international agencies in the late 1980s. A nearby lake was proposed as an alternative water source, but competition for access among area communities was fierce, and securing water rights would have been an expensive, lengthy process involving multiple government agencies (not to mention the possible involvement of local caciques). Nonetheless, the NGO staff knew that the state agricultural ministry had recently launched a pilot project that would partially fund a limited number of campesino cooperatives interested in building greenhouses to grow vegetables for export. The NGO's manager used his expert reputation and connections in the state agricultural ministry to help several households in the community enroll in the program. While the greenhouses did not benefit every family in San Isidro, they did provide a means to conserve limited water resources. Although this solution did not go very far toward addressing the root causes of poverty in San Isidro, the NGO staff reasoned that without professional assistance and the right connections, campesinos might find survival impossible.

The dilemmas that Tulancingo NGOs face point to some of the profound ways in which the terrain of struggle over rural development and democracy has shifted in Mexico. If, as the classical literature holds, forms of mediation are reconfigured in response to structural change, then the mediating dilemmas faced by Tulancingo NGOs may illuminate some of the dynamics of how "actually existing neoliberalisms" (Brenner and Theodore 2002, 349) are forged from existing institutions and social forms. The problems NGO workers face, particularly in constructing legitimate modes of mediation through which to effect change, point to the contingency and path dependency of neoliberalizing projects. Their attempts to find solutions that simultaneously ensure the survival of their organizations (lending legitimacy to their work) and cultivate meaningful forms of social action serve to illustrate the often contradictory processes through which neoliberalizing projects become embedded in specific places.

Conclusion

For nearly seven decades, national mythology—indeed, a sense of Mexicanness itself—was closely tied to an authoritarian corporatist political structure in which intermediaries (intellectuals and caciques alike) not only bridged social groups via cultural idioms of mediation but also helped to legitimize the authority of the state. According to Bartra (2002, 223), the end of the "perfect dictatorship," which shaped the mediation practices described by anthropologists like Wolf, has led to the state's abdication of its previous role as mediator of social change. The policies of intertwined political and economic liberalization mandated by the Washington Consensus have forced the citizens of many countries to reconsider these questions.

In Mexico, as elsewhere, NGOs have taken on intermediary roles, building structural linkages for redistribution of resources and power, as well as facilitating translation of cultural forms between distinct social groups. The project of reconfiguring forms of citizenship in Mexico has been a complicated one. The historical interplay between evolving forms of individualism and corporatism continues to inform this process. In many ways, the great distance that persists between notions of universal rights and the insistence on collective forms of political participation serves to legitimate the intermediary role of NGOs while complicating it further. Indeed, the notion of the "right to have rights" that animated the prodemocracy movement is a prime example of what Tsing (2005) has called "engaged universals," the form taken on by universalisms as they gain traction in particular times and places to become "practical projects accomplished in a heterogeneous world" (8). In contrast to earlier theories of globalization, which assumed the coherence and coordination of global interconnections, Tsing emphasizes the awkwardness and contingency of the material and ideological links through which global norms and forms are brought into being. She calls these moments of awkward engagement between traveling universalisms and the people they mobilize "friction," insisting that the "cultural work of encounter" is central to the production of engaged universals (12). For Tsing, to study such engagements is to examine how particular actors in particular times and places put universalisms to practical use. She warns, however, that the outcomes of the cultural work of encounter, like the labor of mediation performed by Tulancingo NGO workers, can be unpredictable and often contradictory. Indeed, the birthday party guests whose story was told at the beginning of this chapter found themselves caught up in a series of moral and institutional dilemmas that threatened to undo the very changes they sought to cultivate in the Hidalgan countryside.

If we take seriously Wolf's ([1966] 2004) theory that the processes of re-centralization, which accompany major structural shifts, often entail changes to modes of mediation and the emergence of new groups of intermediaries, then examination of how such groups emerge and constitute themselves as intermediaries and how they approach the dilemmas that arise in the process affords valuable insight into complex processes of structural change. Through the course of these dynamics, the limits of the NGO form have become increasingly clear to many of the Tulancingo professionals with whom I worked. Their efforts to overcome these limits by embedding the NGO form within older forms of social networking based on principles of reciprocity are the subject of Chapter 5.

CHAPTER 5

"Bridges of Love"

Building North–South NGO Networks

In the summer of 2004, a strange spectacle confronted the residents of Tulancingo. A large group of visitors from the United States arrived at the central bus terminal loaded down with luggage and expensive cameras. Tulancingo is eager to attract tourists, but the group never checked into a hotel. Instead they were met at the terminal by a large contingent of campesinos who were customarily seen in town only on market days. Their caravan of rusty pickup trucks blocked traffic along the busy street, eliciting honks and curious stares from passing motorists. A group of children bearing flowers and colorful banners clambered down from the truck beds to greet the arriving strangers with hugs and kisses, as if welcoming home prodigal kin. Each visitor was embraced in turn by their hosts, young and old, men and women. They posed for group photos in the middle of the street, seemingly impervious to the commotion. The traffic jam subsided only when the strangers and their luggage were loaded up into the backs of the trucks and whisked away across dusty gravel roads to the small villages where they would spend the next week. Tulancinguenses are well accustomed to witnessing scenes of departure at the bus terminal, the tearful farewells of families come to see off loved ones bound for the capital or the US border. The arrival of so many foreigners, however, appeared as remarkable as the company they kept.

This seemingly singular scenario was part of a ritual of connection aimed at creating and maintaining a transnational network of NGOs. Over the past decade and a half, a variety of visitors has arrived at the central bus station on Los Pinos Street—young activists from Barcelona, Methodist youth from upstate New York, Michigan peace and justice promoters, and German human rights and development advocates, among others. They have journeyed to Tulancingo to renew their ties with Hidalgo Development (HD). From the 1990s on, the organization's relationship with funders and partners from the United States and Europe became crucial to the success of its programs as well as to its institutional survival in an often difficult political and economic climate. HD increasingly relied on the support of its foreign NGO partners to carry out educational programs and organize agricultural cooperatives in areas where rural poverty had been greatly exacerbated by the consequences of neoliberal restructuring and North American economic integration. In the years since NAFTA's opening, cheap, highly subsidized US imports of maize and milk have devastated the local agricultural economy. At the same time, NGOs like HD faced novel challenges, as trends in international aid placed new constraints on local NGOs seeking support via international partnerships. The site visits described above represent crucial points of contact between HD and its foreign NGO partners, where relationships of fictive kinship serve as templates for personalizing and stabilizing organizational networks.

The annual pilgrimage of foreign NGO members to HD project sites in campesino villages was designed as a personal route to institutional alliance. HD's cofounder called this networking strategy "building bridges of love." The exact itinerary of these visits varies from group to group and year to year, but the goal has always been to provide a space in which foreign visitors can share the reality of daily life in campesino communities and forge affectionate personal relationships with campesino families, an experience intended to motivate their future cooperation in HD's development projects. The story of these bridges of love—how and why they are imagined and enacted, the possibilities and limits they engender—is significant because it points to the importance of process and form in the constitution of global networks.

The network has become a central metaphor and model for grasping changes in global social organization. Indeed, the proliferation of transnational NGO networks has been held as symptomatic of such shifts. Nonetheless, there is still need for deeper investigation into the models on which network ties are configured as well as the role of intermediaries in creating and maintaining these ties. This chapter contributes toward that effort by reconsidering some problematic assumptions embedded in the network metaphors that animate contemporary social theory. The case of HD is revealing, in that it both demonstrates the limits of these earlier theories and offers an ethnographic assay of the contingent processes and patterns through which such global connections are produced and maintained. Examining how HD staff build bridges of love with foreign NGO partners yields a new understanding of the production of network ties as a cultural endeavor, involving both affective labor and the creative reworking of extant cultural forms for use in new contexts.

Developing Connections: NGOs and Global Networks

Renewed attention to networks has enabled social theorists to rethink notions of relatedness and distance in the context of uneven and complex global shifts (Knox, Savage, and Harvey 2006). Indeed, the language of networking has become ubiquitous in the social sciences (Castells 1999; Latour 2005; Riles 2000). Transnational NGO networks in particular have been held up as paradigmatic of new forms of social collectivity emerging out of globalization, particularly as evidence of the growth of global civil society (Appadurai 1996, 2000; Castells 1999; Keck and Sikkink 1998). These networks provide both a metaphor for imagining the global and a model for understanding the relationship between agency and structure in an epoch characterized by the reconfiguration of power dynamics simultaneously in multiple social arenas.

As discussed in the Introduction, during the 1990s, the growth of transnational NGO networks seemed to some to represent a counterforce to the alienating dynamics of neoliberalism, a "grassroots globalization" (Appadurai 2000, 1) with liberatory potential. Like the new network theories, much of the early literature on NGO networks tended to be more philosophical than empirical (Fischer 1997; Leve and Karim 2001). With a few notable exceptions (Riles 2000), there has been surprisingly little ethnographic analysis of the configuration of particular network forms or evaluation of the uneven quality of the ties by which NGOs of varying types are linked to one another at multiple scales. While network analysis seemingly promises researchers the ability to uncover latent or emergent global structures, the status of the network as a cultural form deployed both by social scientists and by those whom they study (scientists, activists, government officials, businesspeople, media, educators, etc.) raises methodological problems (Cunningham 1999; Riles 2000). Further challenges are posed by a series of lingering assumptions around the constitution of "the global" itself, which may hamper understanding of the significance of network models and metaphors to contemporary social change. In order to move the theoretical discussion forward, we must closely examine the structures of NGO networks and the processes through which they are produced.

Tsing (2005) contends that the primary constructs through which we conceptualize globalization, including the networked globe, imply first and foremost that we have all become linked into the same universal structure. She argues that, viewed ethnographically, globalization is not in fact a unidirectional process of integration into a preexisting universal system. Rather, it involves forging connections from multiple directions at once via processes of mutual accommodation. "Capitalism, science and politics all depend upon global connections. Each spreads through aspirations to fulfill *universal* dreams and schemes. Yet this is a particular kind of universality: It can only be charged and enacted in the sticky materiality of practical encounters" (Tsing 2005, 1). The nature of the global is not predetermined, but rather is contingent upon the outcome of these frictional interactions between globalizing and localizing projects and their attendant logics of connection (Tsing 2005). The network trope may lead us to assume that the creation of ties among local NGOs and colleagues or donors in other places entails merely plugging in to a preexisting network since it indexes images of rhizomatic, self-organizing systems. However, Knox, Savage, and Harvey (2006, 135) point out that in practice, this fluidity and openness is quite selective, contradicting earlier claims about the inherent spontaneity and flexibility of global civil society networks (Appadurai 2000). In this chapter, I focus on the concrete practices through which north–south NGO networks are constituted, paying special attention to what Juris (2008, 10) terms the "cultural logics of networking" that help to generate those practices in particular contexts.

Appeals to the global are crucial to NGO network organizing efforts (Cunningham 1999). Development NGOs in particular have taken on a global public image as expressions of person-to-person solidarity, across north–south frontiers, intended to counter the harm caused by entrenched structural inequalities. However, some scholars question exactly what is meant by solidarity in this context and whether the existing institutional arrangements through which such acts of solidarity are channeled might in fact work to preserve the very inequalities they are intended to eradicate (Velloso Santisteban 2005). While development experts have lauded NGOs as efficient conduits for aid and pointed to the NGO boom as an indicator of the growth of global civil society, other researchers caution that the implications of this shift may not be so straightforward. NGOs are simultaneously local and transnational, and their forms of intervention into the lives of local populations allow other transnational actors to circumvent states to enact their own programs for development. The line between NGOs, governments, and corporate capital has become increasingly blurred as the number of NGOs has exploded, especially in the global south (Leve and Karim 2001). Dependency on donor funding is a key factor that shapes relationships among participants in transnational networks of development NGOs. In recent years, researchers have begun to problematize issues of power, trust, and accountability that have emerged as northern NGOs have taken on new roles as conduits for aid and partners in local development projects. Accurately charting the large amounts of money channeled through NGOs across the globe is nearly impossible, as most major NGOs receive funds not only from international agencies and private philanthropy but also increasingly through corporate partnerships (Fernando and Heston 1997). Aid is crucial for southern NGOs that cannot rely on domestic funding and must network with donors abroad in order to obtain the necessary funds to carry out their projects. However, most of these "partnerships" are inherently imbalanced. Fowler (1998) argues that effective cooperation between northern and southern NGOs has been disabled by the imposition of a contract-based agenda, which hampers the formation of the trust-based partnerships essential to successful planning and implementation of development projects. Nearly all the flexibility in this model is exercised by INGOs, which renders their local NGO partners vulnerable to a variety of risks, including financial instability and political demobilization (Kapoor 2005).

The structure of upward accountability inherent in such partnerships also allows donors to shape local development agendas by setting funding priorities and promoting competition for funds among formerly allied local groups (Wallace 2003). Ferguson and Gupta (2002) argue that non-state actors like NGOs are inherently implicated in neoliberal modalities of government. In their view, transnational NGO networks may in fact constitute a new mode of "transnational governmentality," which introduces techniques of self-government to devolve both the risks and responsibilities of development interventions onto the local organizations (Ferguson and Gupta 2002, 989). In turn, local NGOs must use these same logics in evaluating, creating, and administrating projects. This aid agenda limits the kinds of transnational partnerships that are possible by determining the circumstances under which these ties are formed and maintained (Fowler 1998). If this model does not inspire confidence on the part of the local NGO, then what are alternative ways of creating networks of trust?

It is precisely the "sticky materiality" of transnational NGO networks that must be investigated in detail if we wish to understand the possibilities and limits of north–south partnerships forged in the contemporary context. If what we are mapping is contact between actors, then how is that contact significant? What does it accomplish, and by what means? It is imperative to push beyond the "generic notion of connection" provided by network tropes (Knox, Savage, and Harvey 2006, 124) to examine how cultural models for creating and managing translocal connections shape the form and intensity of these ties, enabling certain forms of cooperation while disabling others. The recent "cultural turn" among social network analysts has helped to illuminate the "causal role of ideas, beliefs, and values, and of the actors that strive to realize them" (Emirbayer and Goodwin 1994, 1446). Recent work on the significance of affect and the role of intermediaries in creating transnational ties points toward new areas of investigation (Chan 2008; Merry 2006; Richard and Rudnyckyj 2009; Shaw and Charsley 2006). The quality of personal interactions among NGO contacts and the cultural models that inform the configuration of NGO to NGO relationships are both crucial components that must be examined closely in order to deepen our understanding of the structural dynamics of global networks. As Strathern (2001) points out, "Networks rendered contingent on peoples' interactions turn out to have a fragile temporality. They do not last forever; on the contrary, the question becomes how they are sustained and made durable" (523). The case of HD demonstrates that building strong transnational ties among NGOs is a labor-intensive process. Far beyond merely plugging into a preexisting global structure, creating a transnational network from rural Mexico involved reworking extant cultural forms to provide a structure for solidarity capable of sustaining mutual respect and trust among a variety of differently positioned and unequal actors.

The Cultural Labor of Networking

"Here in Hidalgo we are known for our hospitality," Maria, an HD staff member, explained, "especially in the rural communities. People are very open here. We love to have visitors and especially people from outside, in the countryside there is a certain . . . I don't know . . . I feel the visits give HD vitality. And it helps to invigorate, to motivate the people in the communities, knowing that someone from outside has concern for them." It was late afternoon in Tulancingo, and HD's staff was just finishing a communal meal on the first floor of the organization's headquarters. I listened as I cleared our dishes from the table and set up my tape recorder. "So," I asked, "when you invite a foreign group to come and visit, what is it they are coming here to do?" "Well," Raoul replied, "I think that most of the foreigners who come here are looking to feel like part of something larger than themselves. They want to help." Rodrigo paused to stir a spoonful of Nescafé into his mug of hot water and added thoughtfully, "They are also curious about us. They want to know how people in the third world live." His wife, Esperanza, agreed: "They come here to become acquainted with another reality, different from the one they live, as well as to help us with ideas, with money. So we invite them to come and share our reality, to get to know one another as human beings."

Everyone agreed that "sharing realities" was nothing if not difficult. Juan Carlos elaborated,

> At first it is very much on the surface, because the experience can be very disorienting for them. Most of the Europeans arrive with this "conquistador" attitude, they want to be the saviors of the poor stupid Mexicans and teach us how to do things "the right way," but I think in the end they learn more from our culture than we from theirs. Some of the North Americans, well, they come more as tourists, as observers. So we have to teach both groups how to open up and integrate themselves into the communities.

Teaching northern visitors to share of themselves was a long-term prospect requiring patience and persistence on the part of HD staff. The bridges of love on which they sought to build this vision of global solidarity were modeled on the Mexican cultural institution of *compadrazgo*, or ritual coparenthood.

HD received project funding from the Ford Foundation and the United States Agency for International Development (USAID) in the 1980s. In the new millennium, however, international development aid seemed to have dried up as international media attention shifted to humanitarian crises in Asia and Africa. HD was eager to develop partnerships with international NGOs and funding agencies, but conventional institutional alliances did not suit its needs for durable, long-term partnerships. Moreover, prior colonial and neocolonial relationships between Mexicans and citizens of the very countries (Spain and the United States) with whom they were attempting to collaborate instilled HD's staff with a heightened consciousness of the dangers of reproducing historical patterns of power imbalances even as they struggle to level those inequalities through their projects. Those patterns contrasted with their own vision of global solidarity as founded on relationships of reciprocal sharing among people rather than charity or patronage. Maria expressed the idea thusly:

> It is difficult, yes, but necessary because we are struggling for something in common. The point is not to have more paternalism, for them to come here and pity us, to say "look at those poor idiots, let's help them." No, it is to work together, to learn from one another. If they have more possibilities, then they should share what they have just as we share of ourselves.

We should both share willingly, with pleasure. That is the true meaning of solidarity.[1]

Per-project partnerships could not sustain such efforts, and large grants were inaccessible, so in addition to raising its own funds through raffles and the sale of products from cooperatives the group had helped to found, HD also sought out support from smaller groups of interested foreigners. The New Policy Agenda of the 1990s favored formal contractual relations among NGO partners as a means of promoting efficiency, accountability, and mutual trust. In contrast, HD's networking strategy involved intensive personalization to strengthen diffuse ties and make maintenance of long-term cooperation possible, creating a bridge of love across which resources, information, and influence might flow more steadily.

Compadrazgo as a Model for Transnational NGO Networks

Hola comadre!! I have missed you so very much! I try to explain to people in my church and my family how Matt and I have met such an awesome person and how we are now like family but they don't get it. I am so excited about coming back next summer and i will not forget about the "siamese" banana cake. I am sorry that it has taken me so long to write to you. . . . I won't be able to write you again for a while because I am leaving the state again. . . . Thank you all sooo much for everything. I will try to send you pictures of Matt and I. . . . But I have to go now, I will write you again as soon as I can.

Love, Rachel

— Excerpt from e-mail to HD staff member by US NGO solidarity tour participant, July 2004

Recent scholarship on transnational networking overwhelmingly emphasizes the role of the Internet and information technology in shaping network logics, but there is also growing recognition of the importance of face-to-face contact in the constitution of lasting organizational ties (Juris 2008). The cultural logics that generated HD's networking practices were inevitably influenced by changes in communications technology but were also rooted in moral principles of reciprocity and trust embodied in culturally specific institutions. In contrast to cross-border civil society networks based on "the strength of weak ties" (Granovetter 1973; see also Wilson 1998), HD sought to promote trust and long-term cooperation by modeling transnational NGO partnerships on a form of fictive kinship. At human rights conferences and development summits in Mexico and abroad, HD staff attempted to initiate relationships with foreign organizations by enticing their delegates home to the Tulancingo Valley for a visit. Via letters, e-mails, and face-to-face chats, interested foreigners were invited to "share the reality" of the campesino families with whom HD works and experience firsthand their struggles against poverty. Site visits are common in the NGO world as a platform for evaluating the results of development projects and have well-known potential to sway funders' decisions to support a local NGO. But for HD, there was something more to the language of sharing and family within which these invitations were couched. This alternative model of international cooperation was patterned after *compadrazgo*. By entering into metaphorical (and sometimes actual) relationships of *compadrazgo*, members of HD and of foreign NGOs become partners in the development and guidance of village project sites. Transnational networking was thereby transformed from a limited exchange between formal institutional allies into an open-ended act of sharing among kin.

Compadrazgo makes an ideal cultural model for organizing these relationships in three ways: it links large groups of unrelated people into permanent, horizontal, and binding relationships; structures mutual aid; and defines ritual roles of respect and reciprocity from one actor to another. The Mexican system of *compadrazgo* is the result of a process of religious syncretism in which a Spanish practice of baptismal sponsorship (or godparenthood) was conjoined to a preexisting Nahua practice of ritualized friendship (Dávila 1970). As practiced in Spain, *compadrazgo* was a web of interpersonal relationships based on spiritual kinship and mandated by the Catholic Church. The relationship was achieved through the sponsorship of a neophyte in baptism, confirmation, or marriage. Baptismal sponsorship, the prototypical example of this form, involves three sets of persons: the sponsored child, the parents of the child, and the child's sponsor or godparents. As in the godparent complexes of many cultures, the sponsors become like a second set of parents for the child. In contrast to godparent complexes elsewhere, however, the most socially important relationship in the Mexican triad is that between the godparents and the coparents, who are bound in a permanent

Figure 11. Inaugural celebration for a community sewing workshop, built and equipped with donations from one of HD's international partners. Visitors from the partner organization are invited to participate in a traditional dance on the roof of the new workshop.

reciprocal relationship. These two sets of individuals address one another formally as *comadre* or *compadre*, comother or cofather. Coparents, or compadres, are expected to lend one another money, come to one another's aid in the event of illness or emergencies, provide for orphaned godchildren, and offer one another hospitality.

Although *compadrazgo* may be deployed vertically, as a means of acquiring "friends in high places,"[2] it is also used horizontally as a social leveling mechanism, a way of sharing the costs of a celebration or group project. A major celebration such as a wedding may require perhaps twenty sets of godparents, each of which is responsible for furnishing a particular item. Religious tradition requires that godparents be invited to sponsor ritual items (such as the *lazo* used to tie the couple together, the *arras* that symbolize a husband's promise to provide for his future family, and the *copas* the new couple will use to toast their future together at the wedding feast). However, in many parts of rural Hidalgo, godparents are also invited to sponsor other nonreligious aspects of the celebration, such as the wedding photographer, the cake, or the musicians. Personal relationships of *compadrazgo* differ with respect to the degree of ritual formality and the level of expenditure and long-term commitment involved. Collective endeavors also entail enlisting sponsors. Newly constructed village wells and schoolhouses commonly have godparents, as do graduating classes.

Compadrazgo enlarges the immediate group to which an individual belongs beyond the boundaries of the biological family, thereby enhancing his or her economic, spiritual, and social safety net. Unlike kinship ties, however, *compadrazgo* relationships are formed on the basis of choice; the only original requirement for choosing compadres was their status as good Catholics (Foster 1953). Historically, *compadrazgo* has often served as "the social link connecting divergent ethnic groups, disparate social strata, and separate localities," with much greater frequency and hence a stronger influence on social solidarity than affinal ties formed through intermarriage (Mintz and Wolf [1950] 1977, 9). Although it involves a triangle of juniors and seniors, *compadrazgo* may be contrasted with relations of descent in that it usually functions as a relationship between age equals. The most important function of *compadrazgo* is to create social solidarity by both incorporating individuals into a larger cooperative unit and by providing a formal mechanism for configuring relationships of mutual assistance and respect.

Compadrazgo creates solidarity by uniting individuals across lines of ethnicity and social class as well as geographical boundaries. As one member of HD's staff explained to members of a partner NGO visiting from the United States, "With compadres, one is never alone. Here it's not like it is up North. When you get sick or something happens, there you have credit cards. Here, we count on our compadres." Indeed, anthropologists studying rural-to-urban migration in Mexico in the 1970s used social network analysis (SNA) to track how migrant communities used *compadrazgo* to organize relationships of cooperation in new settings (see Adler Lomnitz 1977). Not only was *compadrazgo* highly adaptable, but also, unlike other networking patterns studied by SNA theorists that served to separate in-groups and out-groups, *compadrazgo* was shown to provide crosscutting ties that linked actors from different social classes and locales.

Dávila (1970) argues that an important factor in the functional adaptability of *compadrazgo* is not only its flexibility on the level of the group but also on the individual level. Unlike godparenthood mechanisms elsewhere that provide a basis for the formation of corporate groups[3] or for mobilizing communal action in times of crisis, in this region, *compadrazgo* entails "the development of a selective network of dyadic ties with (the individual) as the center nexus" (Dávila 1970, 403). Because dyads are more easily manipulated than polyadic relationships, the individual maintains a greater degree of control over the initiation, maintenance, and termination of the relationship than would be possible in relation to a polyad such as a corporate kin group, community, or voluntary association. According to Foster (1961),

> No two people have the same combination of compadres. The system represents a net in which ego, represented by a knot, is formally linked to a great many other people, also represented by knots, but only in a few cases are the strands between the knots viable, capable of bearing the load theoretically placed upon them by the ideal functioning of the institution. (1183)

The network model described here is not universal and all-encompassing but rather particular and highly personalized. The production of strong ties requires the maintenance of carefully balanced reciprocal exchanges (*cuidar amistades*) over a long period of time. In order for the "knots" to endure, and thus to bear heavier loads of mutual obligation, regular interaction and exchange are necessary. Equally important is the maintenance of symmetry over the long term. A gift or gesture too grand to be repaid, for example, weakens the tie rather than strengthening it. It may even be interpreted as an attempt to belittle the receiver or to convert the relationship into a clientelistic one. However, exchanges need not be one to one or involve an immediate counterexchange in order to be viewed as balanced. Different categories of tangible and intangible goods may be exchanged over the life of the relationship. According to Adler Lomnitz (1988), the symmetry of the relationship is directly tied to social distance: "The closer the social relation, the greater the *confianza* and consequently the balance of the exchange" (48). While social distance and relative social position of two such parties may be variable over time, underlying moral principles of loyalty and *confianza* are embedded in and embodied through the durable institutions of kinship and *compadrazgo*.

This flexibility makes *compadrazgo* highly adaptable to a variety of social contexts; in fact, it has come to serve as a template for the creation of new forms of social solidarity. Mintz and Wolf ([1950] 1977) mention two such examples: the use of *compadrazgo* to forestall sexual aggression in Puerto Rico and the Huichol tradition of forming *compadrazgos de voluntad*[4] between opposing parties in a dispute in order to prevent the escalation of violent conflict. In a related case, Hirabayashi (1993) demonstrates how Zapotec migrants from Oaxaca rework *paisanazgo*, a traditional form of solidarity based on shared geographical origin, to avoid costly and dangerous interference from outsiders and government officials as they struggle to make a living in Mexico City. He uses Bourdieu's concept of the habitus to describe how this adaptation occurs. According to Hirabayashi, reworking *paisanazgo* is not a matter of simply transferring a traditional pattern or form of mutual aid from country to city. He contends that norms and forms of solidarity are a kind of cultural capital that Zapotecs reproduce as they adapt to life in the metropolis. Rather than mindlessly repeating an ancient script, Zapotec migrants are engaged in structured improvisation. Following Hirabayashi, I argue that the bridges of love HD staff members attempt to create between their NGO and its potential foreign partners are patterned on more traditional forms of *compadrazgo*, which exist as embodied social institutions that may be selectively reshaped to fit new circumstances. HD seeks to enlist foreign NGOs as *padrinos* for villages in which it works, both as sponsors for development projects and more generally as institutional allies.

Bridges of love were created in the context of extended site visits. Generally the trips took place during the summer months, when students and salaried professionals (who make up the majority of the delegations) could take advantage of vacation leave. After arrival and a welcome ceremony in Tulancingo, visiting delegations were transported to a campesino village where they would be staying for the duration of their trip. They were housed and fed in private homes or community facilities.[5] There they joined with local residents to work on development projects[6] and participate in celebrations or local pastimes like soccer or basketball games. Before returning to their home countries, a closing celebration was held for the visitors either in the sponsored project site or at HD's Tulancingo offices.

During these visits, HD staff members served as cultural mediators. They helped to integrate visitors into the campesino communities they visit and to encourage the personal bonds they hoped would motivate foreigners to return and support HD's future projects and/or to serve as advocates and contacts in their home countries. This process was accomplished through particular forms of emotional labor intended to enable visitors to "feel a part of something larger than themselves."[7] However, the work of connection was not without its own anxieties. In order for the relationship between HD and its foreign partners to remain balanced, the possible perception that HD was exchanging love for money must be avoided. The key point HD staffers must convey to visiting foreign NGO members is that the organizations are engaged in nurturing a common project, each apportioning different but equally important contributions toward the overall effort. The labor of bridge building is not just about inducing an emotional effect but rather about affecting a common platform for cooperation—or, as Maria put it in the passage quoted earlier, "struggling for something in common."[8]

Nearly every foreign visitor interviewed about his or her experiences remained deeply impressed by the lengths to which HD staff and community members went to involve them in community life and make them feel, in their words, "at home." Ideally, visitors were matched up with a family upon arrival in the project site and would sleep and eat in that household for the duration of their stay.[9] They would spend time with family members, sharing their household and agricultural chores and learning about their daily routines and struggles. Domestic life became an object lesson in global citizenship. As one HD staff member explained to a US group that was visiting her home village of San Isidro,

> Just as citizens have rights and obligations in their country, in your family you have them too. In your home, everyone loves you and cares for you, but you are expected also to contribute to the family. You can see that here, everyone has their job to do, everyone must fulfill their obligations and show respect to one another. A family that loves one another cooperates together well.

Just as individual visitors were integrated into campesino families as co-operative participants with rights and obligations, the sponsorship of development projects in specific village sites served to structure the institutional relationships between HD, foreign NGOs, and sponsored villages. By participating in community projects, the visitors experienced a shared sense of purpose and attachment to their adopted villages. Furthermore, development projects completed during site visits—like reforestation areas, community buildings, and irrigation systems—became part of the cultural landscape of the village, serving as permanent reminders of the ties between villagers, HD, and foreign NGOs. The opening of Chapter 2 described how the landscape of El Ocote had been transformed through these interventions over the course of decades. The preparations for HD's twenty-fifth anniversary celebration—rehabilitating and inhabiting these spaces—set the stage for a symbolic renewal of those relationships with the international NGOs whose representatives were guests of honor.

These ties were cemented ritually during site visits. In some cases, development projects were named in honor of their foreign NGO *padrinos*. In other cases, the ritual fixing of ties among individuals came to serve as a symbol of the new relationship between the groups to which they belonged. For example, foreigners who are seen to be key figures in their organizations might be invited to become baptismal *padrinos* of the children of HD staff members or prominent residents of project sites. A more common and less formal ritual means of cementing personal relationships forged in the course of NGO site visits built on the Hidalgan folk tradition of *compadrazgo de flores*, a variant of the *compadrazgo de voluntad* noted by Mintz and Wolf ([1950] 1977). According to Hidalgan folklore, the occasion of finding a "double" fruit[10] presents one with an opportunity to invite a close friend to enter into a relationship of *compadrazgo*. The fruit is presented to the potential *comadre* and/or compadre on a platter adorned with flowers, and a rhyming incantation is recited. If the invitation is accepted, the invitees recite a traditional response and, after embracing their new compadres, invite all present to join in a toast. As a symbol of their new relationship, the invitees must return their compadres' offering by presenting them with a cake in the form of the twin fruit with which they were presented. The ritual both symbolizes and affords public recognition of the reciprocal relationship between the two parties. Although foreign visitors who hold key positions in their

NGOs and have developed a relationship with HD over the span of several years might be invited by HD members to become *padrinos de bautizo*, more informal forms of *compadrazgo* such as this one were more commonly used to bind willing outsiders to HD project sites and ensure their return for a later visit. Personal affective ties thus supplement and strengthen institutional affiliation, providing an alternative model for transnational solidarity. Visitors returned home to seek out ways to support HD's antipoverty mission. On an institutional level, foreign NGO partners could raise funds on behalf of HD, sponsor cultural and educational exchanges, or help HD network with other NGOs. Individual veterans of site visits often corresponded with HD staff and/or their campesino hosts and could serve as emergency points of contact for immigrants from "their" villages. In turn, HD incurred an obligation to provide follow-up support (*dar seguimiento*) for village development projects, nurturing them in the absence of foreign partners and collaborating with their partners to plan future projects of mutual interest.

Contrary to the bureaucratic audit culture prevalent among INGOs, these personalized practices, carried out over the long term, provided a basis for trust between HD and its partners. Several such groups have maintained active relationships with HD for over a decade now. Even when some of these foreign NGOs have waned or formally dissolved, individuals who participated in rural site visits, particularly as youth, have returned to Hidalgo to become HD project supporters on their own. As I have argued elsewhere, these bridges of love are not a panacea for the problems encountered by southern NGOs in their quest to create more equitable partnerships with northern colleagues and allies. Indeed,

> Hidalgan NGO workers often worry that their appeals for aid will be misapprehended by potential foreign partners as a simple exchange of love for donations. The term *chantaje emocional*, or emotional blackmail, is used locally to describe such attempts to manipulate the flow of gifts and favours by evoking guilt or pity. The goal . . . is precisely to circumvent pity or superiority on the part of foreign NGO representatives and instead to convert them into solidary subjects. (Richard and Rudnyckyj 2009, 62)

My aim is not to argue for the inherent superiority of personalism over bureaucratic management, especially in Mexico, where the past two decades have been marked precisely by vigorous debates over political accountability and institutional transparency. Rather, this case is intended to demonstrate the significance of cultural patterns and practices of solidarity to the creation of transnational NGO networks.

In recent decades, scholars have struggled to theorize emerging forms of global interconnection as national boundaries are superseded by transnational flows of capital, information, technology, and people. Much of the resulting literature has focused on the proliferation of networks that alternately separate us and link us to one another in ever more complex ways. In particular, transnational networks of solidarity among NGOs have been cited as evidence of a growing globalization from below that theorists hope will counter or circumvent global networks of capitalist accumulation and geopolitical domination (Appadurai 2000, 2002; see also Hardt and Negri 2004). However, critics have charged that in practice, these networks tend to be unstable and thin, and the institutional forms they take are increasingly dictated by the northern INGOs, which set the terms of and priorities for international cooperation (Fischer 1997; Wallace 2003). In many ways, this form of "grassroots globalization" not only fails to counter entrenched global inequalities but may also ultimately contribute to their reproduction. In an international nonprofit regime shaped by flexibilization, increased competition for funding, and an audit culture that tends to place the needs of funders over those of local NGOs or even project participants, HD's staff have come to rely on the power of personalistic relationships to provide the organization with a measure of long-term security. By transforming potential foreign NGO partners into metaphorical (and sometimes literal) compadres, HD gives participants both a shared sense of obligation and a structure for enacting solidarity.

Building Bridges: Network as Process

The significance of networks lies in the work they perform—both the ideological interventions accomplished via the network trope and the complex feats of connection and disconnection undertaken to enable the emergence of contemporary forms of social life in the global age. While it is true that the network trope enables us to grasp anew questions of difference and relatedness across distance, its seductiveness may also lead us to assume that it describes a known, universal structure. Tracing out ethnographically how network models or metaphors are deployed in specific settings yields a very different picture. The cultural labor of networking emerges as a crucial yet undertheorized piece of the puzzle because not only are the form and functioning of global networks predicated on technological or resource infrastructures but they also depend on the quality and configuration of intersubjective ties.

While many scholars have explored how changes to communications and transportation infrastructures have catalyzed the proliferation of global networks, comparatively little research has investigated other influences on network structure. In other words, these theories often fail to account for the human processes through which the global is actually produced. The investigation of kinship networks was once a mainstay of cultural anthropology, yet most studies of kinship and globalization have tended to focus on how kinship models and metaphors have been affected by globalization, rather than how these models and metaphors themselves might be helping to shape global networks. As the case of HD demonstrates, the creation of durable partnerships between northern and southern NGOs is both labor intensive and risky. Even once ties are formed, they may remain highly vulnerable because their maintenance is based both on shifting northern priorities and on southern partners' performance of delicate forms of emotional labor. By examining the cultural labor of networking, we can bring into focus how cultural models of connection are deployed and reworked in response to specific social circumstances and institutional constraints. Close inspection reveals that the politics of NGO partnership is both more complex and more contingent than previously anticipated.

Conclusion

On December 16, 2010, President Felipe Calderón bestowed the third annual Premio Nacional de Acción Voluntaria y Solidaria (National Prize for Volunteerism and Solidarity) on two exemplary Mexican citizens and one NGO during a gala luncheon held at Los Pinos, the presidential residence.[1] On the same day, human rights activist Marisela Escobedo Ortiz was gunned down in front of city hall in the northern capital of Chihuahua. She was leading a protest against the lack of official attention to the victims of mafia-related violence. At the time, an estimated 30,000 people had been killed in the four years since Calderón deployed the Mexican military in a frontal assault on drug cartel leaders. Escobedo Ortiz had begun organizing in response to the murder of her daughter in Ciudad Juárez by the daughter's boyfriend, an associate of one of the most violent mafias, the ex-paramilitary group known as the Zetas. Three judges failed to convict him despite his confession, demonstrating the depths of government corruption and complicity. The murder of Marisela Escobedo Ortiz served as a lightning rod for popular criticism of Calderón's war on the cartels—a war many Mexicans seemed to think he was badly losing. In the speech delivered at Los Pinos, Calderón lauded the assembled NGOs, foundations, and volunteers as "the good guys," who "thankfully outnumber the bad guys," alluding to the narco-mafias. The efforts of NGOs, he insisted, served as the "engine" of democratic reform in Mexico, leading the nation toward reconstruction of the social fabric by cultivating a renewed sense of social solidarity. He admonished the assembled functionaries and cabinet members to "take into account" the proposals and priorities of the "third sector" (Calderón 2010). Calderón's expansion of the state security apparatus as a means of confronting the unresolved contradictions provoked by Mexico's ongoing experiment with neoliberal democracy has been widely criticized, especially his administration's failure to protect victims and activists such as Escobedo Ortiz. However, the growth of the NGO sector—Calderón's good guys—has also increasingly been channeled toward resolving the same contradictions. While the past two PAN administrations have acknowledged the role played by the third sector in enabling opposition electoral victories, they also sought to channel NGOs' organizational efforts into projects more compatible with neoliberal visions of the common good.

In this book, I have tried to place the growth of Tulancingo's third sector in historical perspective, examining the global and local dynamics, institutions, and ideas that created the conditions of possibility for its growth while at the same time taking into account participants' own interpretations of and stories about the changes they have sought to cultivate. I have attempted to discover what NGOs organize in rural Hidalgo, what new problems and possibilities for practicing democracy are created through the modes of civic and social action they mediate, and how these relate to earlier historical forms of civic action. I have asked what sorts of relations of government are nurtured within supposedly nongovernmental organizations and how they are implicated in larger changes on a regional, national, and international scale. This final chapter discusses the broader implications of these developments for understanding how the NGO form acts as a quasi-object and what role NGOs play in the cultivation of citizenship practices in neoliberal democracies.

Delivered in a moment of heightened political, economic, and social insecurity, Calderón's 2010 speech laid out his official vision of active citizenship. According to Calderón, NGO volunteers foment solidarity, one of the greatest virtues of Mexican civic life: "To be in solidarity," he said, "means to be responsible not only for one's own destiny but also for the destiny of others. The moment human beings forget this essential part of their own nature . . . is precisely when we end up with problems like the ones we now face." Despite acknowledging the government's responsibility to provide its citizens with basic services and protections, Calderón declared that the work of NGOs is "more significant" than that of the state because to act charitably on behalf of another outside the realm of one's legal or social obligations is to contribute to "the construction of the common good." He characterized the work of "organized civil society" as central to Mexico's democratic transition, praising the work of NGOs in "pluralizing the public agenda" and reducing barriers to participation in democratic governance. However, his remarks also revealed a slippage between citizenship (concerned with common rights and obligations as well as civic deliberation among equals) and charity (emphasizing voluntary gifts contributed to a particular social cause outside the realm of social obligation) as categories of social action, which has become increasingly common in official discourse. The consequent growth of the third sector has produced deep tensions between an assistential mode of civic action and more radical projects of societal transformation. Calderón's speech therefore encompasses two key issues: the NGO form as an instrument for organizing civil society and the ways that deployment of this form have influenced the public morality of citizenship in Mexico.

The NGO Form

The NGO form provides a means of organizing this active citizenship and rendering it legible at a distance, accomplished primarily through the creation of a new legal regime governing NGO operations in addition to the standardization of international NGO funding practices. It is a quasi-object, an instrument devised for a particular purpose whose deployment in turn has transformed the practices and ideologies of its users. In Mexico, the NGO was preceded by diverse forms of organizing social solidarity, including the *patronato*. The roots of modern NGOs in Hidalgo date to the mid-twentieth century with the importation of US voluntary service organizations under the Good Neighbor program. As a means of organizing solidarity and making claims on the state, the NGO form gained force in the aftermath of the 1985 Mexico City earthquake. In the grassroots struggle for democratic reform during the 1980s and 1990s, Mexican NGOs functioned as an alternative to corrupt political parties by helping to organize the civil society coalitions that pushed for free elections and institutional change. Over the course of these historical shifts, the NGO form became standardized in response to pressure from the state and funders, as well as the desire on the part of many NGOs for a legal means of preserving their autonomy. In turn, NGOs came to participate in the rationalization of social and political change in some unanticipated ways.

The global growth of the third sector in the neoliberal era has been accompanied by a shift away from teleological narratives of national progress associated with the development era toward "metaphors of repair" (Bornstein 2012, 16). During the last thirty years, the neoliberal project has "polarized" Mexico (Dussel Peters 2000), producing contradictions that have led to massive social inequality, increased poverty and dispossession, violence and insecurity, and widespread political abstentionism periodically punctuated by localized uprisings. The upwelling of NGOs was once interpreted as an indication of social stability and civic health, an impression now contradicted by growing violence. Institutional reform over the last decade has been largely directed at securing individual liberties, while issues of redistributive justice raised during the prodemocracy movements of the 1980s and 1990s have remained unresolved and in many places have become more acute. Modes of democratic participation have also come under scrutiny as human rights activism and traditional forms of public social protest are increasingly criminalized, leaving activists vulnerable to intimidation and reprisals (Correas 2007; Fundación para el Debido Proceso Legal 2010).

What has deployment of the NGO form enabled? The formal distinction between NGOs and governmental entities has created an alternative means of organizing social change beyond the traditional party system. This seeming autonomy has lent NGOs legitimacy as intermediaries in processes of change. However, the formalization process and its attendant shifts in accountability structures have also subjected NGOs to new forms of state surveillance and control. In recent years, the Mexican state and the official party system have intensified efforts to rein in NGOs' political impact and control the scope of their operations while also using the NGO form to supplement campaign work (and in some cases to launder money) by creating their own foundations. According to economist and political analyst Jorge Zepeda Patterson (2014), "NGOs give politicians hives." In Mexico, he argues, "hostility against organizations not affiliated with the system is on the rise. In some regions in the worst way: through the simple act of assassinating activists, intimidating NGO workers, and ransacking the offices of those few civic organizations that work for human rights . . . Much more subtle, but equally harmful, is the economic aggression exercised against NGOs in Mexico." This takes the form of selective reductions to public expenditures on public–private partnerships administered by NGOs (the very collaborations once lauded by former president Calderón), the expansion and intensification of elaborate bureaucratic documentation required for NGOs to operate within the law, and the discretionary application of these bureaucratic requisites to prevent certain more radical NGOs from receiving tax-deductible donations or participating in public–private partnerships. Through events like the National Prize for Volunteerism and Solidarity and the creation of special government agencies dedicated to addressing issues originally championed by NGOs and social movements (such as human rights and gender-based violence), the national political apparatus has sought to recapture some of the ground lost to NGOs. At the same time, Mexican NGOs have been forced to negotiate with a variety of actors within and beyond the state in their own quest to be taken into account in decisions that affect them and their constituents. Those negotiations profoundly shape the capacity of local NGOs to openly challenge the neoliberal model, leaving them to confront a political landscape in which activism is dismissed as uncivil while charity stands in for democratic citizenship. To understand how this takes place, it is necessary to examine the connections between public morality and citizenship.

Citizenship and Public Morality

The global economic and political context of the late twentieth century created the conditions of possibility for the NGO boom but it did not entirely determine the direction of changes to the public morality of citizenship that accompanied neoliberal retrenchment in Mexico. Organizers in the Tulancingo River Valley undertook the creation of new NGOs because the existing state and religious institutions seemed to them to be unresponsive to the social problems—poverty, disease, ignorance, environmental degradation, and exploitation—plaguing their *patria* and because they sought to contribute to a more egalitarian vision of the common good in modern Mexico. Working in and through NGOs became a means both to "live with their backs to the state" and to hold state authorities accountable for fulfilling the rights of rural citizens. Becoming intermediaries in processes of change often required them to practice "compromise."[2] While both academic and popular analyses often suggest that NGOs merely provide an outlet for the expression of preexisting desires for and conceptions of community, the case of HD in particular shows how NGOs work as sites of cultural production—of meaning, of subjects, and of the relationships that tie them to one another. It serves as a site of worthwhile intervention for the so-called middle-class martyrs who staff it and whose work contributes to the remaking of a local and translocal sense of belonging and solidarity. For nearly thirty-five years, HD has labored to rework modes of campesino solidarity in the Tulancingo Valley. It has also linked its campesino constituents to urban residents and international agencies and activists in new ways, choosing foreign partners carefully and incorporating them into an economy of affect that strongly resembles traditional networks of fictive kinship. Not all of these attempts have been successful, of course. In its quest to avoid full conscription into the corporate nonprofit institutional model, HD has come up against its own financial and political limits. Further, the mass exodus of young people from the rural regions of Mexico is evidence of the limited efficacy of NGO development projects against the social marginalization unleashed by structural adjustment. Today, the socioeconomic polarization caused by neoliberal reforms is exacerbated by the unprecedented violence of Mexico's narco wars.

Mexico has undergone a cultural transformation in which the contours of the social and the meanings of democracy have been powerfully reworked. The neoliberal project incrementally dismantled the post-Revolutionary social contract and reordered the relationships among state, society, and markets, a process that was interrupted by the Zapatista rebellion and the prodemocracy movement. This was not merely a top-down transformation but rather was constituted through the interplay among multiple actors, giving shape to new forms of power. In the 1990s, renewed debates around citizenship formed at the intersections of three important global dynamics that called into question the nation-state as the reference point for traditional notions of citizenship as both a form of belonging and model for organizing reciprocal relationships of rights and obligations: economic integration coupled with renewed regionalism, the erosion of nation-state sovereignty from above and below, and the withdrawal of the state from its role as a guarantor of social welfare. While orthodox neoliberalism specified the free market as the only necessary arbiter of social relations, the social dislocations brought about by the implementation of neoliberal policies forced the leaders of many countries to seek alternative means of reintegrating their societies.

This dilemma gave rise to a new mode of active citizenship wherein individuals and families participated by doing good for others in the private sphere. In Mexico, early critiques of neoliberalism converged around the need to establish a new development paradigm to rearticulate economic and social change. This notion featured in the campaign rhetoric of Vicente Fox, Mexico's Candidate of Change, although at the time of the 2000 elections, it was unclear how this revisionist neoliberalism would be put into practice. Fox publicly committed to furthering the privatization and decentralization processes begun by his predecessors, but many thought his unprecedented dependence on the support of a coalition of opposition political groups, social movements, and NGOs might force him to take the positions of a wide variety of actors into account.

For many of the Tulancingo NGOs I worked with, the notion that Mexicans should "look out for others" in the private sphere (a phrase popularized by the Mexican Center for Philanthropy, or CEMEFI) was laudable but did not diminish the gap between formal and substantive citizenship manifest in the daily lives of campesinos. While all indeed may be equal before the law, the conditions of rural life had convinced them that not all enjoyed the material and social resources necessary to choose between alternative courses of action or to hold the state accountable for the fulfillment of basic rights. Their anxieties found symbolic expression in the figure of First Lady Marta Sahagún de Fox, whose Vamos México foundation embodied both a shift toward corporate philanthropy and accountability models and troubling new forms of connectivity among NGOs, state agencies, and the political class. In 2003, Vamos México distributed 71,000 used and new bicycles to rural schoolchildren throughout Mexico under the banner of the Programa Ayúdame a Llegar (Help Me to Arrive Program). Sahagún toured the country, handing over the bikes in elaborate ceremonies that were attended by school personnel, parents, children, state officials, and an enormous press corps. She introduced Ayúdame a Llegar to the nation as an antipoverty program, touting the importance of education to developing the human capital of Mexico's future workers and urging Mexicans to participate in the foundation's philanthropic campaigns as a means of looking out for their fellow citizens. These media events were timed to coincide with midterm local and congressional elections that many in Mexico came to view as a referendum on the performance of Sahagún's husband.

Among the program's most exacting critics were the Tulancingo NGOs involved in the human rights and prodemocracy movements of the 1980s and 1990s, whose steadfast efforts had provided the conditions of possibility for Fox's historical electoral victory in 2000. Even those who did not agree with his conservative positions on social issues or his close relationships with Catholic hierarchy had embraced the idea of the *voto útil* (useful vote), forming a strategic coalition to end the seventy-one-year reign of the PRI and open the way for a new social contract. Now, three years later, many were disenchanted with the pace, scale, and direction of the changes taking place under Fox. In this context, Mexican NGOs had expected to be taken into account by the new government. They instead found themselves all but shut out of policy making, competing with one another for shrinking resources while attempting to address the "assemblages of human need" (Ong 2003) left behind by NAFTA and the state's divestment from small-scale agriculture.

As I mentioned in Chapter 4, Sahagún was ridiculed as suffering from "Evita syndrome." In my research with NGO workers, farmers, and government officials in the Tulancingo region, I found that Sahagún's Vamos México elicited two sets of deeply felt anxieties. The first was over the place of collective social rights in neoliberal Mexico, which was cast in terms of the necessary isomorphism of social equality with democracy. The second addressed the proper character of citizen participation in government, and by extension the proper relationship of NGOs to state and capital.

Staff members at HD, for example, criticized Vamos México's Ayúdame a Llegar program as a paternalistic anachronism out of step with Mexico's democratic aspirations. They pointed out that a free and secular education is the constitutional right of every Mexican citizen. Vicente Fox had promised in his campaign to improve both the quality of public education and the people's access to it. Sahagún's appeal to Mexicans to donate money and used bikes to children who had to walk hours to school each day did nothing to address the root causes of the rising dropout rate in rural areas, which, they argued, had less to do with individual transportation woes and more to do with lack of schools, teachers, and materials. Poor school attendance was also tied to the lack of future prospects for rural youth, many of whom left school to look for work in the cities or the United States at younger and younger ages. While "Martita's" rhetoric attempted to represent the relationship between Mexican citizens as produced through the moment of generosity—of looking out for others—HD staffers pointed out other pertinent relationships between donor and recipient. The very existence of social inequality provided the conditions of possibility for Sahagún's philanthropy—both the means to donate and the capacity to promote a particular framing of rural poverty. The Ayúdame a Llegar program, they were fond of pointing out, was funded not only by private donations but also by state taxes and the largesse of corporations that had benefited from Mexican privatization schemes at the expense of the public. Vamos México, they insisted, was taking the people's money so they could turn around and give it right back, but in a way that allowed an unelected authority to both shape the public agenda and skim off a generous transaction fee. Diagnosing Evita syndrome helped Tulancingo NGO workers to make sense of their entrapment in the very processes of change they helped to create.

The voluntaristic model of solidarity actively promoted by organizations like CEMEFI, Vamos México, and the Centro Fox (of which it is now a subsidiary) as a remedy for Mexico's ills is focused on the development of philanthropic subjects rather than the resolution of impunity, injustice or structural inequality. The Centro Fox is a private policy institute led by a cadre of conservative Catholic business leaders, all direct beneficiaries of privatization. One Tulancingo friend mockingly called them "los milionarios de Cristo," referring to the Legionarios de Cristo, an infamous right-wing

Catholic congregation with powerful ties to the PAN. Vamos México was a major recipient of corporate donations from multinationals such as Nestlé, Hasbro, Gruma, UPS, Whirlpool, and Coca-Cola. During Fox's presidency, it created numerous public–private partnerships, leveraging state infrastructure and resources to carry out its own signature programs. The organization was repeatedly accused of financial malfeasance and political influence peddling, and at one point Sahagún was rumored to be using it as a base for launching her own future presidential campaign. Since then, Vamos México has expanded its influence over Mexico's third sector, entering into partnerships with smaller regional NGOs as well as launching a professional certificate program in "social management" marketed to NGO personnel. In the minds of many Tulancingo NGO workers, Vamos México stood for a new wave of Mexican NGOs, organized on the US nonprofit model, run by professionals, and funded through corporate philanthropy. In his 2010 speech, Calderón posited that it is more virtuous for Mexicans to exercise charity toward their fellow citizens than to insist that the state fulfill their rights to justice and basic welfare. The notion of philanthropy as citizenship practice entails the privatization of both social welfare and political representation. Instead of posing problems for democracy, marginalization and exclusion are invoked as opportunities for the entrepreneurial enactment of civic virtue. Although the Foxes have largely faded from Mexico's political spotlight, the Evita syndrome has metastasized, inverting the dreams of democracy that motivated NGO organizers in Tulancingo and across Mexico.

Ferguson (1990) wrote of post–World War II development as an "antipolitics machine," which functioned to depoliticize the allocation of resources by reframing inequality as a technical problem with technical solutions. The NGO boom in Mexico has helped both to pluralize the public agenda and to reframe inequality and dispossession as social rather than political issues. This is not because it has circumvented the political arena per se but rather because it has enabled an incremental transformation of public morality and notions of citizenship. Normative civil society theories of the late twentieth century posited NGOs as organizing a purer form of social and civic agency, free from the corruption and partisanship associated with traditional political parties as well as from the massified character and informality of social movements, in which people could meet as equals and practice solving problems together for the good of all society. A third sector formed by NGOs was imagined to exist autonomously, though history shows that from the beginning, the organizations that gave birth to the modern NGO form existed in dynamic tension with both states and corporate capital. This is not merely true in a structural sense but also in terms of the ways in which NGOs participate in the production of identity and cultural meaning. Because NGOs are not elected, they have the ability to carry out projects of social engineering with little oversight (Fox and Brown 1998). Claims as to the emancipatory potential of an imagined global civil society are countered by a growing number of studies that link the humanitarian mission of NGOs to the renewed imperial ambitions of the United States (Bartholomew and Breakspear 2003; Fischer 1997; Hubbard and Mathers 2004). As more and more socially minded middle-class professionals are displaced from positions in the downsized social welfare apparatus and an increasingly corporatized academia, many migrate to the NGO world as a source of meaningful employment. There they become dependent on the largesse of the very "unelected government" they attempt to critique. This entrapment is a result of financial dependency; it is also linked to the modes through which social activism becomes institutionalized. Some of the Tulancingo NGOs, like HD, have resisted these pressures by refusing to participate in the official national NGO registry or public–private partnerships and by pursuing alternative funding strategies. Despite the celebratory rhetoric of Appadurai (2000, 2002) and others, "grassroots globalization" is neither independent of corporate capital (upon whose philanthropy it increasingly depends and whose left-behind assemblages of human need it is called on to remedy) nor of the state (which regulates its existence and defines the boundaries of civility).

The power of NGOs to cultivate changes, however small, that help to create alternative futures results precisely from their connectivity and cultural intimacy with the forces of state and capital. Wielding detailed knowledge of the limits and possibilities of state bureaucracy and corporate philanthropy, they can sometimes manage to get things done for those they identify as worthy, in ways they identify as feasible. The Evita syndrome represents Tulancingo NGO workers' own consciousness about their compromising position, a partial interpreter of the direction of complex change that has taken place in tandem with neoliberal retrenchment after Fox.

Signs of the growing social unrest caused by decades of structural adjustment and free trade have not entirely doomed the core tenets of the Washington Consensus, but its increasingly obvious limits have become fodder for the formulation of a new development paradigm that seeks to overcome accumulative obstacles by embedding capitalist markets into existing social networks in new ways. This vision animates the current developmental trend that links international agencies, corporations, and NGOs as partners in cultivating social capital through both civil society initiatives and microenterprise programs (Hart 2002b). Just as the entities labeled nongovernmental organizations are precisely governmental in the Foucauldian sense (Ferguson and Gupta 2002), nonprofit organizations are increasingly profitable, working to produce subjects of capital in unexpected ways (Joseph 2000). The push to locate these subjects and practices outside the bounds of official political processes represents an attempt to enforce "coercive harmony" (Nader 1997, 712–715) against the specter of popular revolt and diminishing returns on financial speculation.

Shifts in the political and economic contexts in which NGOs work, as well as the ways in which the efforts of their members have become institutionalized and operationalized by states and capital, have changed the nature of the interventions it is possible for these groups make. The NGO-ization of alternative forms of political and social organizing has received thorough analysis (Alvarez 2009; Choudry and Kapoor 2013), yet what we might call the corporate philanthropization of NGOs has not yet been subjected to the same critical scholarly examination. The strategic circulation of corporate funding through foundations, NGOs, and public–private partnerships that enabled Sahagún to build Vamos México into a powerful tool for personal advancement is part and parcel of larger dynamics that are changing the meaning of citizenship and the public morality of democracies the world over.

The values of reciprocity and trust, necessary to sustaining the social relationships that undergird long-term political stability, have come to be viewed as in need of renewal. Attempts to remake them require a transfiguration of the relations between city and country, rich and poor. Just as colonial governing practices converted indigenous traditions of civic participation and mutual aid into institutions of labor extraction and vocations of Christian charity, Mexican citizens are increasingly called on to relate to one another as philanthropic subjects, converting social crises into opportunities for the enactment of individual civic virtue. This form of civic caring is related to Grewal's (2011) concept of "humanitarian citizenship," in which the revisionist neoliberal ideal of active citizenship is articulated to the funding structures of corporate philanthropy. In the wake of crises and disasters, individuals may choose to save others when governments cannot or will not by donating to relief and development NGOs. This aid practice is a way of enacting bonds of solidarity, often across national boundaries, but may also serve to create new regimes of inclusion and exclusion. When such pastoral practices are encouraged as a substitute for more explicitly political modes of civic action, they work to reinscribe the substantive inequality between giver and recipient into the supposedly egalitarian space of civil society and naturalize the abjection of the rural poor.

In Mexico as elsewhere, while the state is still the center of most mobilization, the fulfillment of social and civil rights is increasingly devolved onto an assemblage of other entities. In these sometimes convoluted and opaque public–private partnerships, the task of organizing and representing society falls to NGOs. For many of the most vulnerable, like rural people who have suffered both natural and governmental disasters, this is yet another way in which fulfillment of their rights is left to the discretion and generosity of self-appointed saviors. They must first be recognized as worthy subjects of aid according to criteria not subject to democratic deliberation or constitutional guarantees. And the upward structures of accountability in these institutional arrangements leave the dispossessed (now coded as victims, not citizens) little recourse. Much of the governance that shapes their everyday lives—health, education, environmental management and resource allocation, economic policy—is transacted in nongovernmental or technocratic arenas that no longer respond to rights-based appeals in familiar ways.

This is a disconcerting development not only for Hidalgan campesinos but also for many of Tulancingo's NGO workers, former champions of democracy and human rights later lauded as Mexico's good guys by a president whose election many questioned as fraudulent. The production of novel forms of networked solidarity, grounded and made meaningful through careful cultural work, is an exciting development made possible at the intersection of Mexico's democratic transition and the global NGO boom. However, in an era when large swathes of the population are rendered increasingly vulnerable, citizenship as a form of recognition and agency seems strangely reserved for only those with philanthropic means, to be enacted at their discretion—a mixed harvest to be sure.

Notes

INTRODUCTION

1. Names of individuals and places, along with identifying details, have been changed to protect the privacy of informants. The names of some active NGOs have also been changed because the purpose of this study is to reveal the possibilities and limits of the NGO form in transforming cultures of citizenship rather than to critique the practices of individual organizations.

2. Pulque is a mildly alcoholic beverage fermented from the juice of the maguey cactus. Traditionally it has been widely consumed by peasants in semiarid regions (such as the plains outside Tulancingo), where fresh water is not easily available. The maguey cactus has been cultivated since the second century CE in the Tulancingo area. In addition to its sap, used for making pulque, the plant provides fiber for rope and papermaking and has many culinary uses. During pre-Columbian times, pulque was a sacred drink, reserved for special occasions and restricted to certain social classes. After the Spanish conquest, its use became secularized and popularized; portions of pulque were included in the daily rations of miners and agricultural workers. During the colonial period, maguey began to be grown on a large scale in haciendas in order to supply the mining industry and the working classes of the capital. In the mid-nineteenth century, the opening of the railway between Veracruz and Mexico City enabled a pulque boom in Hidalgo by enabling cheap transportation to markets in the capital. Pulquerías became popular hangouts in working-class neighborhoods of the city. However, the Revolution destroyed much of the infrastructure that made this trade popular, and pulque's association with rural people and the lower classes led to declining popularity during the heyday of Mexico's modernization "miracle." Today maguey plants are cultivated as boundary markers at the edges of agricultural plots, and most pulque production is carried out as a cottage industry or for household consumption.

3. For third wave democratization theory, see Huntington (1991). For examples of studies of hyphenated democracy, see Paley (2001).

4. The Chicago Boys were a cohort of technocrats who designed and carried

out radical economic reforms in Chile under the Pinochet dictatorship (1973–1990). Many of them trained at the University of Chicago Department of Economics under Milton Friedman in the 1950s and 1960s and were strongly influenced by the anti-Keynesian current. The military dictatorship enabled Friedman and the Chicago Boys, with help from the United States, to forcibly institute radical economic reforms that would become the basis for neoliberal policies promulgated elsewhere in the 1980s and 1990s. See Valdes (1989), Silva (1991), and O'Brien and Roddick (1983). The term "Washington Consensus" was coined in 1989 by economist John Williamson to describe a package of market-based policy recommendations for confronting the economic crises experienced by Latin American countries in the 1980s. These recommendations represented a consensus among neoliberal think tanks and major Washington-based institutions, including the World Bank, International Monetary Fund, and the US government.

5. I have purposely not included the litany of NGO classifications now extant in the literature in this discussion (e.g., GONGO, INGO, BONGO). Most of these are formulated with respect to said organizations' utility to international agencies as mediators for transition processes. Although policy makers find these endless recategorizations useful, I am engaged in a broader theoretical project for which these distinctions have little analytical usefulness. The Tulancingo Valley NGOs discussed in this book are for the most part organizations involved in some way in rural development efforts and are officially classified by the Mexican government as *asociaciones civiles* (civic associations).

CHAPTER I

1. Lorenzo Meyer (2007) has argued that the trajectory of nineteenth-century liberalism in Mexico broadly paralleled that of the late twentieth century. At both of these historical junctures, political reforms became linked to programs for integrating the country into a changing global capitalist system. Moreover, in both instances, the promotion of free markets and individualism ultimately deepened social inequality and exacerbated political tensions.

2. See Engels ([1894] 1951), Lenin ([1899] 1956), Kautsky ([1899] 1988), and Preobrazhensky ([1926] 1965).

3. Byres's (1991) historical analysis of agrarian questions distinguishes three key problematics. The first, *accumulation*, views the countryside as a source of surpluses that could fuel an overall structural transformation; it marks the political and economic significance of the relationship between industry and agriculture, urban and rural (10). The problematic of *production*, also known as the "peasant question," assesses "the extent to which capitalism has developed in the countryside, the forms that it takes, and the barriers that impede it" (10), focusing on changes to labor processes and rural class differentiation. The final problematic is concerned with *political power and processes*, namely "the impact of political forms and forces on the evolution of rural change" (Akram-Lodhi 1998, 138)

4. According to Corrigan and Sayer (1985), this transformation takes place in two interrelated ways: through subjects' elaboration of their experiences (i.e., popular culture) and through the state's attempts to constitute and regulate social identities. Knight (1994b) argues for the importance of viewing the quest for state formation and legitimacy as a long-term process, "arguably begun with the Bourbon era, renewed by Independence and the Reforma, and further accelerated by the 1910 Revolution" (57).

5. According to Escalante Gonzalbo (2001), "Among the cultured urban groups, it was seen as evident that the campesinos could not be citizens; they were serfs or mutineers, detained on the margins of history. For this reason they did not count, except in the good intentions of regeneration" (56–57).

6. Indigenous communities with their own social and economic institutions, legally recognized by the crown and the colonial government of New Spain.

7. During the period of Aztec hegemony in the Tulancingo Valley, the *calpulli* served as the basic social unit. *Calpullis* were organized as corporate lineage groups with common land rights. In addition, they collectively managed a series of religious, educational, and mutual assistance obligations within a territorial ward. Aztec city-states were composed of a series of contiguous *calpullis*, each of which also served as a taxation unit. Reciprocal relations among *calpulli* members and between the *calpulli* and state authorities were embodied in the practice of *faena*, performing collective labor for the public good (which could be ordered by external authorities or organized locally to address community needs).

8. Indeed, as Nader (1990) documents elsewhere in Mexico, presenting a united front to outside authorities (effectively concealing internal tensions or disagreements) was often a means of preserving local autonomy against the threat of intervention.

9. In his account of the cultural zeitgeist of the Porfirian era, Beezley (1987) uses the *corrida de torros*, or bullfight, as a metaphor for the public morality of Mexican society: "This event offers the most obvious expression of the social arrangement in the stands; the sunny and the shady sides represent the basic division within Mexican culture. . . . The poor, the workers, the campesinos and the peones (los de abajo) watch in the sun; the owners, the upper class, the wealthy, the foreigners, the managers, the politicians, and the churchmen (los de arriba) sit in the shade" (5).

10. *Pan o palo* means "bread or stick," the Mexican equivalent of "the carrot or the stick."

11. The language of the original text reveals quite clearly the character of the threat to civic and moral order posed by unruly rural people in the eyes of Hidalgan elites.

12. For more analysis of UN figures on the socioeconomic effects of the bifurcation of Mexican agriculture, see Hewitt de Alcántara (1976).

13. In the Tulancingo Valley, such elections were traditionally held in public as-

semblies, with household heads participating in roll-call voting or collective accla-
mation, often to approve the candidate imposed by local caciques.

14. *Forbes Magazine* headline, quoted in Braig (1997, 247).

15. Herrera Cabañas (1995) draws a parallel between the peasant rebellions of
the latter half of the nineteenth century and those of the 1970s and 1980s in the
Huasteca and Valle del Mezquital regions. In fact, he notes that many of his best
sources on nineteenth-century rural rebellions come from the archives of the Secretary of National Defense, in itself a testament to the remarkable level of military
repression, with little intervention from civil or judicial authorities (10–11).

CHAPTER 2

1. Name withheld; interviewed by Analiese Richard, Tulancingo, September 20,
2002.

2. Rossell, trained as an architect and urban planner, was born in Pachuca but was
educated and spent most of his professional life in Mexico City. Continuing a policy
instituted by his predecessor, Rossell expropriated and redistributed tens of thou-
sands of hectares of land (much of it already unofficially occupied by independent
campesino organizations) to local ejidos, generously indemnifying the ranchers from
whom it was seized with state funds. The second component of the strategy involved
channeling federal development and antipoverty programs like PIDER and SAM
toward the most politically volatile areas of the Huasteca in order to ameliorate class
tensions. Although the carrot of land redistribution and development programs did
help to diminish agrarian strife, Rossell (like other PRI politicians of the era) did not
neglect the stick; during his administration, the 84th Battalion of the Mexican Army
installed a new base in Huejutla, the heart of the conflict zone (Gutiérrez 1990, 48).

3. Many of these communities did not receive electrification until the early 1980s.

4. For a detailed discussion of *envidia*'s function as a social leveling mechanism in
campesino communities, see Foster (1965) and Gregory (1975).

5. The paradox of the permanent subsidy was especially apparent when considering the foundation's pay-per-service model. As the researchers explained in their
report (in language that echoed that of the Echeverría administration), the campesinos' structural disadvantage led to a lack of savings. Hence any amount of money
charged by development organizations for their services would have a negative impact on income level and quality of life. This would directly contradict the foundation's goal of capitalizing the countryside in order to end poverty.

6. Someone with old money, literally a "wealthy person of lineage."

7. The quote is taken from HD's 1984 proposal to the Ford Foundation for a
renewal of the initial 1982 grant.

8. The notion was expressed thusly by one UC member, quoted in minutes of
Encuentro Campesino (1983): *"No se lo que es una cooperativa, lo que si se es que aquí
somos una hermandad y el bistec es parejo."*

9. For a powerful eyewitness account of the quake and its effects on Mexico City, see Poniatowska (1995). For an analysis of the social mobilization following the tragedy, see Eckstein (1990).

10. For example, Nancy Reagan landed in Mexico City shortly after the quake bearing $1 million in aid from the United States.

11. Sergio Aguayo, personal communication, April 13, 2004.

12. These efforts were influenced by Paolo Freire's *Pedagogy of the Oppressed* (1972). Freire's methodology stresses four factors: education as a dialogical experience (people learning together rather than one authority figure acting upon others), praxis (deepening understandings through action for change), conscientization (developing critical consciousness for transforming reality), and situating education within the lived experience of the participants. HD's exchanges, based on this framework, aimed at democratizing technical knowledge and empowering participants to take on more leadership roles in designing and orchestrating projects in communities.

13. Reagan's peace is not (the same as) Jesus' peace (or the promise of "peace on earth, good will to men" with which the angels herald Jesus' birth in Luke 2:14). The liberation theologists' critique contended that Reagan's plan, which entailed a power sharing between the Sandinistas and Contras and a new electoral process, not only ignored the democratic will of the Nicaraguan people but also reinforced the root causes of the poverty and oppression that had led the people to rebel in the first place. Reagan's imposed peace thus represented a cynical mockery of the ideals of "peace with justice" and the "preferential option for the poor."

14. The seed would be sold to Raiz for processing into its signature line of packaged foods, the tender leaves of the plant incorporated into family diets, and the protein-rich stalks fed to cattle to increase dairy production.

CHAPTER 3

1. Preliminary versions of some of the arguments in this chapter appeared in Richard (2008).

2. Although the biofuel ethanol has been produced using maize for decades, the US ethanol industry received a major boost in 2005 when the Energy Policy Act was passed by the US Congress, specifying the inclusion of a minimum amount of renewable fuel in gasoline marketed in the United States. The law, enacted in response to rising petroleum prices and increased concern over global warming, prompted a significant expansion in the number of ethanol processing plants in the US corn belt. This increased productive capacity created a drain on raw materials. More and more surplus maize was diverted from export stocks, and increased demand along with rising transportation costs and bad weather in other growing regions led to rapid jumps in the price of maize on the global market. For a more detailed discussion of this public policy framework and its implications, see Baker and Zahniser (2006).

3. Author's translation. Montemayor's quote is taken from an article on the San Lorenzo mines; however, this phrase has been used to refer to a variety of events over the past several years, including US government mismanagement of post-Katrina relief efforts, the Mexican tortilla crisis, and the wall along the US border.

4. El Niño is a periodic disruption of the ocean–atmospheric system over the tropical Pacific Ocean that produces weather anomalies. During El Niño years, global rainfall patterns are redistributed, resulting in droughts and flooding. El Niño–Southern Oscillation (ENSO) is a global phenomenon in which abnormal warming over the eastern Pacific (associated with El Niño) causes a drop in sea level in the east and a concomitant rise in the west, altering trade wind patterns. A thorough discussion of ENSO is beyond the scope of this book; see Magaña (1999) for an overview of the effects of ENSO on Mexico's climate.

5. The picture is complicated by the ENSO and its effects on the Western Hemisphere Warm Pool, which can produce intensified storm activity in the Gulf of Mexico following an El Niño year, as in the 1999 floods, which were preceded by the strong 1997–1998 El Niño. Detailed data on ENSO only began to be collected in 1976, and Mexico did not begin collecting pertinent regional data until much more recently. However, many top climatologists agree that recent events in the Gulf of Mexico are consistent with the probable outcomes of computer models that demonstrate a synergistic relationship between El Niño and global warming (see Caviedes 2001).

6. See Mathews (2011) for a discussion of the history of "desiccationism" in Mexican forestry.

7. The complete text of the Farm Bill and supporting information is available online (http://www.usda.gov/farmbill).

8. Maseca is a global brand of Gruma, S.A.B. de C.V., a multinational manufacturer of corn flour (*masa seca*) and tortillas, founded in 1949 near Monterrey, Mexico. Industrialized Maize (Maiz Industrializado, SA; MINSA) was created by the federal government in 1949 and became part of the SAM in 1962. An important state official gave away the state-owned company's patented formula for nixtamalized corn flour to his close associate, the owner of Grupo Gruma. MINSA later became part of CONASUPO before being privatized and sold to an industrial consortium, Promotora Empresarial de Occidente, S.A. de C.V. See Ochoa (2001).

9. "Los peces gordos siempre comen a los pequeños" (the big fish always eat the smaller ones). Wealthy and well-connected landowners, businesspeople, and politicians are commonly referred to as *peces gordos*. This traditional proverb is a commentary on human nature and social hierarchy.

10. Author interview, August 2006.

11. The other 10 percent of the land was held either by groups (mostly indigenous) who refused to submit to the PROCEDE process, preferring to continue the practice of collective ownership, or by *ejidos* engaged in ongoing internal disputes or

in boundary conflicts with neighboring *ejidos* or private landowners. Officially, members of *ejidos* may not sell their plots to nonmembers without first securing the permission of other members to legally convert the land to alienable property (*dominio pleno*). In practice, however, *ejidal* lands (especially on the outskirts of growing urban areas) have been sold by individual title holders to third parties for several years now in the Tulancingo area.

12. Author interview, April 2003. *Desclasado*, roughly equivalent to the French *déclassé*, is an insult commonly leveled at people who seem to have forgotten their place in the provincial social hierarchy by those who consider themselves their betters.

13. *Chulo* literally means "good-looking," but in rural Mexico, this connotes an attractive fullness of flesh, whether it is used to describe healthy babies, fat ears of maize, green milpas, or well-built men and women.

14. Author interview, Acatlán, Hidalgo, May 2003.

15. Ibid.

16. Author interview, Tulancingo, Hidalgo, December 2002.

CHAPTER 4

1. Preliminary versions of some of the arguments in this chapter appeared in Richard (2009).

2. The joke is a play on words. "Milpa" refers to maize fields, whereas *mil* means a thousand. The punch line is, "A thousand (pesos) here, a thousand (pesos) there." At the time, a thousand pesos were worth a little under a hundred US dollars.

3. Defined as "political subordination in exchange for material rewards" backed by the threat of coercion, or "the exchange of political rights for social benefits" (Fox 1994, 153).

4. Name withheld; interviewed by Analiese Richard, Tulancingo, May 2003.

5. After a decade of lobbying, a version of this legislation was finally passed by Congress in 2004. See Mexican National Government (2003).

6. See Rivera Flores (2004) for a detailed analysis of how the Fundación Hidalguense (Hidalgan Foundation) was used as an instrument to promote the political career of infamous Hidalgan PRI politician Gerardo Sosa Castelán.

7. In Mexico, universities have long served as political resources and training grounds for future politicians and functionaries. The term *porro* refers to a student (or one who passes as one) whose primary occupation is not studying but rather to ascend the hierarchy of student organizations and accommodate him- or herself within the party structure. Low-ranking *porros* provide support for the party in public marches and events, extort other students, and fight with the *porros* of other parties. Higher-ranking *porros* act as spies, reporting on student activism and other activities to party higher-ups, or infiltrating and manipulating opposition groups. They are usually compensated via direct pay, access to scholarships, or appointment to minor positions.

8. Interview, Tulancingo, Mexico, October 2002.

9. This change was reflected in spatial arrangements, as some NGO offices' large meeting rooms, which once hosted campesino assemblies, were carved up into individual office spaces and in some cases commercial spaces.

10. Most of these projects are aimed at enabling campesinos to purchase expensive equipment intended to increase agricultural productivity (such as feed grinders or in vitro fertilization of livestock) or introducing new cash crops (such as greenhouse vegetables for winter export). They do so by providing grants to cover a percentage of the total proposed investment, or by paying for material costs while campesino cooperatives commit to providing the necessary labor.

11. Interview, Tulancingo, Mexico, June 2003.

12 In reference to the wife of twentieth-century Argentine dictator Juan Domingo Perón.

13. Interview, Tulancingo, Mexico, April 2003.

14. Some NGOs tried to stretch temporary project funding out so that employees would receive at least a nominal salary at all times. Others, however, only hired employees on a temporary basis. Many NGO workers were involved in sidelines that helped them make ends meet. One man I knew sold agricultural inputs in the countryside. Another drove a taxi between periodic stints of employment by NGOs and government agencies. Some female NGO workers, like other women in Tulancingo, were actively engaged in the informal economy, selling everything from jewelry and household linens to makeup and nutritional supplements. Sidelines were common in Tulancingo during my fieldwork, but now professionals, like NGO workers and schoolteachers, seem to be participating in unprecedented numbers.

15. Although I heard this assertion frequently, no NGO worker with whom I spoke could name such an open private sector position in the Tulancingo region. In fact, several of those with whom I spoke had long been seeking such a post in vain.

16. Interview, Tulancingo, Mexico, October 2002.

CHAPTER 5

1. Informant interview, Tulancingo Mexico, 2003.

2. This form is associated with clientelistic relationships, as in the relationships of *cacicazgo* discussed in Chapter 2.

3. The classic example here would be the Balkan *kumstvo* described in Hammel (1968), which serves to link corporate kin groups and is inherited agnatically.

4. *Compadrazgos de voluntad* (voluntary *compadrazgos*) are entered into on an ad hoc basis rather than in the context of a formal life-crisis ritual.

5. These include schoolhouses or village meeting rooms where present. On occasion the empty homes of migrant workers currently in the United States may be used for this purpose.

6. This mostly entails manual labor like digging ditches, planting trees, and mix-

ing and helping to pour concrete. Lack of agricultural skills and sometimes language skills generally prevents foreign visitors from taking up other tasks.

7. Informant interview, 2002.

8. See Richard and Rudnyckyj (2009) for a more detailed discussion of this dilemma.

9. Groups with younger members are often housed all together in the vacant homes of absent emigrants or are partnered up with more outgoing or experienced visitors and housed with families.

10. These fruits themselves are referred to as *cuates*. These are usually conjoined fruits, vegetables, or maize. The symbolic power of these fruits is grounded in the fact that they grow together, side by side, accompanying one another through life.

CONCLUSION

1 A small portion of this chapter appeared in an earlier form in Richard (2013).

2 After Li's (1999) use of the term to denote political processes that involve both coming to a mutual understanding and placing one's self in a position of risk or difficulty.

References

Adler Lomnitz, Larissa. 1977. *Networks and Marginality: Life in a Mexican Shanty-town*. New York: Academic Press.

———. 1988. "Informal Exchange Networks in Formal Systems: A Theoretical Model." *American Anthropologist* 90 (1): 42–55.

Aguilar Valenzuela, Rubén. 1997a. "Apuntes para una historia de las organizaciones de la sociedad civil en México." *Cuadernos de la sociedad civil* 1 (2): 9–31.

———. 1997b. "Las ONG de Desarrollo y la Democracia Interna: Una Aproxima-cion [Development NGOs and internal democracy: An approximation]." In *La democracia de los de abajo* [Democracy from below], edited by Jorge Alonso and Juan Manuel Ramirez Saíz, 293–315. Mexico City: La Jornada Ediciones, Con-sejo Electoral del Estado de Jalisco.

Akram-Lodhi, A. Haroon. 1998. "The Agrarian Question, Past and Present." *Journal of Peasant Studies* 25 (4): 134–149.

Alonso, Ana Maria. 2005. "Territorializing the Nation and 'Integrating the Indian': 'Mestizaje' in Mexican Official Discourses and Public Culture." In *Sovereign Bodies: Citizens, Migrants, and States in the Postcolonial World*, edited by Thomas Blom Hansen and Finn Stepputat, 39–60. Princeton, NJ: Princeton University Press.

Alvarez, Sonia E. 2009. "Beyond NGO-ization? Reflections From Latin America." *Development* 52 (2): 175–184.

Amat, Patricia, Mark Fried, Katherine Daniels, Simon Ticehurst, and Katia Maia. 2003. *Make Trade Fair for the Americas: Agriculture, Investment, and Intellectual Property*. Rio de Janiero: Oxfam International.

Appadurai, Arjun. 1996. *Modernity at Large: Cultural Dimensions of Globalization*. Minneapolis: University of Minnesota Press.

———. 2000. "Grassroots Globalization and the Research Imaginary." *Public Culture* 12 (1): 1–19.

———. 2002. "Deep Democracy: Urban Governmentality and the Horizon of Politics." *Public Culture* 14 (1): 21–47.

193

Arroyo Picard, Alberto. 2003. "Lecciones del TLCAN: El alto costo del 'libre' comercio (Resumen ejecutivo)." Mexico City: Red Mexicana de Acción Frente al Libre Comercio.

Baker, Allen, and Steven Zahniser. 2006. "Ethanol Reshapes the Corn Market." *Amber Waves* 4 (2): 30–37.

Barkin, David. 2006. "Building a Future for Rural Mexico." *Latin American Perspectives* 33 (2): 132–140.

Barry, Tom. 1995. *Zapata's Revenge: Free Trade and the Farm Crisis in Mexico*. Boston: South End Press.

Bartholomew, Amy, and Jennifer Breakspear. 2003. "Human Rights as Swords of Empire." *The Socialist Register 2004: The New Imperial Challenge*, edited by Leo Pantich and Colin Leys, 125–145. New York: Monthly Review Press.

Bartra, Armando. 1996. "A Persistent Rural Leviathan." In *Reforming Mexico's Agrarian Reform*, edited by Laura Randall, 173–184. New York: M. E. Sharpe.

Bartra, Roger. 2002. *Blood, Ink, and Culture: Miseries and Splendors of the Post-Mexican Condition*. Durham, NC: Duke University Press.

Becerra-Acosta, Juan Pablo. 2007. "La tortilla, vergüenza del Estado." *Milenio*, January 7, http://jalisco.milenio.com/.

Becerril, Andrea. 2007. "Pírricos beneficios del acuerdo sobre la tortilla: Ramirez López." *La Jornada*, January 25. http://www.jornada.unam.mx/.

Beezley, William H. 1987. *Judas at the Jockey Club and Other Episodes of Porfirian Mexico*. Lincoln: University of Nebraska Press.

Bellamy, Richard. 2008. *Citizenship: A Very Short Introduction*. Oxford: Oxford University Press.

Bernal, Victoria, and Inderpal Grewal, editors. 2014. *Theorizing NGOs: States, Feminisms and Neoliberalism*. Durham, NC: Duke University Press.

Bizberg, Ilán. 2010. "Una democracia vacía. Sociedad civil, movimientos sociales y democracia." I. Bizberg F. Zapata (coord.), *Movimientos sociales*, México, Colmex. http://cei.colmex.mx/PDFs/Prof% 20Bizberg/Movimientos. pdf.

Burdick, J., and W. Hewitt. 2000. *The Church at the Grassroots in Latin America: Perspectives on Thirty Years of Activism*. Westport, CT: Greenwood Publishing Group.

Bornstein, Erica. 2012. *Disquieting Gifts: Humanitarianism in New Delhi*. Stanford, CA: Stanford University Press.

Boyer, Christopher Robert. 2003. *Becoming Campesinos: Politics, Identity, and Agrarian Struggle in Postrevolutionary Michoacán, 1920–1935*. Stanford, CA: Stanford University Press.

Braig, Marianne. 1997. "Continuity and Change in Mexican Political Culture: The Case of PRONASOL." In *Citizens of the Pyramid: Essays on Mexican Political Culture*, edited by Wil G. Pansters, 247–278. Amsterdam: Thela.

Brazil, Eric. 2001. "Sending Dollars to Latin America, Wiring Money Home Cheaply." *San Francisco Chronicle*, June 24. http://www.sfgate.com/.

Brenner, Neil, and Nik Theodore. 2002. "Cities and the Geographies of 'Actually Existing Neoliberalism.'" *Antipode* 34 (3): 349–379.

Brown, Wendy. 2003. "Neo-Liberalism and the End of Liberal Democracy." *Theory and Event* 7 (1): 1–25.

Buve, Raymond. 1997. "Between Ballots and Bullets: Long-Term Trends in Nineteenth Century Mexican Political Culture." In *Citizens of the Pyramid: Essays on Mexican Political Culture*, edited by Wil G. Pansters, 41–65. Amsterdam: Thela Publishers.

Byres, T. J. 1991. "The Agrarian Question and Differing Forms of Capitalist Agrarian Transition: An Essay with Reference to Asia." In *Rural Transformation in Asia*, edited by Jan Breman and Sudipto Mundle, 3–76. Delhi: Oxford University Press.

Cabildo, Miguel. 2003. "Vivirán paises ricos en la intranquilidad, dice CNC." *La Jornada*. Mexico City.

Calderón, Felipe. 2010. "Palabras del presidente Calderon en el *Premio Nacional de Accion Voluntaria y Solidaria*." *Los Pinos*, December 16. http://www.presidencia.gob.mx.

Camera de Diputados, Republica de México. 2004. *Gaceta Parliamentaria. Año VII*, 1486, April 29. http://gaceta.diputados.gob.mx.

Cansino, Cesar. 2004. "El síndrome de Evita." *El Universal*, February 15. http://www2.eluniversal.com.mx/.

Carlsen, Laura. 2007. *NAFTA Free Trade Myths Lead to Farm Failure in Mexico*. Washington, DC: Center for International Policy.

Carothers, Thomas. 2002. "The End of the Transition Paradigm." *Journal of Democracy* 13 (1): 5–21.

Carroll, Thomas F. 1992. *Intermediary NGOs: The Supporting Link in Grassroots Development*. West Hartford: Kumarian.

Caviedes, Cesar N. 2001. *El Niño in History: Storming Through the Ages*. Gainesville: University Press of Florida.

Centeno, Miguel Ángel. 1994. *Democracy Within Reason: Technocratic Revolution in Mexico*. University Park: Pennsylvania State University Press.

Chan, Stephanie. 2008. "Cross-Cultural Civility in Global Civil Society: Transnational Cooperation in Chinese NGOs." *Global Networks* 8 (2): 232–252.

Chevalier, Jacques M., and Andres Sánchez Bain. 2003. *The Hot and the Cold: Ills of Humans and Maize in Native Mexico*. Toronto: University of Toronto Press.

Choudry, Aziz, and Dip Kapoor. 2013. *NGO-ization: Complicity, Contradictions, and Prospects*. London: Zed Books.

Comisión Nacional de Derechos Humanos (CNDH). 2001. "Informe especial sobre las quejas en materia de desapariciones forzadas ocurridas en la década de los 70 y principios de los 80." http://www.cndh.org.mx/lacndh/informes/espec/desap70s/index.html.

Comaroff, Jean, and John L. Comaroff. 2000. "Millennial Capitalism: First Thoughts on a Second Coming." *Public Culture* 12 (2): 291–343.

Cooke, Bill, and Uma Kothari. 2001. *Participation: The New Tyranny?* London: Zed.

Cornelius, Wayne, Ann L. Craig, and Jonathan Fox. 1994. "Mexico's National Solidarity Program: An Overview." In *Transforming State–Society Relations in Mexico: The National Solidarity Strategy*, edited by Wayne A. Cornelius, Ann L. Craig, and Jonathan Fox, 3–28. San Diego: Center for US–Mexican Studies, University of California, San Diego.

Correas, Oscar. 2007. "The Criminalization of Social Protest in Mexico and Latin America." Paper presented at the annual meeting of the the Law and Society Association, Berlin, Germany, July 25.

Corrigan, Philip. 1994. "State Formation." In *Everyday Forms of State Formation: Revolution and Negotiation of Rule in Modern Mexico*, edited by Gilbert M. Joseph and Daniel Nugent, xviii–xix. Durham, NC: Duke University Press.

Corrigan, Philip, and Derek Sayer. 1985. *The Great Arch: English State Formation as Cultural Revolution*. Oxford: Basil Blackwell.

Cunningham, Hilary. 1999. "The Ethnography of Transnational Social Activism: Understanding the Global as Local Practice." *American Ethnologist* 26 (3): 583–604.

Dagnino, Evelina. 2003. "Citizenship in Latin America: An Introduction." *Latin American Perspectives* 30 (2): 3–17.

Das, Veena. 1996. *Critical Events: An Anthropological Perspective on Contemporary India*. New York: Oxford University Press.

Dávila, Mario. 1970. "Compadrazgo: Fictive Kinship in Latin America." *Readings in Kinship and Social Structure*, edited by Nelson H. Graburn, 396–406. New York: Harper & Row.

Davis, Mike. 2001. *Late Victorian Holocausts: El Niño Famines and the Making of the Third World*. London: Verso.

Deakin, Nicholas. 2001. *In Search of Civil Society*. London: Palgrave.

de la Peña, Guillermo. 1981. *A Legacy of Promises: Agriculture, Politics and Ritual in the Morelos Highlands*. Austin: University of Texas Press.

———. 2007. *Derechos indígenas y ciudadanía étnica: Derechos y políticas sociales*. Mexico City: UNAM-Miguel Ángel Porrúa.

de la Tejera, Beatriz, Angel Santos, and Raul García. 2007. "Maíz en Mexico: De una política pública de dependencia y vulnerabilidad hacia una política de soberanía alimentaria con la sociedad." Paper presented at Congress of the Latin American Studies Association, Montreal, Canada, September 5–8.

de Vries, Pieter. 2002. "Vanishing Mediators: Enjoyment as a Political Factor in Western Mexico." *American Ethnologist* 29 (4): 901–927.

Díaz, Henry F., and David W. Stahle. 2007. "Climate and Cultural History in the Americas." *Climatic Change* 83 (1–2): 1–8.

Douglas, Mary. 1975. *Implicit Meanings*. London: Routledge & Kegan Paul.

Dresser, Denise. 1994. "Bringing the Poor Back In: National Solidarity as a Strategy of Regime Legitimation." In *Transforming State–Society Relations in Mexico: The National Solidarity Strategy*, edited by Wayne A. Cornelius, Ann L. Craig, and Jonathan Fox, 143–166. San Diego: Center for US–Mexican Studies, University of California, San Diego.

Dussel Peters, Enrique. 2000. *Polarizing Mexico: The Impact of Liberalization Strategy*. Boulder, CO: Lynne Rienner Publishers.

Eckstein, Susan. 1990. "Poor People vs. the State and Capital: Anatomy of a Successful Community Mobilization for Housing in Mexico City." *International Journal of Urban and Regional Research* 14 (2): 274–296.

Emirbayer, Mustafa, and Jeff Goodwin. 1994. "Network Analysis, Culture, and the Problem of Agency." *American Journal of Sociology* 99 (6): 1411–1454.

Endfield, Georgina H., and Isabel Fernández-Tejedo. 2006. "Decades of Drought, Years of Hunger: Archival Investigations of Multiple Year Droughts in Late Colonial Oaxaca." *Climatic Change* 75 (4): 391–419.

Endfield, Georgina H., and Sarah L. O'Hara. 1997. "Conflicts Over Water in the 'Little Drought Age' in Central Mexico." *Environment and History* 3 (3): 255–272.

———. 1999. "Degradation, Drought, and Dissent: An Environmental History of Colonial Michoacán, West Central Mexico." *Annals of the Association of American Geographers* 89 (3): 402–419.

Engels, Friedrich. (1894) 1951. *The Peasant Question in France and Germany. Selected Works of Marx and Engels*. Vol. 2. Moscow: Foreign Language Publishing House.

Escalante Gonzalbo, Fernando. 1992. *Ciudadanos imaginarios*. Mexico City: El Colegio de Mexico.

———. 2001. "La dificultad del liberalismo mexicano." *Revista internacional de filosofía política* 18: 83–98.

Escobar, Arturo. 1995. *Encountering Development: The Making and Unmaking of the Third World*. Princeton, NJ: Princeton University Press.

Escobar Ohmstede, Antonio. 2004. *Desastres agrícolas en México: Catálogo histórico II: Siglo XIX (1822–1900)*. Mexico City: Centro de Investigaciones y Estudios Superiores en Antropología Social/Fondo de Cultura Económica.

Ferguson, James. 1990. *The Anti-Politics Machine: "Development," Depoliticization, and Bureaucratic Power in Lesotho*. Minneapolis: University of Minnesota Press.

Ferguson, James, and Akhil Gupta. 2002. "Spatializing States: Toward an Ethnography of Neoliberal Governmentality." *American Ethnologist* 29 (4): 981–1002.

Fernando, Jude L., and Alan Heston, eds. 1997. *NGOs: Charity and Empowerment:*

The Annals of the American Academy of Social and Political Science. London: Sage Publications.

Fidler, Stephen. 2001. "Migrants Spur Growth in Remittances." *Financial Times*, May 17, 17.

Fischer, William. 1997. "Doing Good? The Politics and Anti-Politics of NGO Practices." *Annual Review of Anthropology* 26:439–464.

Flores, Margarita, Raquel Araujo, Edith Betancourt, and Diana Liverman. 1996. "Comportamiento de la superficie potencialmente apta para el cultivo del maíz de temporal ante un cambio climático." In *Memorias del segundo taller de estudio de país: México, México ante el cambio climático, 8 a 11 mayo, 1996*, edited by Instituto Nacional de Ecología, 179–184. Cuernavaca: Universidad Nacional Autónomo de México.

Florescano, Enrique. 1969. *Precios del maíz y crisis agrícolas en México (1708–1810)*. Mexico City: Colegio de México.

Florescano, Enrique, and Susan Swan. 1995. *Breve historia de la sequía en México*. Xalapa: Universidad Veracruzana.

Foley, Michael W. 1991. "Agenda for Mobilization: The Agrarian Question and Popular Mobilization in Contemporary Mexico." *Latin American Research Review* 26 (2): 39–74.

Forment, Carlos. 2002. "La sociedad civil en el Perú del siglo XIX: Democrática o disciplinaria." In *Ciudadanía politica y formación de las naciones: Perspectivas históricas de América Latina*, edited by Hilda Sabato, 202–230. Mexico: Fondo de Cultura Económica, El Colegio de México.

———. 2003. *Democracy in Latin America, 1760–1900, vol. 1, Civic Selfhood and Public Life in Mexico and Peru*. Chicago: University of Chicago Press.

Foster, George M. 1953. "Cofradia and Compadrazgo in Spain and Spanish America." *Southwestern Journal of Anthropology* 9 (1): 11–12.

———. 1961. "The Dyadic Contract: A Model for the Social Structure of a Mexican Peasant Village." *American Anthropologist* 63 (6): 1173–1192.

———. 1965. "Peasant Society and the Image of Limited Good." *American Anthropologist* 67 (2): 293–315.

Foucault, Michel. 1991. "Governmentality." In *The Foucault Effect: Studies in Governmentality*, edited by Graham Burchell, Colin Gordon, and Peter Miller, 87–104. Chicago: University of Chicago Press.

———. 2000. *Power*. New York: New Press.

Foweraker, Joseph. 1993. *Popular Mobilization in Mexico: The Teachers' Movement, 1977–1987*. London: Cambridge University Press.

Fowler, Alan F. 1998. "Authentic NGDO Partnerships in the New Policy Agenda for International Aid: Dead End or Light Ahead." *Development and Change* 29 (1): 137–159.

Fox, Jonathan. 1994. "The Difficult Transition from Clientelism to Citizenship: Lessons from Mexico." *World Politics* 46 (2): 151–184.

Fox, Jonathan, and L. David Brown. 1998. *The Struggle for Accountability: The World Bank, NGOs, and Grassroots Movements*. Cambridge, MA: MIT Press.

Fox, Jonathan, and Luis Hernández. 1992. "Mexico's Difficult Democracy: Grassroots Movements, NGOs and Local Government." *Alternatives* 17 (2): 165–208.

Fraser, Nancy. 2003. "From Discipline to Flexibilization? Rereading Foucault in the Age of Globalization." *Constellations* 10 (2): 160–171.

Freire, Paolo. 1972. *Pedagogy of the Oppressed*. Harmondsworth: Penguin.

Friedrich, Paul. 1986. *The Princes of Naranja: An Essay in Anthrohistorical Method*. Austin: University of Texas Press.

Fundación para el Debido Proceso Legal (DPLF). 2010. *Criminalización de los defensores de derechos humanos y de la protesta social en México*. Mexico City: Fundación para el Debido Proceso Legal.

Galarza Mercado, Juan Manuel, César Miramonte Piña, Maria Soledad Cruz Delgado, Martha Magdalena Gómez Valdez, Martha Elena Ortiz Pulido, Ana Maria Entzana Tadeo, Clara Yasmín Juárez Hernández, and Veronica Santillan Moctezuma. 2004. *Situación actual y perspectivas del maíz en México*. Mexico City: SAGARPA.

Gagnon, Jean-Paul, and Mark Chou. 2014. "Why Democratic Theory?" *Democratic Theory* 1 (1): 1–8.

García Acosta, Virginia, Juan Manuel Pérez Zevallos, and América Molina del Villar. 2003. *Desastres agrícolas en México: Catálogo histórico I: Epocas prehispanicas y coloniales (958–1822)*. Mexico City: Centro de Investigaciones y Estudios Superiores en Antropología Social/Fondo de Cultura Económica.

Geertz, Clifford. 1960. "The Javanese Kijaji: The Changing Role of a Cultural Broker." *Comparative Studies in Society and History* 2 (2): 228–249.

Gilbert, Dennis. 2007. *Mexico's Middle Class in the Neoliberal Era*. Tucson: University of Arizona Press.

Gill, Richardson B. 2006. "Living in a Physical World: Cataloging Natural Disasters in Mexico." *Culture and Agriculture* 28 (1): 66–84.

Gledhill, John. 2000. *Power and Its Disguises: Anthropological Perspectives on Politics*. Sterling, VA: Pluto Press.

Gobierno del Estado [de] Hidalgo, Secretaria de Desarrollo Social. 1993. *Monografía del Estado de Hidalgo*. Vol. 2. Pachuca: Instituto Hidalguense de la Cultura.

González Graf, Jaime, and Carlos Camacho Alfaro. 1983. *Una evaluación de la estrategia de la Fundación Mexicana para el Desarrollo Rural*. Mexico City: Instituto Mexicano de Estudios Politicos, AC.

Goodale, Mark, and Nancy Postero. 2013. *Neoliberalism, Interrupted: Social Change and Contested Governance in Contemporary Latin America*. Stanford, CA: Stanford University Press.

Gordon, Sara. 1998. "Entre la filantropía y el mercado: La Fundación Mexicana para el Desarrollo Rural." In *Organizaciones civiles y políticas públicas en México y Centroamérica*, edited by José Luis Mendez, 293–319. Mexico City: Porrúa.

Grandin, Greg. 2006. *Empire's Workshop: Latin America, the United States, and the Rise of the New Imperialism*. New York: Owl Books.

Granovetter, Mark. 1973. "The Strength of Weak Ties." *American Journal of Sociology* 78 (6): 1360–1388.

Gregory, James R. 1975. "Image of Limited Good, or Expectation of Reciprocity?" *Current Anthropology* 16 (1): 73–92.

Grewal, Inderpal. 2011. "Humanitarian Citizenship and Race: Katrina and the Global War on Terror." Lecture presented at Rapoport Center for Human Rights and Justice, Austin, TX, September 9.

Grindle, Merilee. 1981. "Official Interpretations of Rural Underdevelopment: Mexico in the 1970s." Working Paper in US–Mexican Studies. La Jolla: Center for US–Mexican Studies, University of California, San Diego.

Gutiérrez, Irma Eugenia. 1990. *Hidalgo: Sociedad, Economía, Política y Cultura*. Mexico City: Universidad Nacional Autónoma de México.

Hale, Charles A. 1989. *The Transformation of Liberalism in Nineteenth Century Mexico*. Princeton, NJ: Princeton University Press.

———. 1991. *Las transformaciones del liberalismo en México a fines del siglo XIX*. Mexico City: Vuelta.

Hall, Stuart, and David Held. 1990. "Citizens and Citizenship." In *New Times: The Changing Face of Politics in the 1990s*, edited by Stuart Hall and Martin Jacques, 173–195. New York: Verso.

Hammel, Eugene A. 1968. *Alternative Social Structures and Ritual Relations in the Balkans*. Englewood Cliffs, NJ: Prentice-Hall.

Handelman, Howard. 1997. *Mexican Politics: The Dynamics of Change*. New York: St. Martin's Press.

Hardt, Michael, and Antonio Negri. 2004. *Multitude: War and Democracy in the Age of Empire*. New York: Penguin.

Hart, Gillian. 2002a. *Disabling Globalization: Places of Power in Post-Apartheid South Africa*. Berkeley: University of California Press.

Hart, Gillian. 2002b. "Geography and Development: Development/s Beyond Neoliberalism? Power, Culture, Political Economy." *Progress in Human Geography* 26 (6): 812–822.

Harvey, David. 1995. "Globalization in Question." *Rethinking Marxism* 8 (4): 1–17.

———. 2005. *A Brief History of Neoliberalism*. Oxford: Oxford University Press.

Hellman, Judith A. 1988. *Mexico in Crisis*. New York: Holmes & Meier.

Henriques, Gisele, and Raj Patel. 2004. *NAFTA, Corn, and Mexico's Agricultural Trade Liberalization*. Silver City: Interhemispheric Resource Center.

Herrera Cabañas, Arturo. 1995. *Los Movimientos Campesinos en el Estado de Hidalgo, 1850–1876.* Pachuca: Gobierno del Estado de Hidalgo.

Herzfeld, Michael. 1997. *Cultural Intimacy: Social Poetics in the Nation-State.* New York: Routledge.

Hevia de la Jara, Felipe. 2009. "De progresa a oportunidades: Efectos y límites de la corriente cívica en el gobierno de Vicente Fox." *Sociológica* 24 (70): 43–81.

Hewitt de Alcántara, Cynthia. 1976. *Modernizing Mexican Agriculture: Socioeconomic Implications of Technological Change, 1940–1970.* Geneva: United Nations Research Institute for Social Development.

Hirabayashi, Lane Ryo. 1993. *Cultural Capital: Mountain Zapotec Migrant Associations in Mexico City.* Tucson: University of Arizona Press.

Hubbard, Laura, and Kathryn Mathers. 2004. "Surviving American Empire in Africa: The Anthropology of Reality Television." *International Journal of Cultural Studies* 7 (4): 441–459.

Huntington, S. P. 1991. "Democracy's Third Wave." *Journal of Democracy* 2 (2): 12–34. International Center for Not-for-Profit Law (ICNL). 2012. "NGO Law Monitor: Mexico." May 8, 2013. http://www.icnl.org/research/monitor/mexico.pdf.

Jiménez Román, Arturo, and Laura Elena Maderey Rascón. 2004. "Modificaciones del ciclo del agua en la cuenca del Río Panuco ante el cambio climático global." *Revista Geográfica* 135:38–55.

Joseph, Gilbert M., and Daniel Nugent, eds. 1994. *Everyday Forms of State Formation: Revolution and the Negotiation of Rule in Modern Mexico.* Durham, NC: Duke University Press.

Joseph, Miranda. 2000. *Against the Romance of Community.* Minneapolis: University of Minnesota Press.

Juris, Jeffrey. 2008. *Networking Futures: The Movements Against Corporate Globalization.* Durham, NC: Duke University Press.

Kapoor, Dip. 2005. "NGO Partnerships and the Taming of the Grassroots in Rural India." *Development in Practice* 15 (2): 210–215.

Kautsky, Karl. (1899) 1988. *The Agrarian Question.* London: Zwann.

Keck, Margaret E., and Kathryn Sikkink. 1998. *Activists Beyond Borders: Advocacy Networks in International Politics.* Ithaca, NY: Cornell University Press.

Knight, Alan 1994a. "Solidarity: Historical Continuities and Contemporary Implications." In *Transforming State–Society Relations in Mexico: The National Solidarity Strategy,* edited by Wayne Cornelius, Ann L. Craig, and Jonathan Fox, 29–45. San Diego, Center for US–Mexican Studies: University of California, San Diego.

———. 1994b. "Weapons and Arches in the Mexican Revolutionary Landscape." In *Everyday Forms of State Formation: Revolution and the Negotiation of Rule in*

Modern Mexico, edited by Gilbert Joseph and Daniel Nugent, 24–68. Durham, NC: Duke University Press.

Knox, Hannah, Mike Savage, and Penny Harvey. 2006. "Social Networks and the Study of Relations: Networks as Method, Metaphor and Form." *Economy and Society* 35 (1): 113–140.

LaShaw, Amanda. 2012. "How Progressive Culture Resists Critique: The Impasse of NGO Studies." *Ethnography* 0 *(00):* 1–22.

Latour, Bruno. (1991) 1993. *We Have Never Been Modern*. Translated by C. Porter. Cambridge, MA: Harvard University Press.

———. 2005. *Reassembling the Social: An Introduction to Actor-Network-Theory*. Oxford: Oxford University Press.

Lenin, Vladimir I. (1899) 1956. *The Development of Capitalism in Russia: The Process of the Formation of a Home Market for Large-Scale Industry*. Moscow: Foreign Languages Publishing House.

Leve, Lauren, and Lamia Karim. 2001. "Privatizing the State: Ethnography of Development, Transnational Capital, and NGOs." *Political and Legal Anthropology Review (PoLAR)* 24 (1): 53–58.

Li, Tania Murray. 1999. "Compromising Power: Development, Culture, and Rule in Indonesia." *Cultural Anthropology* 14 (3): 295–322.

Lomnitz , Claudio. 2001. *Deep Mexico, Silent Mexico: An Anthropology of Nationalism*. Minneapolis: University of Minnesota Press.

Magaña, Víctor O., ed. 1999. *Los impactos de El Niño en México*. Mexico City: Centro de Ciencias de la Atmósfera, Universidad Nacional Autónoma de México.

Magazine, Roger. 2003. "An Innovative Combination of Neoliberalism and State Corporatism: The Case of a Locally Based NGO in Mexico City." *Annals of the American Academy of Political and Social Science* 590:243–256.

Mallon, Florencia E. 1995. *Peasant and Nation: The Making of Postcolonial Mexico and Peru*. Berkeley: University of California Press.

Mathews, Andrew. 2011. *Instituting Nature: Authority, Expertise, and Power in Mexican Forests*. Cambridge, MA: MIT Press.

Menes Llaguno, Juan Manuel. 1976. *Fuentes para la historia de la tenencia de la tierra en el Estado de Hidalgo: Indice de documentos del ramo de tierras del Archivo General de la Nación*. Pachuca: Centro Hidalguense de Investigaciones Historicas, A.C.

———. 2006. *Historia mínima del Estado de Hidalgo*. Mexico City: Porrua.

Merry, Sally Engle. 2006. "Transnational Human Rights and Local Activism: Mapping the Middle." *American Anthropologist* 108 (1): 35–51.

Mexican National Government. 2003. *Ley federal de fomento a las actividades realizadas por organizaciones de la sociedad civil* [Federal law of support for the activities undertaken by civil society organizations], Diario Oficial de la Federación Mexicana, February 9, 2004. http://www.dof.gob.mx/.

Meyer, Lorenzo. 2007. "The Second Coming of Mexican Liberalism: A Comparative Perspective." In *Cycles of Conflict, Centuries of Change: Crisis, Reform, and Revolution in Mexico*, edited by Elisa Servin, Leticia Reina, and John Tutino, 271–304. Durham, NC: Duke University Press.

Mintz, Sidney W., and Eric R. Wolf. (1950) 1977. "An Analysis of Ritual Co-Parenthood (Compadrazgo)." In *Friends, Followers, and Factions: A Reader in Political Clientelism*, edited by Steffen W. Schmidt, Laura Guasti, Carl H. Landé, and James C. Scott, 1–15. Berkeley: University of California Press.

Miraftab, Faranak. 1997. "Coqueteando con el enemigo: Desafíos de las ONG para el desarrollo y el empoderamiento." *Cuadernos de la sociedad civil* 1 (2): 33–57.

Montemayor, Carlos. 2005. "Desastres naturales y desastres gubernamentales." *La Jornada*, October 19, http://www.jornada.unam.mx/.

Moreno, Jenalia. 2002. "Middle Class Drowns in a Sea of Haves, Have-Nots in Mexico." *Houston Chronicle*, September 1, 1.

Nader, Laura. 1969. "Up the Anthropologist: Perspectives Gained from Studying Up." In *Reinventing Anthropology*, edited by Dell H. Hymes, 284–311. New York: Pantheon Books.

———. 1980. "The Vertical Slice: Hierarchies and Children." In *Hierarchy and Society*, edited by Gerald M. Britain and Ronald Cohen, 31–43. Philadelphia: Institute for the Study of Human Issues.

———. 1990. *Harmony Ideology: Justice and Control in a Zapotec Mountain Village*. Stanford, CA: Stanford University Press.

———. 2002. *The Life of the Law: Anthropological Projects*. Berkeley: University of California Press.

Natal, Alejandro, Patricia Greaves, and Sergio García. 2002. *Recursos privados para fines públicos: Las instituciones donantes Mexicanas*. Mexico City: Centro Mexicano para la Filantropía (CEMEFI).

O'Brien, Phil, and Jackie Roddick. 1983. *Chile, the Pinochet Decade: The Rise and Fall of the Chicago Boys*. London: Latin American Bureau.

Ochoa, Enrique C. 2001. *Feeding Mexico: The Political Uses of Food since 1910*. Wilmington, DE: Scholarly Resources.

Ocádiz, Roberto. 1962. *Tulancingo y sus alrededores*. Mexico: Cámara de Diputados, XLIX Legislatura.

Olvera Rivera, Alberto J. 1997. "Transformaciones económicas, cambios políticos, y movimientos sociales en el campo: Los obstáculos a la democracia en el mundo rural." In *La Democracia de los de abajo en México*, edited by Jorge Alonso and Juan Manuel Ramírez Saíz, 65–89. Mexico City: Centro de Investigaciones Interdisciplinarias en Humanidades UNAM.

———. 1999a. "Introducción." In *La sociedad civil: De la teoría a la realidad*. Edited by Alberto J. Olvera Rivera, 1–26. Mexico City: El Colegio de Mexico.

———. 1999b. "Los modos de recuperacion contemporanea de la idea de sociedad civil" [Contemporary modes of recuperating the idea of civil society]. In *La socie-*

dad civil: De la teoría a la realidad [Civil society: From theory to reality], edited by Alberto J. Olvera Rivera, 27–54. Mexico City: El Colegio de Mexico.

Ong, Aihwa. 2003. *Buddha Is Hiding: Refugees, Citizenship, the New America*. Berkeley: University of California Press.

Ortega Pizarro, Fernando. 2001. "CCE: El poder del dinero." *Proceso*, November 18.

Ortner, Sherry. 2006. *Anthropology and Social Theory: Culture, Power, and the Acting Subject*. Durham, NC: Duke University Press.

Palacios, Guillermo. 1999. *La pluma y el arado: Los intelectuales pedagogos y la construcción sociocultural del "problema campesino" en México, 1932–1934*. Mexico City: Centro de Estudios Historicos, Colegio de Mexico, Division de Estudios Politicos, Centro de Investigacion y Docencia Economicas.

Paley, Julia. 2001. *Marketing Democracy: Power and Social Movements in Post-Dictatorship Chile*. Berkeley: University of California Press.

Padilla, José. 2007. "Cae primer helado del año." *La Ruta*, October 24, A1.

Peck, Jamie, and Adam Tickell. 2002. "Neoliberalizing Space." *Antipode* 34 (3): 380–404.

Pérez, Matilde. 2006. "El campo sobrevive por las remesas: Agricultores." *La Jornada*, November 27. http://www.jornada.unam.mx/.

Poniatowska, Elena. 1995. *Nothing, Nobody: The Voices of the Mexico City Earthquake*. Philadelphia: Temple University Press.

Populorum Progressio. 1967. *Encyclical of Pope Paul VI on the Development of Peoples*. March 26. http://w2.vatican.va/.

Preobrazhensky, Evgenii. (1926) 1965. *The New Economics*. Oxford: Oxford University Press.

Press, Irwin. 1969. "Ambiguity and Innovation: Implications for the Genesis of the Culture Broker." *American Anthropologist* 71 (2): 205–217.

Putnam, Robert D. 2000. *Bowling Alone: the Collapse and Revival of American Community*. New York: Simon & Schuster.

Reina, Leticia, Elisa Servin, and John Tutino. 2007. "Crises, Reforms, and Revolutions in Mexico, Past and Present." In *Cycles of Conflict, Centuries of Change: Crisis, Reform, and Revolution in Mexico*, edited by Elisa Servin, Leticia Reina, and John Tutino, 1–22. Durham, NC: Duke University Press.

Richard, Analiese. 2008. "Withered Milpas: Governmental Disaster and the Mexican Countryside." Journal of Latin American and Caribbean Anthropology 13(2): 387–41.

———. 2009. "Mediating Dilemmas: Local NGOs and Rural Development in Neoliberal Mexico." *Political and Legal Anthropology Review* 32 (2): 166–194.

———. 2013. "'Taken into account': Democratic Change and Contradiction in Mexico's Third Sector." In *Neoliberalism Interrupted: Social Change and Contested*

Governance in Contemporary Latin America, edited by Mark Goodale and Nancy Postero, 137–166. Stanford, CA: Stanford University Press.

Richard, Analiese, and Daromir Rudnyckyj. 2009. "Economies of Affect." *Journal of the Royal Anthropological Institute, n.s.*, 15 (1): 57–77.

Riles, Annelise. 2000. *The Network Inside Out*. Ann Arbor: University of Michigan Press.

Rivera Flores, Alfredo. 2004. *La sosa nostra: Porrismo y gobierno coludidos en Hidalgo*. Mexico City: Porrua.

Rodriguez, Victoria. 1997. *Decentralization in Mexico: From Reforma Municipal to Solidaridad to Nuevo Federalismo*. Boulder, CO: Westview Press.

Rose, Nikolas. 1999. *Powers of Freedom: Reframing Political Thought*. Cambridge: Cambridge University Press.

Rus, Jan, and Miguel Tinker Salas. 2006. "Mexico 2006–2012: High Stakes, Daunting Challenges." *Latin American Perspectives* 33 (2): 5–15.

La Ruta. 2004. "Tambien profesionistas tienen que ir en busca del 'sueño americano'" [Professionals must also leave in search of the American dream]. March 18, 1.

Sabato, Hilda. 2001. "On Political Citizenship in Nineteenth Century Latin America." *American Historical Review* 106 (4): 1290–1315.

Salinas de Gortari, Carlos. n.d. "Modernización con apego a nuestros valores." In *Discursos de campaña*. Vol. 4. Mexico City: PRI.

Schryer, Frans J. 1990. *Ethnicity and Class Conflict in Rural Mexico*. Princeton, NJ: Princeton University Press.

Schuller, Mark. 2012. *Killing with Kindness: Haiti, International Aid, and NGOs*. New Brunswick, NJ: Rutgers University Press.

Scott, James C. 1977. *The Moral Economy of the Peasant: Rebellion and Subsistence in Southeast Asia*. New Haven, CT: Yale University Press.

Secretaría de la Reforma Agraria (SRA). 2006. *Programa de certificación de derechos ejidales y titulación de solares (PROCEDE), memoria técnica 1993–2006*. Pachuca, Hidalgo: Secretaría de la Reforma Agraria.

Serres, Michel. (1980) 2007. *The Parasite*. Translated by Lawrence R. Sher. Minneapolis: University of Minnesota Press.

Shaw, Alison, and Katharine Charsley. 2006. "*Rishtas:* Adding Emotion to Strategy in Understanding British Pakistani Transnational Marriages." *Global Networks* 6 (4): 405–421.

Shefner, Jon. 2007. "Rethinking Civil Society in the Age of NAFTA: The Case of Mexico." *Annals of the American Academy of Political and Social Science* 610 (1): 182–200.

Silva, Patricio. 1991. "Technocrats and Politics in Chile: From the Chicago Boys to the CIEPLAN Monks." *Journal of Latin American Studies* 23 (2): 385–410.

Smith, Brian H. 1990. *More Than Altruism: The Politics of Private Foreign Aid.* Princeton, NJ: Princeton University Press.

Sociedad Agricola Mexicana. 1906. *Segundo Congreso Agricola de Tulancingo.* Mexico City: Tipografía Particular de la Sociedad Agrícola Mexicana.

Sonnenfeld, David A. 1992. "Mexico's 'Green Revolution,' 1940–1980: Towards an Environmental History." *Environmental History Review* 16 (4): 28–52.

Sponsel, Leslie. 1992. "The Environmental History of Amazonia: Natural and Human Disturbances, and the Ecological Transition." In *Changing Tropical Forests: Historical Perspectives on Today's Challenges in Central and South America,* edited by Harold K. Steen and Richard P. Tucker, 233–251. Durham, NC: Forest Historical Society.

Strathern, Marilyn. 2001. "Cutting the Network." *Journal of the Royal Anthropological Institute* 2 (3): 517–535.

Thompson, Ginger. 2002. "Free Market Upheaval Grinds Mexico's Middle Class." *New York Times,* September 2, A3.

Tsing, Anna. 2005. *Friction: An Ethnography of Global Connection.* Princeton, NJ: Princeton University Press.

Valdes, Juan Gabriel. 1989. *La Escuela de Chicago: Operacion Chile.* Buenos Aires: Grupo Zeta.

Valdespino Castillo, Roberto. 1992. *Hidalgo a traves de sus gobernantes.* Queretaro: Talleres de Grafica Empresarial.

Vargas, A. 2006. *Diagnóstico de la cadena maíz-tortilla.* Mexico City: Consejo Nacional de Productores de Maíz, A.C.

Vargas González, Pablo E. 1998. *Hidalgo: Las dificultades de la transición política.* Guadalajara, Jalisco: Universidad de Guadalajara, Universidad Autónoma del Estado de Hidalgo.

Vaughan, Mary Kay. 1997. *Cultural Politics in Revolution: Teachers, Peasants, and Schools in Mexico, 1930–1940.* Tucson: University of Arizona Press.

Velloso Santisteban, Agustín. 2005. "The Poor Will Always Be With Us—And So Will NGOs." *Development in Practice* 15 (2): 200–209.

Verduzco, Gustavo, Regina List, and Lester Salamon. 2002. *Perfil del sector no lucrativo en México.* Mexico City: Centro Mexicano Para la Filantropía (CEMEFI) and Johns Hopkins University Institute for Policy Studies, Center for Civil Society Studies.

Wallace, Tina. 2003. "NGO Dilemmas: Trojan Horses for Global Neoliberalism?" *The Socialist Register 2004: The New Imperial Challenge,* edited by Leo Panitch and Colin Leys, 202–219. New York: Monthly Review Press.

Williams, Raymond. 1973. *The Country and the City.* Oxford: Oxford University Press.

Williamson, John. 1989. *Voluntary Approaches to Debt Relief.* Washington, DC: Institute for International Economics.

Wilson, Tamar Diana. 1998. "Weak Ties, Strong Ties: Network Principles in Mexican Migration." *Human Organization* 57 (4): 394–403.

Wolf, Eric R. 1956. "Aspects of Group Relations in a Complex Society: Mexico." *American Anthropologist* 58 (6): 1065–1078.

———. 1959. *Sons of the Shaking Earth*. Chicago: University of Chicago Press.

———. (1966) 2004. "Kinship, Friendship, and Patron–Client Relations in Complex Societies." In *The Social Anthropology of Complex Societies*, edited by Michael Banton, 1–22. New York: Routledge.

———. 2001. *Pathways of Power: Building an Anthropology of the Modern World*. Berkeley: University of California Press.

Yar, Majid. 2004. "'Community': Past, Present, and Future." *Electronic Journal of Social Issues* 2 (1).

Zárate Hernández, Jose Eduardo. 1997. *Procesos de identidad y globalización económica: El Llano Grande en el sur de Jalisco* [Processes of identity and economic globalization: The Great Plain of southern Jalisco]. Zamora: El Colegio de Michoacan.

Zepeda Patterson, Jorge. 2014. "La crucifixión de las ONG." *El Pais*, September 24. http://internacional.elpais.com/.

Zulema, Maria Cecilia. 1999. "La prensa agrícola del Porfiriato como fuente para la historia económica." *Signos Historicos* 1 (2): 59–88.

Index

Comisión Nacional de Derechos
Humanos (CNDH), 67
Commodity Credit Corporation (CCC),
107
communism, 65–66, 86, 88
compadrazgo (ritual coparenthood), 32,
158, 159–68, 190nn2,4
ConAgra, 107
CONASUPO. *See* National Company
for People's Sustenance
confraternities (*cofradias*), 32
consciousness of catastrophe, 97, 98, 99,
101, 109, 114
Cooke, Bill, 15
Cornelius, Wayne, 59
corporatism, 30, 34, 44–47, 111; of PRI,
46, 50, 53, 55, 56, 58, 59, 67, 77, 96,
101, 110, 117, 125, 126, 127, 138, 139–
40, 141, 149
Correas, Oscar, 173
Corrigan, Philip, 25, 26, 185n4
Cortés, Hernán, 17, 19
Craig, Ann L., 59
credit, 67–68, 71, 73, 79, 107
Cristero rebellion, 44
CSC. *See* Civil Society Council
cuates, 166, 191n10
Cuban revolution, 65–66
cultivation as metaphor, 21–23
Cunningham, Hilary, 154, 155

Das, Veena, 102
Dávila, Mario, 160, 163
Davis, Mike, 99
Deakin, Nicholas, 15, 95
de la Madrid, Miguel, 55–56
de la Peña, Guillermo, 124, 125, 126,
137, 140, 141
de la Tejera, Beatriz, 106, 107, 108
democracy, 21, 30, 183n3; in Mexico, 1,
7, 8, 12–16, 19, 22, 23, 28–29, 34, 38,
56, 59, 64, 89, 90–91, 94, 97, 102, 103,
117, 118, 119, 122, 123, 127, 128, 130,
131, 132, 133, 135–36, 138, 141, 142,
144, 149, 171, 172, 173, 175–76, 177,
178, 179, 182; and neoliberalism, 7–16,
20, 22, 171, 175–76; and NGOs, 6–7,
9–16, 20, 64, 79, 81, 87, 89, 90–91, 94,
103, 109, 122, 123, 125, 127, 128, 130,
133, 135–36, 138, 141, 142, 144, 147,

148, 149, 171, 172, 173, 174, 176, 177,
179, 182
Democratic Revolutionary Party (PRD),
19
de Vries, Peter, 126, 137
Díaz, Henry K., 100
Díaz, Porfirio, 19, 27, 40–42, 98, 103,
185n9
discourse of desiccation, 97, 99, 101, 102,
109–10, 115–18, 119
Douglas, Mary, 102
Dresser, Denise, 58, 59, 108
drug cartels, 60–61, 170–71, 175
Duran, Marcelino, 30
Dussel Peters, Enrique, 173

Earth Summit of 1992, 10
Echeverría, Luis, 49, 50, 51–52, 53, 54,
66–67, 79, 85, 186n5
Eckstein, Susan, 187n9
ejidos, 1, 19, 44, 51, 67–68, 76, 78, 80, 94, 98,
103, 114, 122, 185n13, 188n11; and PRI,
2–3, 45, 46–47, 52, 54, 186n2; privatization of, 57, 105, 108, 110, 111, 116, 118
El Barzón, 138
El Campo No Aguanta Más movement,
98, 111, 112, 118
elites, 17, 28, 29, 30, 31, 39–40, 69–71,
81, 185nn9,11, 188n9; hacendados,
2–3, 18–19, 19, 32, 35, 36, 40, 41, 42,
45, 103; and neoliberalism, 8, 13–14;
political elites, 22, 64, 130–31, 133
El Ocote, 1, 3, 4, 5, 45, 62–63, 112, 166
Emirbayer, Mustafa, 156
Endfield, Georgina M., 100, 103
Engels, Friedrich, 184n2
entrepreneurship: among caciques, 136,
137–38, 143; among campesinos,
57, 63, 67–68, 74, 75–76, 77, 82–83;
among NGO workers, 123, 127, 136,
137, 142, 146, 147
Escalante Gonzalbo, Fernando, 26–27,
28, 31, 32, 34, 38, 185n5
Escobar, Arturo, 10
Escobar Ohmstede, Antonio, 103
Escobedo Ortiz, Marisela, 170–71
ethanol, 97, 102, 117, 187n2
Evita syndrome, 145, 177, 178, 179, 180

faena, 32, 59, 62, 76, 185n7